SJP

Database Projects in Access
for Advanced Level
for Advanced Level

Julian Mott and Ian Rendell

Hodder & Stoughton
A MEMBER OF THE HODDER HEADLINE GROUP

Orders: please contact Bookpoint Ltd, 130 Milton Park, Abingdon, Oxon
OX14 4SB. Telephone: (44) 01235 827720.
Fax: (44) 01235 400454. Lines are open from 9.00 to 6.00, Monday to Saturday,
with a 24-hour message answering service.
You can also order through our website www.hodderheadline.co.uk.

British Library Cataloguing in Publication Data
A catalogue record for this title is available from The British Library

ISBN 0 340 81201 X

First published 2003
Impression number 10 9 8 7 6 5 4 3 2 1
Year 2009 2008 2007 2006 2005 2004 2003

Typeset by Tech-Set Ltd, Gateshead, Tyne & Wear.
Printed in Great Britain for Hodder & Stoughton Educational, a division of
Hodder Headline Ltd, 338 Euston Road, London NW1 3BH by
J W Arrowsmith, Bristol

CONTENTS

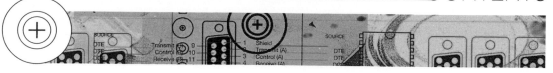

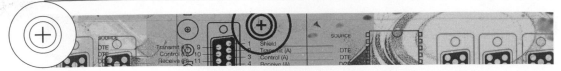

Aims

The book is aimed at a number of Advanced courses of study within the National Qualifications Framework currently available in schools and colleges and supported by AQA, OCR and Edexcel.

The book covers all the key software skills required in practical components of specifications where a study of databases using Microsoft Access is required.

The materials in this book support the following courses of study:

○ the coursework components for students studying **A/S** and **A levels** in **ICT**;
○ the mandatory unit in Database Design for students studying the **Advanced VCE** in **ICT**;
○ the Computing project component for students studying **A/S** and **A levels** in **Computing**.

The book also offers advice and support materials to assist students in documenting the systems they have developed. Students are taken through the process of analysing, designing, implementing, testing and evaluating solutions to problems using a software package.

The materials and approach used in the book may also be applicable to students on many courses in further and higher education where a study of databases through Microsoft Access is necessary.

Teacher's resources

Julian Mott and Ian Rendell have written two coursework books:

○ Spreadsheet Projects in Excel for Advanced Level;
○ Database Projects in Access for Advanced Level.

Materials used in the books can be freely downloaded from the web site www.hodderictcoursework.co.uk

Advanced features of Access

The following advice is intended only for guidance. Teachers should use this in conjunction with the Specification and Examiners' Reports to ensure the correct features are being used appropriately.

Use of these features alone does not guarantee high marks. It is down to how the student uses them to solve an ICT problem and documents the solution.

Projects at this level of study in Microsoft Access are likely to include some of the following features:

- simple input masks and data validation;
- related tables;
- select and parameter queries;
- data entry using fully customised forms;
- list boxes or combo boxes to facilitate data entry;
- output fully tailored to user requirements;
- macros to automate commonly used features;
- a switchboard;
- subforms to display information in related tables;
- update, append and delete queries;
- forms and reports based on multi-table queries;
- customised reports with use of logos, headers and footers to show grouped data and calculated totals;
- customised menus and interfaces by removing toolbars and automating features.

Students are expected to go beyond implementing a single table database. Solutions should be relational and used in a relational manner.

Solutions do not need to be over-complicated. Three or four tables are sufficient at this level.

Students should work towards the production of fully automated and customised solutions that hide the software from the user. Wizards should be seen as the starting point on which students develop their solutions.

As more and more records are added, data will build up. The clearing out of old data should be considered. For example, in a school library system how long will details of loans be stored?

Students should also consider the cyclic nature of their solutions. For example, how will the library system handle those pupils in years 11 and 13 at the end of the school year? Procedures at the end of the year, start of the season or end of term might be considered and reflected in solutions.

Programming and the use of Visual Basic are not usually within the spirit of the specifications or the systems promoted in this book. The chosen software package should drive the solution and not Visual Basic code. However, students may wish to enter modules with code from routines researched and found in books or other media but this must be acknowledged at all times.

Access 2002/2000/97 issues

It is not necessary to have the latest software version. All the materials in this book are compatible with all versions. If you are new to Access 2002 (sometimes called Access XP) and prefer the desktop feel of Access 2000 you can right click on the desktop and change the Appearance properties to Windows Classic. All the screen images in this book have been produced in Access 2002.

What's the difference between Access 2000 and Access 2002?

Access 2002 has much the same look, feel and functions as its previous versions Access 97 and Access 2000. Briefly Access 2002 offers:

- multiple Undo and Redo;
- support for Access 2000 file formats making it easier to work between software versions;
- new keyboard shortcuts;
- Pivot Tables and Pivot Charts;
- easier editing of subforms or subreports;
- speech and handwriting recognition.

A more detailed account of the differences can be found using the Help menu in Access 2002 or by going to www.microsoft.com

Probably the biggest change is the introduction of the task pane (common to all Microsoft Office XP suite applications). The task pane (see Figure 0.1) appears on the right-hand side of the Access application window when you use certain features in Access. The task pane gives you quick access to your files.

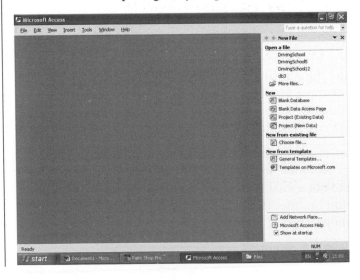

Figure 0.1

Which file format should I use – Access 2000 or Access 2002?

If this is the first database you have set up in Access then this should not really be an issue. However, if you have been working in an earlier version of Access or indeed the version you use at work/school differs from the one that you use at home then you need to give the file format a little thought.

By default, databases created in Access 2002 are created in Access 2000 format. This means your files are compatible with Access 2000.

If you feel you are only going to ever work in Access 2002 then you can set the default file format to Access 2002.

1   From the **Tools** menu select **Options**.
2   Click the **Advanced** tab in the **Options** dialog box and from the drop-down choose the file format **Access 2002** (see Figure 0.2).

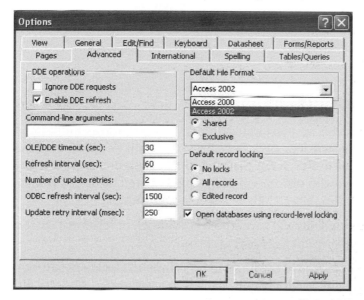

Figure 0.2

If you develop your database in Access 2002 it is easy to convert it to Access 97 or Access 2000 format.

○   Load your database and in the Database Window select **Tools, Database Utilities, Convert Database** and click on the version type required (see Figure 0.3).

Figure 0.3

How to use this book

The book assumes students have a working knowledge of Windows and Windows-based software. Students will have been introduced to databases via the National Curriculum or the study of ICT at Key Stage 3 and Key Stage 4. It is expected that students will be familiar with the concept of files, records and fields and will have practical experience of simple searching and sorting techniques.

It is also assumed that students will have studied the design of relational databases through a theory component in their course of study.

The book can be used as a formal teaching aid by lecturers, or students can work independently through the self-study units in class or away from the classroom.

Part 1 takes the student through the development of a system with each unit building on the range of features in Access. The system is based around a driving school, is fictitious and has been designed to incorporate as many features as is possible for demonstration purposes only. The units are best worked through in sequence.

Units 1 to 15 set up a working system, using features which might be expected from students at this level. Units 16 to 20 show how to develop this system further.

Part 2 covers the major issues in documenting coursework projects and offers pointers, hints and examples of good practice.

Part 3 offers a range of useful tips and features in Access to support the units and should provide interesting reading. These could be used as further activities for students. It is hoped that they can be the starting point for finding out even more about Access.

A note to students and lecturers

It is important to note that the system used in the text is not being put forward for a particular grade at any level. The system is fictitious and is aimed at showing the student the potential of Microsoft Access and how software features can be incorporated to produce a working ICT system.

All exam boards provide exemplar materials, support and training. It is vital that students in conjunction with their tutors are guided by the specifications.

The documentation of ICT solutions at this level follows the systems life-cycle approach of analysis, design, implementation, testing and evaluation. Again though, different specifications and different solutions will have a different emphasis.

A word of caution. Students must on no account copy materials in text books and submit them for examination. Moderators, examiners and the exam boards are very aware of published exemplar materials. You will be penalized severely.

Choosing a coursework project

Don't try to do everything. Using every single feature of Access would almost certainly lead to a very complicated and contrived project. It is better to choose a problem which involves some of the advanced features rather than all of them in the solution.

Don't try to do too much. It is easy to be over ambitious. Computerising the payroll, income tax, national insurance and pension records of a county council or producing a stock control system for a multinational company is unrealistic at this level. It is best to stick to something that you know you can achieve.

Don't try to do too little. However, the opposite is also true. A shopping list or a list of friends' birthdays would be too simple at this level. If you can set the system up in a few lessons, it is likely the project chosen does not have enough scope.

Do try to find a real problem and real user. It is best to choose a real problem with a real end-user. You will find a real problem far more interesting and challenging. The user could be one of your parents or a friend or neighbour. They could be a member of staff in your school or college. The local painter, gardener, handyman, fancy-cake maker, plumber, mobile hairdresser often provide a source of ideas. Having a real user does make analysis, testing and evaluating your solution all the easier. *For some courses a real end-user is essential.*

Ideas for projects

Car hire

A car hire company wants to store details of customers, cars for hire, pricing structure and future bookings. The system might produce timetables for cars on hire, details of car availability, reports on when a particular car has been hired and invoices for customers.

UCAS applications

A school's head of sixth form wants to store records of application by Year 13 students for courses at universities, including applications and offers. The system might produce full information on any student, full lists of applicants, details of who has not yet applied, details of offers and details of students who have not yet had an offer. The system would offer online access to student records for the head of sixth form and print weekly update reports.

The school library

A school library wants to store details of pupils, reference books, books that can be borrowed and loans. The system might produce details of books currently on loan, details of books that are overdue, reports on which books are available, reports on when a particular book has been borrowed and letters for pupils reminding them that a book is overdue.

Sports club membership

A sports club wants to store membership details electronically. The system might produce membership lists, details of who has and who hasn't paid their subscriptions and send out letters to members about meetings. The system could also store details of bookings of the club's facilities such as squash courts or fitness equipment but potentially there are two separate systems here.

Work experience placements

A school wants to store details of work experience placements including names of pupils, employers, who is going to which employers and any special details. The system might produce details of which pupils will not be in school on a certain day, lists for staff, details of which pupils can be visited and when, including a contact name, pupils who have not yet got a placement finalised and individual letters to employers and pupils telling them of arrangements.

Stock control

A fast food outlet wants to computerise its stock control. The system might store details of current stock levels, deliveries and today's sales. It might produce sales reports and stock reports, update stock levels automatically and produce orders for new stock.

ICT inventory

A school ICT department wants to keep an inventory of all its hardware on computer. The system might store details of hardware including purchase date, serial numbers, repairs and maintenance details, location and guarantee expiry. It might produce reports for internal audit, health and safety, service records and repair and maintenance history for each hardware item.

The driving school

A driving school wants to store details of lesson bookings including names of students and instructors. The system might produce timetables for all instructors for all days, details of when an instructor is available for a lesson, print records of students and produce membership cards.

School assessment records

A school wants to store details of pupil assessment records including names, teachers, marks, subjects and dates. The system might produce full results for any assessment, full information on any pupil, chart progress in a subject, compare performance in different subjects and print an automatic report for parents.

The dry-cleaning shop

A dry-cleaning company wants to store details of customers, items deposited for cleaning and charges for customers. The system might produce reports on what items have been brought in today, reports on when a particular customer has used the shop, show sales figures day-by-day or week-by-week and produce invoices for customers.

School options

A school wants to store details of the option choices for Year 9 pupils, including names of pupils, options available, and who has opted for which subjects. The system might produce details of how many pupils have opted for each subject, produce pupil lists for each subject, produce subject lists for each pupil and reports on pupils who have not yet made their choices.

Shoe repair shop

A shoe repair shop wants to store details of shoes brought in for repair, type of repair needed, as well as names and contact details of customers. The system might produce reports on work in hand, work completed, allocate collection tickets to customers, store sales details and produce invoices for customers.

School play seat booking

A school wants to produce tickets for its school play on computer and store details of the tickets sold for the various performances. The system might include what seats are available, the times and dates of performances, the cost of tickets, which ones have been sold. It should be able to produce up-to-the-minute reports on sales and income and produce diagrams to show which seats have not been sold for each performance.

Hotel room availability

A local hotel wants to set up an automated booking system. The system will store details of customers, rooms available, prices and bookings. Rooms must not be double booked. The system might produce reports on bookings, room availability and customer invoices.

Hairdressers' salon

A small hairdressers needs to be able to store appointment details. The system will store details of customers, stylists, requirements and bookings. Times for each booking must reflect the needs of the stylist. The system might produce reports on bookings and availability.

Local garage

A garage wants to store details of repairs electronically. The system will store details of customers, cars, MOT testing, servicing and repairs and bookings. The system might produce timetables for this week, reports on garage availability and customers for whom a service or MOT is due.

Sandwich shop

A sandwich shop takes orders from customers every morning, makes the sandwiches and delivers them to local shops, offices and factories. They want an electronic system to store details of orders and provide reports on what sandwiches must be produced, ingredients needed and delivery lists.

Watch repairer

A watch repairer who runs his own business wants more accurate reports on repairs to be carried out. He wants to store details of customers, watches to be repaired and charges for customers. The system might produce reports on what items have been brought in today and show sales figures day-by-day or week-by-week.

Project timetable

A project timetable helps you ensure that the workload is spread evenly throughout the project period, allowing for other factors such as module tests in ICT and other subjects, holidays and half-terms, workloads in other subjects etc. You should break your project up into sub-tasks and draw up the timetable at the start and try to stick to it. If you don't you can end up with too much to do at the last minute. This means that deadlines cannot be met and the final sections are rushed and only get low marks.

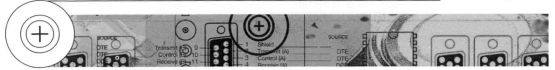

The development of a system

Unit 1 The Pass-It Driving School

The system covered by this book is based on a local driving school. The driving school caters for many students in the surrounding villages. The school has a number of full-time and part-time instructors.

When a student starts a course of lessons they are issued with a membership card and allocated an instructor. Students can book lessons through their instructor or by phoning the driving school office. Students usually book lessons of one or two hours though they can book longer sessions if they wish.

The school offers different types of lesson: Introductory, Standard, Pass Plus or the Driving Test. Fees are charged depending on the type of lesson booked. The driving school organises the practical and theory test for the students and if successful the students can go on to a Pass Plus course.

The system will have four related tables: Student, Instructor, Lesson Type and Lesson. Details are shown in Table 1.1.

STUDENT TABLE	INSTRUCTOR TABLE	LESSON TABLE	LESSON TYPE TABLE
Student ID	Instructor ID	Lesson No	Lesson Type
Title	Title	Student ID	Cost
Surname	Surname	Instructor ID	
Forename	Forename	Date	
Address 1	Address 1	Start Time	
Address 2	Address 2	Length of Lesson	
Address 3	Address 3	Collection Point	
Address 4	Address 4	Drop-Off Point	
Tel No	Home Tel No	Lesson Type	
Date of Birth	Mobile No		
Sex			
Theory Test Date			
Passed Theory Test			
Practical Test Date			
Passed Practical Test			
Pass Plus Req			
Issued Card			

Table 1.1

The development of a system

The system will allow the user to book, cancel and cost driving lessons. Details of all students and their test dates will be stored, enabling quick access and easy editing. Contact details for instructors working for the school will also be stored.

A range of search options will allow the user quickly to locate details of students and/or lessons. Full reporting menus will be implemented with options of weekly or daily lesson timetables for specified instructors. Student and instructor reports will also be offered. Further options will include the automatic:

- issue of membership cards;
- increase or decrease of lesson price ranges;
- processing of students who leave the school after passing their test;
- filing of all lessons taken for later reference.

All user interfaces will be fully customised with user-friendly menus.

⊕ Unit 2 Getting started

Microsoft Access is a database management system. It allows the user to store and manipulate data.

The main components of an Access database are:

○ tables
○ queries
○ forms
○ reports
○ macros
○ pages
○ modules

The Pages component allows data to be saved in web format for publishing on the web. The Modules component gives the developer access to Visual Basic for Applications. Neither component is covered in this book.

Tables

Access stores data in tables. A table is organised in rows (called records) and columns (called fields).

For example, in a student table a row would store the information about one particular student. This is called a record. Each column would contain details about each student such as forename, surname etc. These are called fields.

Library No	Surname	Forename	Sex	Year	Form
1	Sahota	Sanjot	Female	11	S
2	Gillanders	Mark	Male	13	R
3	Randall	David	Male	11	T
4	Smith	Paul	Male	11	T
5	Webster	Stephanie	Female	10	H
6	Askham	Stephanie	Female	12	I
7	Dayaram	Sunil	Male	13	O
8	Holland	Amanda	Female	11	N
9	Mace	Rebecca	Female	11	N
10	Cooper	Harry	Male	13	J
11	Dilkes	Gemma	Female	13	J
12	Payne	Karen	Female	12	O
13	Pearson	Kathryn	Female	10	P

Record: 14 of 14

Figure 2.1

The development of a system

Typically a system will consist of more than one table. For example, in a school library the database might be made up of a student table, a book table and a loan table. The student table is shown in Figure 2.1.

Access is often referred to as a relational database. Relationships can be defined between tables and used to support the searching and processing of data. A relational database will have at least two tables that are linked together.

Queries

A query is a way of asking questions about the data in your tables according to certain criteria. The user may wish to display a list of appointments for a particular day or output customers who owe payments. In the example shown in Figure 2.2 a query has produced a list of students in Year 11. This is known as a **Select Query**.

Library No	Surname	Forename	Sex	Year	Form
1	Sahota	Sanjot	Female	11	S
3	Randall	David	Male	11	T
4	Smith	Paul	Male	11	T
8	Holland	Amanda	Female	11	N
9	Mace	Rebecca	Female	11	N

Record: ◀◀ ◀ 1 ▶ ▶▶ ▶✳ of 5

Year 11 Search : Select Query

Figure 2.2

You will notice that there are five records in the output from this query. In the original table there were 13 records. Five of the 13 pupils are in Year 11.

Queries in Access offer a powerful processing tool. Later you will meet action and parameter queries. Queries can also be used to take data from more than one table and perform calculations on data.

Forms

Forms are used mainly to display the records in a table in a user-friendly way. Through a form you can enter and edit records more easily.

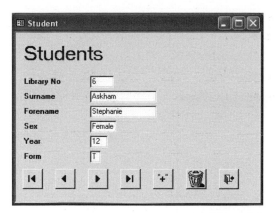

Figure 2.3

Forms are fully customisable. You can add buttons and controls, edit the appearance and include images (see Figure 2.3).

Reports

Reports are used to print information from your database. They provide professional looking output from a table or query. They can be fully customised and can display summary information (see Figure 2.4).

Year 11 Students

Library No	Surname	Forename	Sex	Year	Form
1	Sahota	Sanjot	Female	11	S
3	Randall	David	Male	11	T
4	Smith	Paul	Male	11	T
0	Holland	Amanda	Female	11	N
9	Mace	Rebecca	Female	11	N

Figure 2.4

Macros

A macro is a set of one or more actions that perform a particular operation. You can use macros to add buttons to print a report, open a form and perform other commonly used tasks. Macros help you in fully automating and customising your system.

Starting Access

○ To start Access click on **Start, Programs, Microsoft Access**. The Microsoft Access application window appears as shown in Figure 2.5.

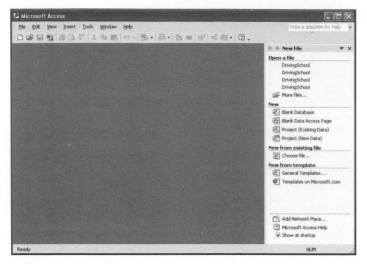

Figure 2.5

On the right of the screen is the task pane. From here you can either open an existing database, create a new database or use a range of pre-defined databases.

The databases you have most recently used appear in the upper half of the pane.

The Database Window

When you open an Access database the **Database Window** is displayed. The **Database Window** is the control centre of your application.

In Access 2002 the Database Window looks very similar to that shown in Figure 2.6. It has a slightly different feel from the Database Window in earlier versions of Access but has all the same features and functions.

The Database Window operates in a very similar way whichever version of the software you use.

From the Database Window you can access any of the components in your database by clicking on the object tabs. For example, in the screenshot in Figure 2.6 the Tables tab is selected ready to create a new table.

You would also click on this tab to open an existing table or edit an existing table.

Similarly, by clicking on the **Queries, Forms, Reports, Macros** or **Modules** tabs, you can open, edit or create queries, forms, reports, macros or modules.

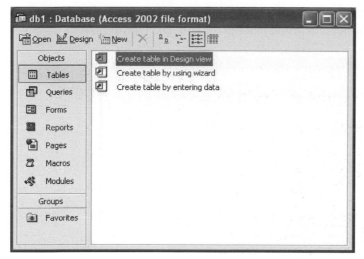

Figure 2.6

The Database Window Toolbar

Figure 2.7

- **Open** allows you to open a table, query or form
- **Design** allows you to enter Design View to set up a table, query, form, report or macro
- **New** allows you to set up a new table, query, form, report or macro
- **Delete** allows you to delete an object in the Database Window
- The remaining icons offer display options in the Database Window

Toolbars

The toolbars in Access change dynamically depending on which mode you are working in.

For example, if you are designing a table, there is a **Table Design** toolbar, as in Figure 2.8.

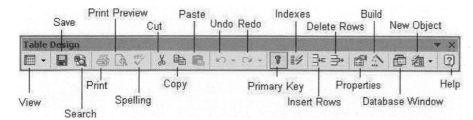

Figure 2.8

If you are viewing a form, there is a **Form View** toolbar. If the toolbar is not on the screen, click on **View, Toolbars** and choose from the menu (see Figure 2.9).

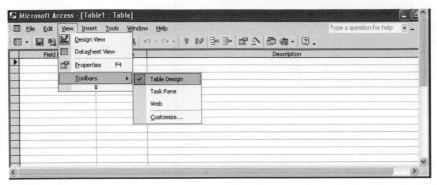

Figure 2.9

⊕ Unit 3 Setting up the tables

In Units 3 and 4 you will learn how to set up the tables that are needed to store the data for the Pass-It Driving School. The Driving School system is based on four tables.

- **Student**
- **Instructor**
- **Lesson**
- **Lesson Type**

In this Unit you will set up the **Student Table**. In Unit 4 you will enter the data and set up the remaining tables.

There are two stages to designing a table:

- Define the field names that make up the table and declare the data type for each.
- Set the field properties for each field name.

Defining the field names and data types

Access needs to know the name of each field in each table and what sort of data to expect. For example, in the Student table, the Student's telephone number might have as its **Field Name**: Tel No. You also need to tell Access whether the **Data Type** is number, text, date/time, currency, etc. In this case it is text.

Setting the field properties

Once you have named the table and defined each field with its data type, you can control the fields further by setting **Field Properties**. These properties tell Access how you want the data stored and displayed. For example a date could be displayed 19/06/94, 19th June 1994 or 19-Jun-94.

Setting up the Student table

1   Load **Microsoft Access**.

2   Select **Blank Database** in the task pane (see Figure 3.1).

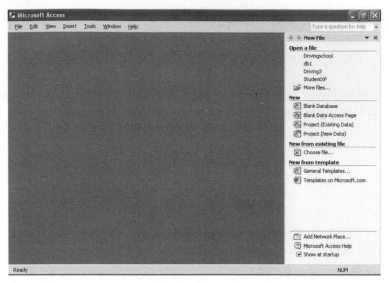

Figure 3.1

The **File New Database** Window appears as in Figure 3.2.

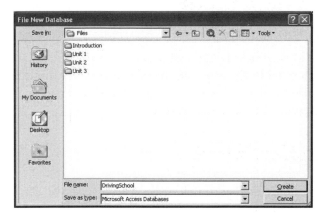

Figure 3.2

3 Use the Save In drop-down box to locate where you want to save your database. Name the file **DrivingSchool** and click on **Create**.

The Database Window loads. This is the control centre from which you can design tables, queries, forms, reports and macros. See Figure 3.3.

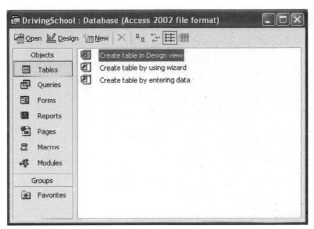

Figure 3.3

4   Click on **Tables** (it should already be selected) and click on **New**.

The **New Table** window will appear. See Figure 3.4.

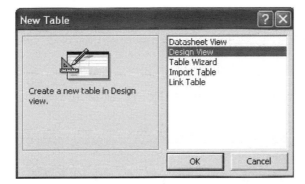

Figure 3.4

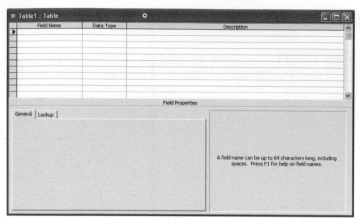

Figure 3.5

5   Click on **Design View** and then **OK**.

The **Table Design** window appears as shown in Figure 3.5.

Once you are in Table Design view you can start entering the details of the fields needed in the table. The small column to the left of the Field Name column is called the Row Selector column.

Defining the Field Names and Data Types

1   Enter the first Field Name: **Student ID** and press TAB or ENTER to move to the **Data Type** field.

After entering the Field Name you will notice that Field Properties are displayed in the lower half of the window. We will enter these later.

2   Click on the drop down and select **AutoNumber** (see Figure 3.6).

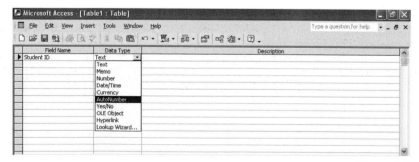

Figure 3.6

3   In the **Description Field** enter **Student's ID number**. This is optional and only for information.

4   Complete the Field Names and Data Types as shown in Figure 3.7 for the Student table.

FIELD NAME	DATA TYPE
Student ID	AutoNumber
Title	Text
Surname	Text
Forename	Text
Address 1	Text
Address 2	Text
Address 3	Text
Address 4	Text
Tel No	Text
Date of Birth	Date/Time
Sex	Text
Theory Test Date	Date/Time
Passed Theory Test	Yes/No
Practical Test Date	Date/Time
Passed Practical Test	Yes/No
Pass Plus Req	Yes/No
Issued Card	Yes/No

Figure 3.7

5   Set the Student ID field to be the key field by clicking on the row selector for this field and clicking on the **Primary Key** icon of the **Table Design** toolbar or click on **Edit, Primary Key**. A small picture of a key appears to the left of the Field Name (see Figure 3.8).

Microsoft Access - [Table1 : Table]

File   Edit   View   Insert   Tools   Window   Help

Field Name	Data Type		Description
Student ID	AutoNumber	Student's ID Number	

Figure 3.8

6   Your **Table Design** window should appear as in Figure 3.9. Save the table by closing the window or by choosing **File, Save**. The **Save As** dialogue box will appear. Name the table **Student**.

Field Name	Data Type	Description
Student ID	AutoNumber	Student's ID Number
Title	Text	
Surname	Text	
Forename	Text	
Address 1	Text	
Address 2	Text	
Address 3	Text	
Address 4	Text	
Tel No	Text	
Date of Birth	Date/Time	
Sex	Text	
Theory Test Date	Date/Time	
Passed Theory Test	Yes/No	
Practical Test Date	Date/Time	
Passed Practical Test	Yes/No	
Pass Plus Req	Yes/No	
Issued Card	Yes/No	

Figure 3.9

Naming tables

Note   When saving tables some Access users like to start the name with tbl, e.g. **tbl student**. They would start queries with qry, forms with frm, reports with rpt and macros with mcr. You may wish to consider using this naming convention.

Editing the table structure

If the **Table Design** toolbar is not already on the screen insert it by clicking **View, Toolbars, Table Design** (see Figure 3.10).

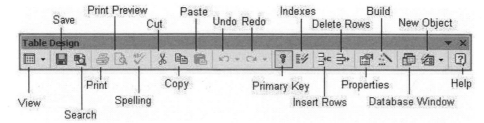

Figure 3.10

During the course of setting up the table it is probable you will make a mistake or decide to make a change to your table's structure. You have a number of editing options available.

Inserting a field

Click on the row selector of the field below the insertion point.

Press the INSERT key on the keyboard or click the **Insert Rows** icon on the toolbar.

Deleting a field

Click on the row selector of the field to delete.

Press the DELETE key on the keyboard or click the **Delete Rows** icon on the toolbar.

Moving a field

Click on the row selector of the field you wish to move.

Click again and drag to its new position – a black line marks the insertion point.

Changing the primary key field

You can only have one primary key. If you have set the wrong field as the primary key, remove it as follows:

Click on the row selector of the correct field.

Click on **Edit, Primary Key** or click the **Primary Key** icon on the toolbar.

Setting the field properties

When you click on a field in Design View its field properties are displayed in the lower half of the window.

We will go through each field in the Student table and set its Field Property including input masks where appropriate.

Student ID

1   From the Database Window click on **Tables**, select the **Student** table and click on **Design.**

2   The Student ID field should be the one selected. If not, click in the row selector for Student ID.

3 In the Field Properties set **Field Size** to **Long Integer** (it probably already is). See Figure 3.11.

General	Lookup	
Field Size	Long Integer	
New Values	Increment	
Format		
Caption		
Indexed	Yes (No Duplicates)	

Figure 3.11

Title

The Title field can only have the values Mr, Mrs, Miss and Ms. We can use the **Lookup Wizard** whenever we want to restrict the data entered into a field to certain values.

1 Click on the **Title** field name. See Figure 3.12.

	Field Name	Data Type	Description
🔑	Student ID	AutoNumber	Student's ID Number
▶	Title	Text ▼	
	Surname	Text	
	Forename	Memo	
	Address 1	Number	
	Address 2	Date/Time	
	Address 3	Currency	
	Address 4	AutoNumber	
	Tel No	Yes/No	
	Date of Birth	OLE Object	
	Sex	Hyperlink	
	Theory Test Date	Lookup Wizard...	
	Passed Theory Test	Yes/No	
	Practical Test Date	Date/Time	

Figure 3.12

2 In the **Data Type** column click on **Lookup Wizard**. See Figure 3.13.

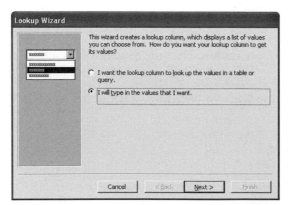

Figure 3.13

3   Click on **'I will type in the values that I want.'** and click on **Next**. See Figure 3.14.

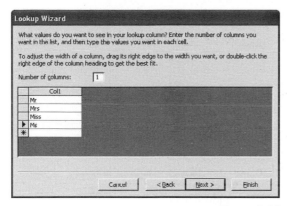

Figure 3.14

4   Enter **Mr, Mrs, Miss** and **Ms** into the column, press TAB to move to the next row. Click on **Next**. See Figure 3.15.

Figure 3.15

5   Click on **Next** and then click on **Finish**.

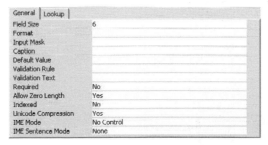

Figure 3.16

6   In the **Field Properties** set the Field Size to 6. See Figure 3.16.

7   If you click on the **Lookup** tab you will see the screen shown in Figure 3.17.

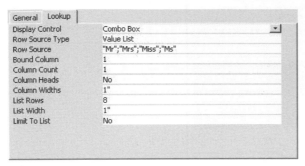

Figure 3.17

When you wish to enter data into this field a combo box (drop-down box) will give you the choice of Mr, Mrs, Miss or Ms.

Surname, Forename, Address 1 and Address 2

1   Select the Field Name: Surname and set the Field Size to 20, repeat for Forename.

2   Select the Field Name: Address 1 and set the Field Size to 30, repeat for Address 2.

Address 3

The Pass-It Driving School is based in Derby. It is likely that students will live in Derby. It will save time if we set the default value for the Address 3 field to Derby.

1   Click on the **Address 3** field.

2   In the **Default Value** box of the Field Properties, enter **Derby**. Access inserts speech marks around the text.

3   Set the Field Size to 20. See Figure 3.18.

General	Lookup	
Field Size	20	
Format		
Input Mask		
Caption		
Default Value	"Derby"	
Validation Rule		
Validation Text		
Required	No	
Allow Zero Length	Yes	
Indexed	No	
Unicode Compression	Yes	
IME Mode	No Control	
IME Sentence Mode	None	

Figure 3.18

Note

More information on Default Values can be found at the end of Unit 4.

Address 4

The **Address 4** field is the student's postcode.

1   Click on the **Address 4** field name.

2   Set the Field Size to 10.

3   Click on the **Format** property box and enter > as shown in Figure 3.19.

This will convert any lower case letters entered into upper case, e.g. de34 2qy will become DE34 2QY. Later you will see how to set an Input Mask to make entering postcodes easier.

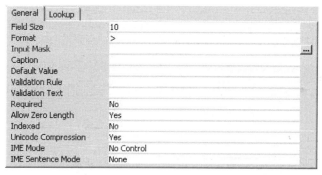

Figure 3.19

Tel No

Select the Field Name: **Tel No** and set the Field Size to 15.

Note

Telephone numbers cannot be a number field as they are likely to include a space, brackets or a preceding zero.

Date of Birth

The student table uses three Date/Time fields. We will use the **Short Date** format for each, e.g. 19/06/94.

1   Select the **Date of Birth** field.

2   Click on the **Format** box in the Field Properties.

3   A drop down list appears. Choose **Short Date**. See Figure 3.20.

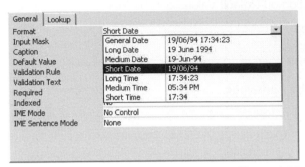

Figure 3.20

It is also possible to use the Input Mask wizard to set a placeholder --/--/-- for each date entered.

4   Click in the **Input Mask** property box and click the three dots icon at the end of the row or the **Build** icon on the **Table Design** toolbar; you will be asked to save your table first. The Input Mask Wizard window is shown as in Figure 3.21.

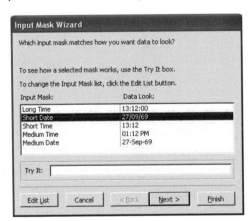

Figure 3.21

5   Select the **Short Date** option and click on **Next**.

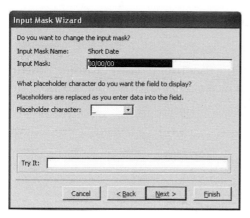

Figure 3.22

6 A choice of placeholders is offered. Click on **Next** and then click on **Finish** (see Figure 3.22).

The field properties are set as shown in Figure 3.23.

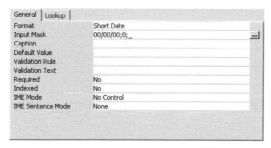

Figure 3.23

7 Repeat this for the other two Date/Time fields, **Theory Test Date** and **Practical Test Date**.

Note   More information on Input Masks can be found at the end of Unit 4.

Sex

The Sex field can only have the values M and F. We can use the Validation Rule box in the Field Properties only to allow M or F.

1 Click on the **Sex** Field Name.

2 In the **Validation Rule** box enter **M or F**.

3   In the **Validation Text** box enter **Sex must be either M or F**.

4   Save your table as **Student**.

This is the error message that will appear if the user tries to enter anything other than M or F into this field. The field properties will appear as shown in Figure 3.24.

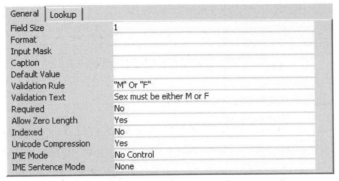

General	Lookup
Field Size	1
Format	
Input Mask	
Caption	
Default Value	
Validation Rule	"M" Or "F"
Validation Text	Sex must be either M or F
Required	No
Allow Zero Length	Yes
Indexed	No
Unicode Compression	Yes
IME Mode	No Control
IME Sentence Mode	None

Figure 3.24

It is of course equally possible to have used the Lookup Wizard for this field property and limit the choices to M or F.

Note   More information on Validation Rules can be found at the end of Unit 4.

Passed Theory Test, Passed Practical Test, Pass Plus Req and Issued Card fields.

All the above fields have already been set to **Yes/No** field types and no further field properties are required.

⊕ Unit 4 Entering the data

In this unit we are going to enter the data into the **Student** table and set up the remaining tables needed to complete the system.

There are two modes for working with tables. So far we have worked in **Design View**.

Design View is used to set up new tables, to edit the structure and to define validation checks and input masks.

To enter new data you have to switch to **Datasheet View**.

In the Database Window select the **Student** table and click **Open** on the toolbar to open the table in **Datasheet View** as shown in Figure 4.1.

Student ID	Title	Surname	Forename	Address 1	Address 2	Address 3	Address 4
(AutoNumber)						Derby	

Figure 4.1

You can switch between modes by selecting **View**, **Design View** from the menu.

Entering data into the Student Table

Enter details of the first student Robert Brammer as given in Figure 4.2. Use TAB or ENTER to move between fields.

Student ID	Title	Surname	Fore-name	Address 1	Address 2	Address 3	Address 4	Tel No	Date of Birth	Sex	Theory Test Date	Passed Theory Test	Practical Test Date	Passed Practical Test	Pass Plus Req	Issued Card
1	Mr	Brammer	Robert	10 Plymouth Drive	Stenson Fields	Derby		DE28 9LO	01332 885304	27/7/83	M	12/05/02	Yes	12/06/02	Yes	No	No

Figure 4.2

You will notice a number of features as you enter the data.

○ The Student ID which is an AutoNumber field, is entered automatically.
○ The Title field has a drop-down box set up by the lookup table wizard (see Figure 4.3).

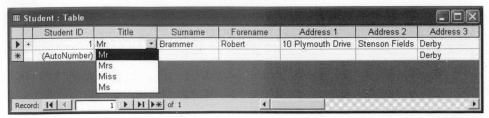

Figure 4.3

○ Data entered into the Sex field is validated and any invalid entries rejected (see Figure 4.4).

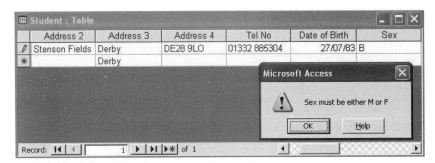

Figure 4.4

○ Placeholders appear in the fields where you have set input masks to make data entry easier.
○ Enter data into Yes/No fields by ticking the check box for Yes and leaving unchecked for No (see Figure 4.5).

Student ID	Title	Surname	Forename	Passed Theory Test	Practical Test Date
1	Mr	Brammer	Robert	☑	12/06/02
2	Mr	Jenkins	Steven	☑	15/12/02

Record: ◀◀ ◀ | 1 | ▶ ▶▶ ▶※ of 10

Figure 4.5

○ When you have entered the last field in a record a blank record appears underneath to enter the next record. Don't worry if your table finishes with a blank record. Microsoft Access will ignore it.
○ When a new record is created, the Address 3 field is set to Derby. This can still be edited.
○ Data is saved as soon as it is entered. Adjust the column widths by dragging out the column dividers.
○ Navigation buttons appear at the bottom of the screen allowing you to scroll through the records (see Figure 4.6).

Figure 4.6

Useful keys for entering data

KEY	ACTION
TAB key, ENTER or right arrow	Move to next field
SHIFT + TAB key or left arrow	Move to previous field
Down arrow	Move to next record
Up arrow	Move to previous record
HOME	Move to start of field
END	Move to end of field

Undo

Press ESC to quit editing a record.

Use the **Undo** icon to undo the last action.

Deleting records

To delete a record, click on the record selector and press DELETE.

Complete the **Student** table by entering the data as shown in Figure 4.7. Remember to save frequently.

Student ID	Title	Surname	Fore-name	Address 1	Address 2	Address 3	Address 4	Tel No	Date of Birth	Sex	Theory Test Date	Passed Theory Test	Practical Test Date	Passed Practical Test	Pass Plus Req	Issued Card
1	Mr	Brammer	Robert	10 Plymouth Drive	Stenson Fields	Derby	DE28 9LO	01332 885304	27/7/83	M	12/05/02	Yes	12/06/02	Yes	No	No
2	Mr	Jenkins	Steven	37 Woodfield Close	Etwall	Derby	DE49 5PQ	01283 539264	14/05/83	M	14/05/02	Yes	15/12/02	No	No	No
3	Miss	Fowler	Sarah	19 Sea View Road	Mickleover	Derby	DE34 8NT	01332 293751	05/06/84	F	12/04/02	Yes	05/08/02	Yes	No	No
4	Mr	Beswood	Michael	25 Lundie Close	Allestree	Derby	DE45 5AF	01332 752410	15/02/84	M	22/07/02	Yes	24/10/02	No	No	Yes
5	Miss	Williams	Charlotte	21 Church Street	Littleover	Derby	DE33 8RD	01332 293184	30/03/83	F	23/06/02	Yes	17/12/02	No	Yes	Yes
6	Mr	Windsor	David	86 Milford Road	Allenton	Derby	DE5 4PT	01332 389144	18/04/84	M	02/07/02	Yes	31/10/02	No	No	Yes
7	Mrs	Trueman	Mary	156 Station Road	Allestree	Derby	DE45 9HS	01332 347810	27/10/83	F	07/02/02	Yes	28/09/02	No	No	Yes
8	Ms	Spencer	Victoria	73 Mayfield Road	Stenson Fields	Derby	DE28 9VB	01332 832024	20/12/82	F	16/08/02	Yes	03/10/02	No	No	Yes
9	Mr	Watson	Greg	7 Derwent Close	Etwall	Derby	DE49 8HU	01283 552594	17/06/83	M	21/06/02	Yes	21/12/02	No	Yes	Yes
10	Ms	Jones	Lucy	183 Uttoxeter Road	Allenton	Derby	DE5 2CN	01332 668228	28/05/84	F	31/03/02	Yes	10/09/02	No	Yes	Yes

Figure 4.7

Closing the table

When you have finished entering the data, close the table by clicking on the **Close** icon (see Figure 4.8). You will return to the Database Window with the name of the table highlighted.

Address 3	Address 4	
Derby	DE28 9LO	Close
Derby	DE49 5PQ	

Figure 4.8

Setting up the Instructor table

You now need to set up a second table called **Instructor** to store the details of the instructors. Set it up with the structure as shown in Figure 4.9.

FIELD NAME	DATA TYPE	OTHER INFORMATION
Instructor ID	AutoNumber	Set as Primary Key field
Title	Text	Lookup table values Mr, Mrs, Ms, Miss Field Size 6
Surname	Text	Field Size 20
Forename	Text	Field Size 20
Address 1	Text	Field Size 30
Address 2	Text	Field Size 30
Address 3	Text	Default value = 'Derby' Field Size 20
Address 4	Text	Field Size 10 and set Format to >
Home Tel No	Text	Field Size 15
Mobile No	Text	Field Size 15

Figure 4.9

Save the table as **Instructor** and switch to **Datasheet View** mode to enter this data (see Figure 4.10).

Instructor ID	Title	Surname	Forename	Address 1	Address 2	Address 3	Address 4	Home Tel No	Mobile No
1	Mr	Jones	Doug	57 Swanmore Road	Etwall	Derby	DE65 6LU	01283 122541	07720 521478
2	Mr	Batchelor	Arnold	13 Gairloch Close	Etwall	Derby	DE34 5FG	01283 552147	07980 352145
3	Mr	Smith	Andrew	5b Sunrise Road	Littleover	Derby	DE45 4ED	01332 521452	07980 525214

Figure 4.10

Setting up the Lesson Type table

The third table will be the **Lesson Type** table, storing details of the lessons and the cost of each lesson. The structure is shown in Figure 4.11.

FIELD NAME	DATA TYPE	OTHER INFORMATION
Lesson Type	Text	Set as Primary Key field Field Size 25
Cost	Currency	

Figure 4.11

Save the table as **Lesson Type** and enter the data as shown in Figure 4.12.

LESSON TYPE	COST
Introductory	£12.00
Pass Plus	£17.00
Standard	£15.00
Test	£25.00

Figure 4.12

The Lesson table

The fourth table will be the **Lesson** table. This is the table that links all the other tables together and stores details of lessons booked with the driving school. It is shown in Figure 4.13.

FIELD NAME	DATA TYPE	OTHER INFORMATION
Lesson No	AutoNumber	Set as Primary Key field
Student ID	Number	Long Integer
Instructor ID	Number	Long Integer
Date	Date/Time	Format: Short Date and set Input Mask
Start Time	Date/Time	Format: Short Time and set Input Mask
Length of Lesson	Number	Integer and set validation rule as 'Between 1 and 8'
Collection Point	Text	Default value = 'Home Address' Field Size 30
Drop-Off Point	Text	Default value = 'Home Address' Field Size 30
Lesson Type	Text	Lookup table values (see below): Introductory, Standard, Pass Plus, Test Field Size 25

Figure 4.13

Note

When you run the Lookup Wizard choose to type the values in, but you could look up the values from the table Lesson Type.

Save the table as **Lesson** and enter the data as shown in Figure 4.14.

Lesson No	Student ID	Instructor ID	Date	Start Time	Length of Lesson	Collection Point	Drop-Off Point	Lesson Type
1	1	1	30/07/02	08:00	1	Home Address	City Centre	Standard
2	2	1	30/07/02	09:00	2	Derby Station	Home Address	Standard
3	2	2	31/07/02	12:00	1	Home Address	Home Address	Introductory
4	3	1	31/07/02	13:00	2	John Port School	Home Address	Standard
5	4	3	01/08/02	18:00	1	Home Address	Home Address	Test
6	5	1	31/07/02	08:00	1	Home Address	Home Address	Introductory
7	6	2	30/07/02	12:00	1	Home Address	Home Address	Standard
8	7	1	30/07/02	11:00	1	Home Address	Home Address	Standard
9	8	1	30/07/02	12:00	3	Home Address	Home Address	Standard
10	1	1	31/07/02	11:00	1	Home Address	Home Address	Standard
11	9	2	02/08/02	10:00	1	Home Address	Home Address	Standard

Figure 4.14

We do not need to store the name of the student or the name of the instructor in the Lesson table. These are already stored elsewhere. The next unit shows you how to link these tables together.

Further information on setting up tables

This section provides a little more detail on a number of the functions you met during setting up the Student table. In particular:

- Data types;
- Field properties;
- Input Masks;
- Format field properties;
- Default field properties;
- Validation Rules.

Data types

Access has different data types available to store different kinds of data. They are shown in Table 4.1.

DATA TYPE	MEANING
Text	This is the default setting. Used for shorter text entries. Can be a combination of text, numbers, spaces and symbols. Maximum length 255 characters but you can set it to fewer using the Field Size property.
Memo	Used for longer text entries. Maximum length 65,535 characters!
Number	Used to store numeric data.
Date/Time	This stores a date or a time or a date and the time. There are several formats for a date/time field.
Currency	Monetary values. Normally in the UK this will be set to pounds and work to two decimal places.
AutoNumber	An AutoNumber field will number records automatically as you enter more data. The field acts as a counter. Duplicates are avoided and so AutoNumber fields are ideal as the key field. An AutoNumber cannot be edited and when an AutoNumber record is deleted Access does not allow you to go back and reuse this number.
Yes/No	Only allows logical values such as Yes/No, True/False.
OLE Object	An object linked to or embedded in a Microsoft Access table. This might be an image or a sound or a file created in another package such as Microsoft Excel or Microsoft Word.
Hyperlink	A hyperlink address. This can be linked to: 1. An object in your Access file, e.g. another table. 2. Another locally stored file. 3. A web page. 4. An e-mail address.
Lookup Wizard	This data type creates a lookup table so that you can choose a value from a drop-down box.

Table 4.1

Field properties

Table 4.2 describes the range of field properties:

PROPERTY	DESCRIPTION
Field Size	This is used to fix the maximum length of a text field. The default value is 50 characters. The maximum length is 255.
Format	This fixes how data can be displayed, for example dates can be displayed in many different forms such as 13/01/01 or 13 Jan 01 or 13 January 2001.
Input Mask	This sets a pattern for the data to be entered into this field.
Caption	This is the field label in a form or report. You are not likely to need to use this property.
Default Value	This is the value entered into the field when the record is created. It is usually left blank but can be very powerful.
Validation Rule	This defines the data entry rules.
Validation Text	This is the error message if data is invalid.
Required	This indicates whether an entry must be made or not. If an entry is required, it is best not to set this property until the database is fully working.
Indexed	This allows data to be stored in the order of this field, which speeds up searches.
Allow Zero Length	This is used with text fields to decide whether records in that field are allowed to contain zero length or empty text strings
Unicode Compression	This is a method of compressing the data entered in this field.
IME Mode	Input Method Editor, which allows special character input.
IME Sentence Mode	Allows special character input.

Table 4.2

Setting input masks

Input masks make data entry easier. They display on screen a pattern for the data to be entered into a field.

For example you maybe given the prompt --/--/-- to enter the date.

They are suitable for data that always has the same pattern such as dates, times, currency and also for codes like National Insurance numbers, stock numbers or postcodes.

Characters for input masks you are likely to use are as follows:

0	A number (0–9) must be entered
9	A number (0–9) may be entered
#	A number, + or – sign or space may be entered
L	A letter A–Z must be entered
?	A letter A–Z may be entered
A	A letter or digit must be entered
a	A letter or digit may be entered
C	Any character or space may be entered
&	Any character or space must be entered
<	All characters to the right are changed to lower case
>	All characters to the right are changed to upper case

Examples of input masks

A **National Insurance number** in the UK must be of the form **AB123456C**. All letters are in capitals. Its input mask would be >**LL000000L** (it must be two letters followed by six numbers and one letter).

A **postcode** consists of one or two letters, then one or two numbers, then a space, a number and two letters. All the letters must be capital letters. Examples are **B1 1BB** or **DE13 0LL**. The input mask would be >**L?09 0LL**.

Car registration numbers such as W125 HGS could have >**L000 LLL** as an input mask. For new registrations of the form FN03 ANJ the input mask would be >**LL00 LLL**.

A **driving licence no.** of the form BESWO150282 MB9BM could have >**LLLLL#000000#LL0LL** as an input mask.

For **product codes** of the format A2C-123-4567, a possible input mask might be **AAA-000-0000**.

Input masks are very powerful and need a lot of thought. It is possible to use the Input Mask Wizard to set up an input mask for a field. At this stage you may wish to ignore input masks unless you know the exact format of the input data.

The Format field property

The formats supplied with Access will suit practically all your needs. However it is possible to set a custom format of your own. Two commonly used examples follow:

>   will change text entered in the field to upper case
<   will change text entered in the field to lower case

> **Note** There is a significant difference between the Format and Input Mask field property. The Format property affects the data in the field after it is entered, e.g. if you enter 14/07/99 into a Long Date format field, it will appear as 14th July 1999.

The Input Mask property controls and restricts data entry. An Input Mask set to --/--/-- will only accept dates in the format 14/07/99.

The default field property

Default values are added automatically when you add a new record. For example in a table of names and addresses you might set the County field to Derbyshire. Derbyshire then appears automatically each time a new record is added and the user can either leave it or change it to something else.

You can also use expressions in this field property. Typically =**Date**() will return the current date from your PC.

In a Library Book Loaning system, the default value for the **Date of Loan** field could be set to =**Date**() and, similarly, for the **Date of Return** the default value could be set to =**Date**()+**14** (assuming a 14-day loan period).

Setting validation rules

Validation rules allow you to control the values that can be entered into a field.

By setting the validation text property you can choose the message that is displayed if the validation rule is broken.

You set up a validation rule by typing an expression into the field properties (see Figure 4.15).

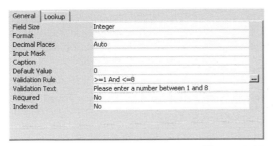

Figure 4.15

In the example above the user will be forced to only enter numbers between (and including) 1 and 8.

If they do not the Validation Text message is displayed as shown in Figure 4.16.

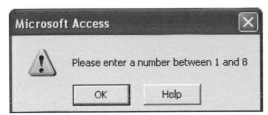

Figure 4.16

A number of comparison operators are available in Access. See Tables 4.3 and 4.4.

OPERATOR	MEANING
<	Less than
<=	Less than or equal to
>	Greater than
>=	Greater than or equal to
=	Equal to
<>	Not equal to
IN	Test for 'equal to' any item in a list
BETWEEN	Test for a range of values; the two values separated by the AND operator
LIKE	Tests a Text or Memo field to match a pattern string of characters

Table 4.3

The development of a system

EXAMPLES OF VALIDATION RULE SETTINGS	POSSIBLE VALIDATION TEXT
>8000	Please enter a salary greater than £8000
<#01/01/01#	You must enter dates before January 1st 2001
>Date()	The date returned must be after today's date!
'S' or 'M' or 'L'	Sizes can only be S, M or L
Between 0 and 36	Goals scored cannot be greater than 36!
Like 'A????'	Code must be five characters beginning with A
<20	Age of student must be less than 20
IN('A','B','C')	Grades must be A, B or C

Table 4.4

⊕ Unit 5 Defining the relationships

In this section we will define and create the relationships linking the four tables.

The links that need setting up are shown in Figure 5.1.

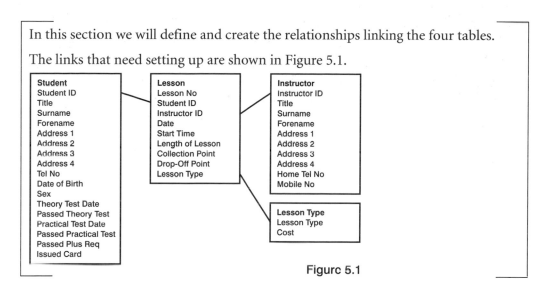

Figurc 5.1

Adding the tables

1   In the Database Window open the **Relationships** window by any of these three methods.

   ○ Right click anywhere in the window and select **Relationships**.
   ○ Click on the **Relationships** icon on the **Database** toolbar if showing (see Figure 5.2).
   ○ Click on **Tools, Relationships** from the menu bar.

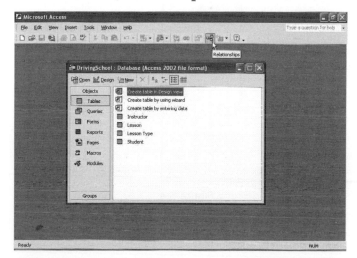

Figure 5.2

If it is the first time you've established a relationship then the Show Table dialogue box will appear (see Figure 5.3).

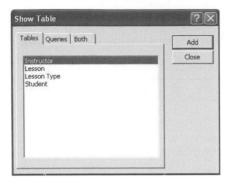

Figure 5.3

Note

If the Show Table window is not present display it by clicking on **Relationships, Show Table** from the menu or click on the **Show Table** icon.

2   Click on the **Instructor** table and click on **Add**.

3   Add the other three tables and then **Close** the window.

4   In the **Relationships** window rearrange the position of the tables by dragging and resizing the table windows (see Figure 5.4).

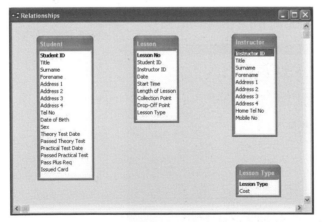

Figure 5.4

Setting the links

1   Click on **Instructor ID** in the **Instructor** table.

2   Drag it on top of **Instructor ID** in the **Lesson** table and let go. The **Edit Relationships** dialogue box appears (see Figure 5.5).

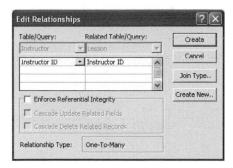

Figure 5.5

3   Check the **Enforce Referential Integrity** box and then check the **Cascade Delete Related Records** box. Click on **Create**.

A link called the **Relationship Line** is set up between the two tables.

4   Click on the **Student ID** field in the **Student** table and drag it on top of the **Student ID** field in the **Lesson** table.

5   Check the **Enforce Referential Integrity** box and then check the **Cascade Delete Related Records** box. Click on **Create**.

6   Repeat the process for the **Lesson Type** field, dragging it from the **Lesson Type** table to the **Lesson** table and check **Enforce Referential Integrity** and **Cascade Delete Related Records**.

The Relationship window should now look like Figure 5.6.

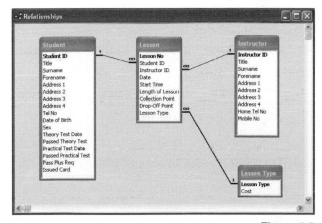

Figure 5.6

The number 1 and the infinity symbol mean that all three relationships are one-to-many. A **Student ID** can appear only **one** time in the **Student** table as it is a unique ID. However a **Student ID** can appear **many** times in the **Lesson** table as the student will need many lessons.

Similarly the **Instructor ID** can only appear once in the **Instructor** table but many times in the **Lesson** table. The **Lesson Type** can appear only once in the **Lesson Type** table but many times in the **Lesson** table.

7   Save your layout by clicking **File, Save** from the menu and confirming the option as shown in Figure 5.7.

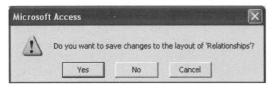

Figure 5.7

Note

As a rule the field you use to create a relationship must be of the same type. However when you create a relationship between tables using an AutoNumber field, the related field must be Numeric and set to Long Integer.

Referential integrity

Referential integrity is a system of rules that Microsoft Access uses to ensure that relationships between records in related tables are valid and that you don't accidentally delete or change related data.

For example with Referential Integrity set you would not be able to book a lesson for a Student ID 46 as no student with ID number 46 appears in the Student table. Similarly you could not book a lesson for an instructor who was not present in the Instructor table.

Cascading Updates and Deletes

Cascading Updates and Deletes affect what Access does with the data when you update or delete a record in a table that is related to other records in other tables.

If Cascade Delete is set, then when you delete a record in the Primary table all related data in other tables is deleted. For example if a student is deleted from the Student table then all related records for that student in the Lesson table would also be deleted.

Note

We have checked Cascade Delete at this point in the development of the system, as we will need it later in the units.

Deleting relationships

If you wish to delete a relationship:

1 Open the Relationship window as before.

2 Click on the Relationship Line of the relationship you wish to delete and press the DELETE key. Alternatively you can right click on it and choose delete.

If you wish to delete a field that contains a relationship, you will have to delete the relationship first.

Editing relationships

You can edit relationships by going to the Relationship window and double clicking on the Relationship Line of the relationship you wish to edit.

⊕ Unit 6 Select queries

In the previous units you set up tables to store information about the students, instructors and lesson bookings in the Pass-It Driving school.

In this section you will use queries to search and sort the data in your tables according to certain criteria. Queries provide an easy way of asking questions of your database and producing useful information.

For example we might want to:

○ find details of lessons booked on a given date;
○ find contact details for a student whose lesson needs to be cancelled;
○ view details of instructors' names and addresses.

There are a number of different types of query available in Access:

○ Select Query
○ Parameter Query
○ Multi-Table Query
○ Action Query
○ Crosstab Query

We will start by taking you through basic select and parameter queries progressing to a query involving more than one table. You will meet the other query types as you work through the units.

As with many other parts of Microsoft Access, there is a wizard to help you design simple queries. We shall first look at setting up a query without the wizard.

Query 1 Finding details of lessons booked on a given day

There are usually five steps involved in planning a query:

○ choosing which tables to use;
○ choosing the fields needed in your query;
○ setting the criteria to produce the output required;
○ running the query;
○ saving and/or printing the results.

1   Load the **DrivingSchool** database.

2   In the Database Window click on **Queries** and select **New** (see Figure 6.1).

Figure 6.1

3   In the **New Query** window select **Design View** and click on **OK** (see Figure 6.2).

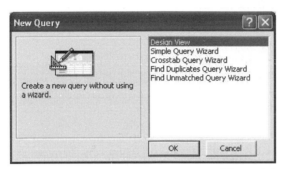

Figure 6.2

4   In the **Show Table** window select the table **Lesson**, click on **Add** and then **Close**
the window (see Figure 6.3).

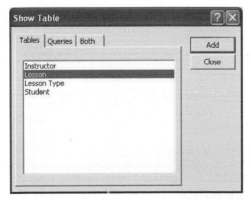

Figure 6.3

The **Query Design View** window is now shown.

The window is in two sections. The upper section contains the field list for the table used in the query and the lower section contains the QBE (Query by Example) grid where you design the query. Primarily it consists of five rows (see Figure 6.4).

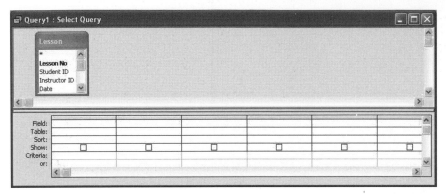

Figure 6.4

Field	Contains the names of the fields needed for your query.
Table	Holds the name of the table containing the selected field.
Sort	Offers ascending, descending sort options.
Show	Allows you to hide fields from the output.
Criteria	This is where you enter the criteria for your search.

You can maximise the window and use the scroll bars in the usual way. You can resize the upper/lower panes by dragging the dividing line between them up or down.

5   If the Query Design toolbar is not showing, click on **View**, **Toolbars**, **Query Design** (see Figure 6.5).

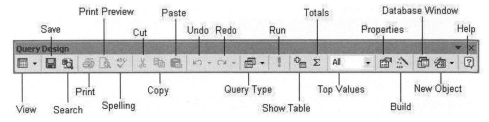

Figure 6.5

The next stage is to select the fields needed in our query.

6   Double click on **Lesson No** in the **Lesson** table field list. Then double click on each of the next five fields in turn: **Student ID, Instructor ID, Date, Start Time, Length of Lesson**. The fieldnames will appear in the grid as shown in Figure 6.6.

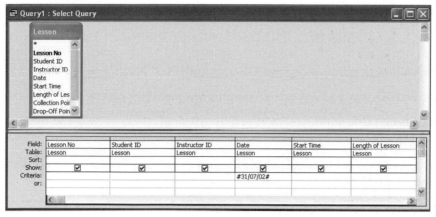

Figure 6.6

7   Now select the criteria by entering **31/07/02** in the criteria row of the fourth (Date) column of the QBE grid. Access surrounds the data with a #.

If you have added a field by mistake, click at the top of the column in the QBE grid to select the column and then press DELETE.

8   To run your query click on the **Datasheet View** icon, the **Run Query** icon or choose from the menu **Query, Run**. There should be four lessons (see Figure 6.7).

Lesson No	Student ID	Instructor ID	Date	Start Time	Length of Lesson
3	2	2	31/07/02	12:00	1
4	3	1	31/07/02	13:00	2
6	5	1	31/07/02	08:00	1
10	1	1	31/07/02	11:00	1

Record: 14 ◄ | 1 ► ►I ►¥ | of 4

Figure 6.7

9   Once the Query has been run it can be printed using **File, Print**.

10   Save the query as **Lessons 31 July Query** by clicking on the save icon on the toolbar.

Selecting fields in Query Design View

There are a number of other ways of selecting a field from the Field list in the Query Design window. You need to select the one that suits you best.

o   In each field cell on the grid is a drop down list from which fields can be chosen.
o   Double click on the title bar in the Field List table. This highlights all the field names. Click on any one (not the *) and drag them to the field cell on the grid. On releasing the mouse button all fields will be entered into the grid.
o   Highlight the field in the Field List table and drag it to the field cell on the grid.

Query 2 Finding the contact details for a student, e.g. student named Watson

1   In the Database Window click on **Queries** and select **New**.

2   In the **New Query** window select **Design View** and click on **OK**.

3   In the **Show Table** window select the table **Student**, click on **Add** and then **Close** the window.

The next stage is to select the fields needed in our query. We will add them to the QBE grid by dragging and dropping each field.

4   Select **Student ID** in the **Student** table and drag it to the field cell.

5   Drag and drop the fields **Surname, Forename** and **Tel No** in the same way. The fieldnames will appear in the grid as below (see Figure 6.8).

6   Now select the criteria by entering **Watson** in the criteria row of the **Surname** column. Access puts in the quotation marks.

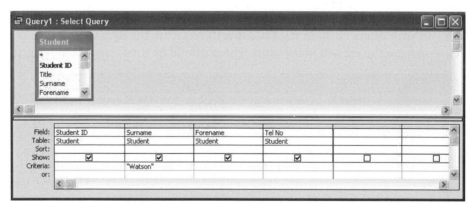

Figure 6.8

7   To run your query click on the **Datasheet View** icon, the **Run Query** icon or, from the menu, select **Query, Run**. The details are shown below (see Figure 6.9).

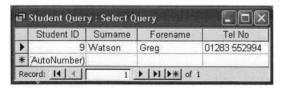

Figure 6.9

8   Save your query as **Search for Student Query**.

Some further hints

Adding and removing tables

○ To remove a table from the Query Design grid, double click the title bar of the field list box and press DELETE.

○ To add a table to the Query Design grid click on the **Show Table** icon or select from the menu, **Query, Show Table** and add the tables required.

○ To clear the QBE grid from the menu select **Edit, Clear Grid**.

Renaming the field headings

You can give a different name to the column titles in the query grid.

In the field row, click the start of the field name, type in the new name followed by a colon, e.g. **Telephone number: Tel No.**

Changing the order of the fields chosen

Click the field selector at the top of the column.

Drag the field to the new location (see Figure 6.10).

Figure 6.10

As you drag the field a solid bar appears showing where the relocated field will appear.

Deleting a query

Queries that are only used once are not really worth saving.

In the Database Window select the query to delete and press the DELETE key.

Query 3   Producing a list of instructors' names and addresses

We will use the Query Wizard to design the next query.

1   In the Database Window click on **Queries** and select **New**.

2   In the **New Query** window select **Simple Query Wizard** and click on **OK**.

| The development of a system |

The Simple Query Wizard dialogue box is displayed.

3   Select the table **Instructor** from the Tables/Queries drop-down list.

4   Select the field **Instructor ID** in the Available Fields and click the right arrow >.

5   Repeat this process for the fields **Surname, Forename, Address 1, Address 2, Address 3**, and **Address 4** as shown below (see Figure 6.11).

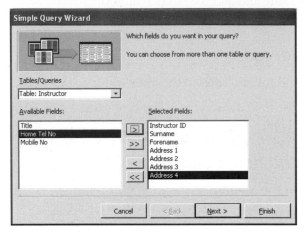

Figure 6.11

6   Click on **Next,** name the query **Instructor Addresses Query** and click on **Finish** (see Figure 6.12).

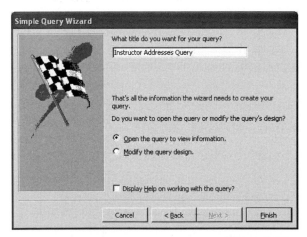

Figure 6.12

The resulting query opens in Datasheet View as shown in Figure 6.13, giving the details of the Instructors' names and addresses.

Figure 6.13

From the menu you can now select **View, Design View** to show the QBE grid (see Figure 6.14) and refine your query if needed. For example, click on the drop-down list in the Sort cell of the Surname field to choose either ascending or descending sort order.

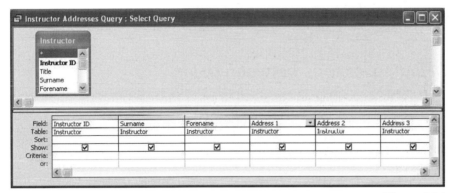

Figure 6.14

⊕ Unit 7 Further queries

Unit 6 introduced you to simple **Select** queries and the Query Design window. In this unit you will be shown how to take **Select** queries further and introduced to **Parameter** queries.

Selecting records in ranges

Suppose we wish to view lessons between certain dates or print a list of lessons for the coming week.

You can select a range of records using the operators <, >, <=, >=, +, –, BETWEEN, AND and NOT.

Query 1 Finding lessons between dates

1   In the Database Window click on **Queries** and select **New**.

2   In the **New Query** window select **Design View** and click on **OK**.

3   In the **Show Table** window select the table **Lesson**, click on **Add** and then **Close** the window.

4   Add the fields **Lesson No, Student ID, Instructor ID, Date** and **Collection Point**.

5   In the criteria row of the **Date** column enter >**30/07/02 And** <**02/08/02** as shown in Figure 7.1.

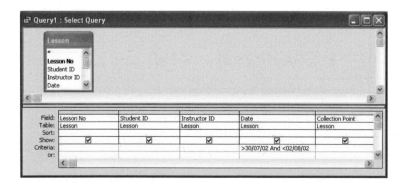

Figure 7.1

6   Run the query to view the records and then save the query as **Dates Query** (see Figure 7.2).

Query1 : Select Query				
Lesson No	Student ID	Instructor ID	Date	Collection Point
3	2	2	31/07/02	Home Address
4	3	1	31/07/02	John Port School
5	4	3	01/08/02	Home Address
6	5	1	31/07/02	Home Address
10	1	1	31/07/02	Home Address

Record: 1 of 5

Figure 7.2

Note   This query could also have been designed by entering the expression **Between 31/07/02 and 01/08/02** in the criteria row of the **Date** field cell. The expression includes the stated dates.

Using multiple criteria

It is possible to specify criteria in more than one field. For example you may want to see details of a specific instructor's lessons on a certain date. This is sometimes known as an AND search because it involves the Instructor ID field and the Date field.

Query 2   Finding lessons for an instructor on a given date

1   In the Database Window click on **Queries** and select **New**.

2   In the **New Query** window select **Design View** and click on **OK**.

3   In the **Show Table** window select the table **Lesson**, click on **Add** and then **Close** the window.

4   Add the fields **Student ID, Instructor ID, Date, Start Time, Collection Point** and **Lesson Type** (see Figure 7.3).

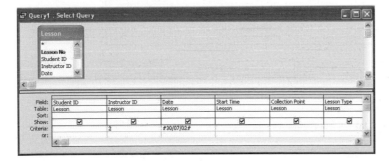

Figure 7.3

5 In the criteria row of the **Instructor ID** column enter **2** and enter **30/07/02** in the criteria cell for **Date**.

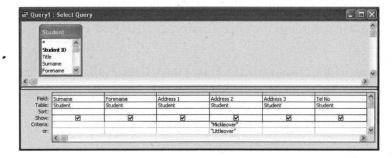

Figure 7.4

6 Run the query to view the records shown in Figure 7.4. Save your query as **And Query**.

You may wish to look for records which meet one criterion OR another. For example you may wish to view students who live in one area or another. This is sometimes known as an OR search.

1 In the Database Window click on **Queries** and select **New**.

2 In the **New Query** window select **Design View** and click on **OK**.

3 In the **Show Table** window select the table **Student**, click on **Add** and then **Close** the window.

4 Add the fields **Surname**, **Forename**, **Address 1**, **Address 2**, **Address 3** and **Tel No** as shown in Figure 7.5.

5 In the criteria row of the **Address 2** column enter **Mickleover** and enter **Littleover** in the row below.

Figure 7.5

6 Run the query to view the records and then save as **Or Query** (see Figure 7.6).

Surname	Forename	Address 1	Address 2	Address 3	Tel No
Fowler	Sarah	19 Sea View Road	Mickleover	Derby	01332235751
Williams	Charlotte	21 Church Street	Littleover	Derby	01332293184
				Derby	

Record: 1 of 2

Figure 7.6

Using the Date() function

You will often want to search for records with the current date. For example, you may want to view today's lessons at the driving school. You can do this using your computer's system clock and the Date function.

Query 3 Finding today's lessons

1 In the Database Window click on **Queries** and select **New**.

2 In the **New Query** window select **Design View** and click on **OK**.

3 In the **Show Table** window select the table **Lesson**, click on **Add** and then **Close** the window.

4 Add the fields **Lesson No, Student ID, Instructor ID, Date** and **Start Time** as shown in Figure 7.7.

5 In the criteria row of the **Date** column enter **=Date()**.

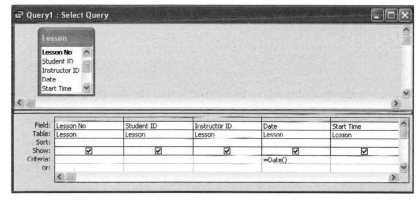

Figure 7.7

6 Run the query to view the records and save it as **Today's Lessons Query**.

Note To run this query you will have to change some of the lessons in the lesson table to the current date·

The date function is a powerful tool in query work and will form the basis of a number of queries later in the units.

Parameter queries

All the queries so far have been select queries. **Select queries** are not very useful if you have to run the query frequently and use different criteria each time.

Parameter queries overcome this problem by allowing you to enter the criteria each time the query is run.

On running the query a dialogue box will appear asking you to enter the details (see Figure 7.8).

Figure 7.8

In the example shown you would enter the date and the records matching the criteria shown would be displayed.

Query 4   Looking up a student's details

1   Load the **DrivingSchool** database.

2   In the Database Window click on **Queries** and select **New**.

3   In the **New Query** window select **Design View** and click on **OK**.

4   In the **Show Table** window select the table **Student**, click on **Add** and then **Close** the window.

5   Select **Student ID** in the **Student** Table and drag it on to the QBE grid.

6   Drag and drop the fields **Surname, Forename, Address 1, Address 2, Address 3, Address 4, Tel No, Date of Birth** and **Sex** in the same way. The fieldnames will appear as in Figure 7.9.

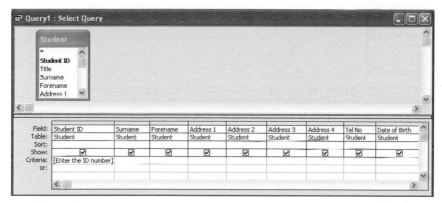

Figure 7.9

7   In the criteria cell for the **Student ID** field type in [**Enter the ID number**]. The square brackets are required.

8   Run the query and enter **2** in the dialogue box as shown in Figure 7.10.

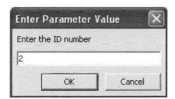

Figure 7.10

9   The query will display the details of Student number 2. Save your query as **Search by Student ID Query**.

Query 5   Looking up a student's lessons

1   In the Database Window click on **Queries** and select **New**.

2   In the **New Query** window select **Design View** and click on **OK**.

3   In the **Show Table** window select the table **Lesson**, click on **Add** and then **Close** the window.

4   Select **Student ID** in the **Lesson** table and drag it on to the field cell (see Figure 7.11).

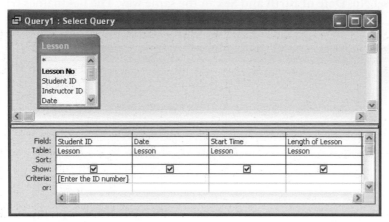

Figure 7.11

5   Drag and drop the fields **Date**, **Start Time** and **Length of Lesson** in the same way. The fieldnames will appear in the grid as in Figure 7.11.

6   In the criteria cell for the **Student ID** field type in [**Enter the ID number**]. The square brackets are required.

7   Run the query and enter **2** in the dialogue box as shown in Figure 7.12.

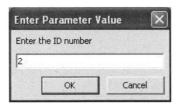

Figure 7.12

The query will display the lessons for Student number 2. Save your query as **Student Lesson Query**.

Query 6   Searching for lessons on any date

1   In the Database Window click on **Queries** and select **New**.

2   In the **New Query** window select **Design View** and click on **OK**.

3   In the **Show Table** window select the table **Lesson**, click on **Add** and then **Close** the window.

4   Add the fields to the QBE grid as shown in Figure 7.13.

5 In the criteria row of the **Date** column type in [**Please enter the Date**]. The square brackets here are vital.

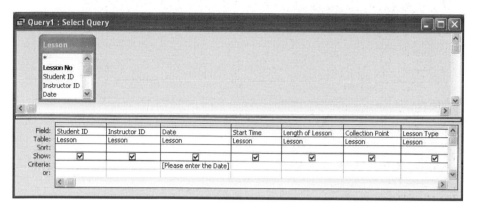

Figure 7.13

6 Run the query and enter **02/08/02** in the dialogue box (see Figure 7.14).

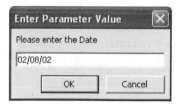

Figure 7.14

7 The result of the query is shown in Figure 7.15. Save your query as **Search on Lesson Date Query**.

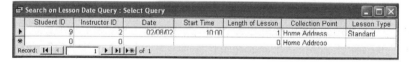

Figure 7.15

Query 7   Searching for an instructor's lessons by date

1 In the Database Window click on **Queries** and select **New**.

2 In the **New Query** window select **Design View** and click on **OK**.

3 In the **Show Table** window select the table **Lesson**, click on **Add** and then **Close** the window.

4   Add all the fields to the grid by double clicking the title bar of the **Field List** table and dragging the highlighted fields to the field cell (see Figure 7.16).

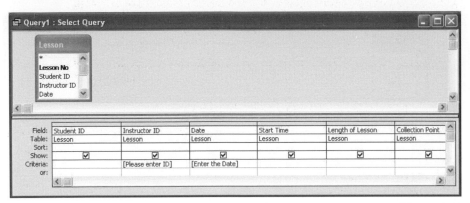

Figure 7.16

5   Remove fields **Lesson No**, **Drop-off Point** and **Lesson Type** by clicking the column selector and selecting from the menu **Edit**, **Delete Columns**.

6   In the criteria cell for the field **Instructor ID** type in [**Please enter ID**].

7   In the criteria cell for the field **Date** type in [**Enter the Date**].

8   Run the query and enter **1** for the **Instructor ID** (see Figure 7.17).

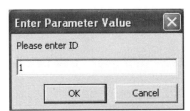

Figure 7.17

9   Enter **30/07/02** for the date (see Figure 7.18).

Figure 7.18

10 The result of the query is shown in Figure 7.19.

Student ID	Instructor ID	Date	Start Time	Length of Lesson	Collection Point
1	1	30/07/02	08:00	1	Home Address
2	1	30/07/02	09:00	2	Derby Station
7	1	30/07/02	11:00	1	Home Address
8	1	30/07/02	12:00	3	Home Address

Record: 1 of 4

Figure 7.19

11 Save your query as **Instructor Lessons by Date Query**.

The following queries set up in Units 6 and 7 were only for demonstration purposes:

○ **Lessons 31 July Query;**
○ **Search for Student Query;**
○ **Instructor Addresses Query;**
○ **Dates Query;**
○ **And Query;**
○ **Or Query.**

They are not needed as part of the Pass-It Driving School System. It is a good idea to go to the Database Window and delete them now.

⊕ Unit 8 Setting up multi-table queries

In Units 3 and 4 you designed four tables: Student, Instructor, Lesson and Lesson Type. You later learned how to set up relationships between those tables.

For example, when you book a lesson you do not want to have to key in the student's name and address every time when it is stored in the student table.

In this section you will see how to base your queries on more than one table and start to use the relationships you have set up. In addition you will see how you can use queries to do calculations.

Lesson No	Student ID	Instructor ID	Date	Start Time	Length of Lesson
3	2	2	31/07/02	12:00	1
4	3	1	31/07/02	13:00	2
6	5	1	31/07/02	08:00	1
10	1	1	31/07/02	11:00	1

Record: 1 of 4

Figure 8.1

At the start of Unit 6 you set up a query called **Lesson 31 July Query** to output the lessons booked on a given date.

The output is shown in Figure 8.1 based on the **Lesson** table. If we wanted the output to include the students' names we would have to base the query on the **Lesson** table (which stores the details of the lessons, dates and ID numbers) and the **Student** table (where the students' names are stored).

Query 1   To produce a list of lessons together with student names

1   Load the **DrivingSchool** database.

2   In the Database Window click on **Queries** and select **New**.

3   In the **New Query** window select **Design View** and click on **OK** (see Figure 8.2).

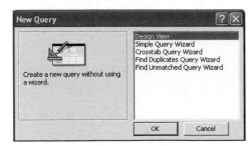

New Query

Design View
Simple Query Wizard
Crosstab Query Wizard
Find Duplicates Query Wizard
Find Unmatched Query Wizard

Create a new query without using a wizard.

OK   Cancel

Figure 8.2

4   In the **Show Table** window select the table **Lesson** and click on **Add** (see Figure 8.3).

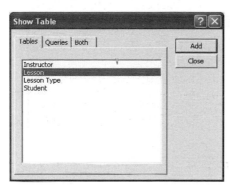

Figure 8.3

5   Select the table **Student**, click on **Add** and then **Close** the window.

6   The **Query Design View** window is now shown in Figure 8.4 with the two tables and their relationships.

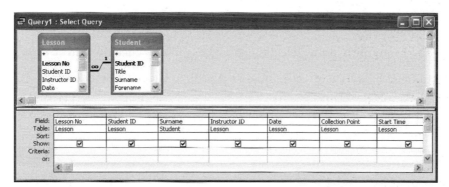

Figure 8.4

7   From the **Lesson** table drag and drop the fields **Lesson No, Student ID, Instructor ID, Date, Collection Point** and **Start Time** into the field cells.

8   From the **Student** table drag and drop the **Surname** field.

9   Move its position by clicking on the column header and dragging to a position after the **Student ID** column. Alternatively you could have entered the fields in the order shown.

10   Run the query and save it as **Lesson and Names Query**.

11 The results of your query are shown in Figure 8.5.

Lesson No	Student ID	Surname	Instructor ID	Date	Collection Point	Start Time
1	1	Brammer	1	30/07/02	Home Address	08:00
10	1	Brammer	1	31/07/02	Home Address	11:00
2	2	Jenkins	1	30/07/02	Derby Station	09:00
3	2	Jenkins	2	31/07/02	Home Address	12:00
4	3	Fowler	1	31/07/02	John Port School	13:00
5	4	Beswood	3	01/08/02	Home Address	18:00
6	5	Williams	1	31/07/02	Home Address	08:00
7	6	Windsor	2	30/07/02	Home Address	12:00
8	7	Trueman	1	30/07/02	Home Address	11:00
9	8	Spencer	1	30/07/02	Home Address	12:00
11	9	Watson	2	02/08/02	Home Address	10:00

Record: ⏮ ◀ 1 ▶ ⏭ ▶* of 11

Figure 8.5

Query 2   Searching for an instructor's lessons

This query will enable us to key in an Instructor ID and find all their lessons.

1 In the Database Window click on **Queries** and select **New**.

2 In the **New Query** window select **Design View** and click on **OK**.

3 In the **Show Table** window select the table **Lesson** and click on **Add**.

4 Select the table **Instructor**, click on **Add** and then **Close** the window.

5 The Query Design grid is now shown in Figure 8.6 with the two tables and their relationships.

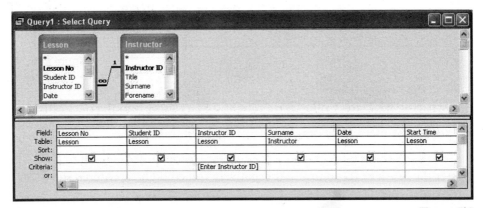

Figure 8.6

6 From the **Lesson** table drag and drop the fields **Lesson No, Student ID, Instructor ID, Date** and **Start Time**.

7 From the **Instructor** table drag and drop the **Surname** field.

8 Move its position by clicking on the column header and dragging to a position after the **Instructor ID** column.

9 In the criteria cell of the **Instructor ID** type [**Enter Instructor ID**].

10 Run the query and enter **2** in the dialogue box (see Figure 8.7).

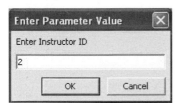

Figure 8.7

11 The query produces a list of lessons for Instructor ID 2 as shown in Figure 8.8.

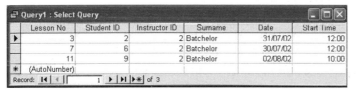

Figure 8.8

12 Save the query as **Instructor Search Query**.

Query 3 Viewing all lessons with full details of instructor and student names

We will use the Query Wizard to design the next query.

1 In the Database Window click on **Queries** and select **New**.

2 In the **New Query** window select **Simple Query Wizard** and click on **OK**.

The Simple Query Wizard dialogue box is displayed.

3 Select the **Lesson** table from the Tables/Queries drop-down box.

4   Click the double right arrow >> to put all the fields in the selected fields area (see Figure 8.9).

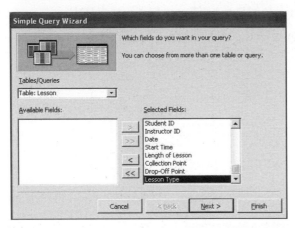

Figure 8.9

5   Select the **Instructor** table from the Tables/Queries drop down.

6   Select fields **Surname** and **Forename** and add to the selected fields by clicking the right arrow >.

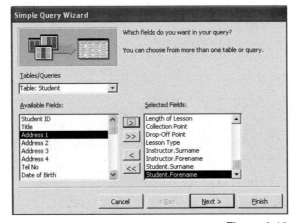

Figure 8.10

7   Select the **Student** table from the Tables/Queries drop-down menu and add the fields **Surname** and **Forename** to the selected fields (see Figure 8.10).

8   Click on **Next**, choose **Detail**, click on **Next** again, call the query **Full Details Query** and click on **Finish**.

The resulting query opens in Datasheet View (see Figure 8.11), giving full details of the lessons, the students and instructors along with their names. (You will need to drop into Design View to position names alongside IDs.)

Lesson No	Student ID	Instructor ID	Date	Start Time	Length of Lesson	Collection Point	Drop-Off Point	Lesson Type
1	1	1	30/07/02	08:00	1	Home Address	City Centre	Standard
2	2	1	30/07/02	09:00	2	Derby Station	Home Address	Standard
3	2	2	31/07/02	12:00	1	Home Address	Home Address	Introductory
4	3	1	31/07/02	13:00	2	John Port School	Home Address	Standard
5	4	3	01/08/02	18:00	1	Home Address	Home Address	Test
6	5	1	31/07/02	08:00	1	Home Address	Home Address	Introductory
7	6	2	30/07/02	12:00	1	Home Address	Home Address	Standard
8	7	1	30/07/02	11:00	1	Home Address	Home Address	Standard
9	8	1	30/07/02	12:00	3	Home Address	Home Address	Standard
10	1	1	31/07/02	11:00	1	Home Address	Home Address	Standard
11	9	2	02/08/02	10:00	1	Home Address	Home Address	Standard

Figure 8.11

We are now going to develop two more queries which will be used later in these units.

Query 4 Viewing full details of lessons on a certain date

1   Open the **Full Details Query** in Design View.

2   In the criteria row of the **Date** column, type [**Please enter the date**] (see Figure 8.12).

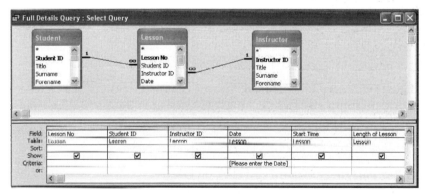

Figure 8.12

3   Use **File, Save As** to save the query as **Full Details by Date Query**.

When you run this query you will be prompted for a date. Access will display full details of the lessons on that date along with the names of the students and instructors.

Query 5 Viewing full details of lessons this week

1   Open the **Full Details by Date Query** in Design View again.

2   In the criteria row of the **Date** column enter **Between Date() and Date()+7**. This
will return all lessons booked in the next seven days starting from the current
date (see Figure 8.13).

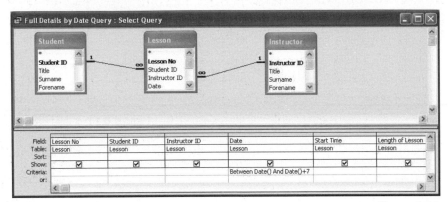

Figure 8.13

3   Use **File, Save As** to save the query as **Next Week's Lessons Query**.

4   To test the query adjust the dates in your table or adjust the time clock on your
PC.

Query 6 Adding a calculated field to a query

A calculated field is an added field in a query that displays the results of a calculation.
For example, if we multiply together the hourly rate for each lesson and the length of
each lesson, we can use the query to work out the cost of each lesson.

1   In the Database Window click on **Queries** and select **New**.

2   Select the **Simple Query Wizard** and click on **OK**.

3   Click on the **Lesson** table and click on the double arrow >> to select every field.

4   Select the **Lesson Type** table and click on the field **Cost**. Click on the single arrow
> to select just this field.

5   Select the **Instructor** table and click on the field **Forename**. Click on the single
arrow to select just this field. Add the **Surname** field also.

6   Select the **Student** table and click on the field **Forename**. Click on the single
arrow to select just this field. Then add the **Surname**, **Address 1** and **Address 2**
fields as well.

7   Click on **Next**. Click on **Next** again and call the query **Lesson Cost Query**. Click on **Finish**.

8   Switch to **Design View**. You will need to rearrange the tables by dragging to more suitable positions (see Figure 8.14).

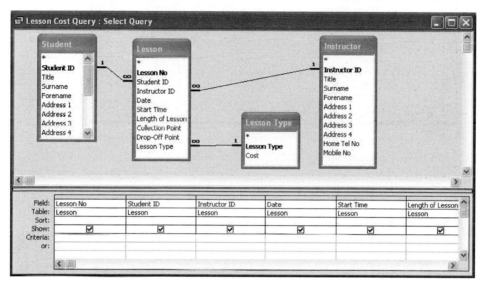

Figure 8.14

9   Using drag and drop, rearrange the order of fields in the QBE grid so that **Instructor ID** comes after **Lesson No**, followed by **Instructor Forename** and **Surname**, then **Student ID** followed by **Student Forename, Surname, Address 1** and **Address 2**.

10 Scroll to the right and find the first blank column of the QBE grid. If there is no blank column, select the last field and click on **Insert, Columns**.

11 In the field row of the blank column enter **TotalCost: [Length of lesson]*[Cost]** (see Figure 8.15).

Collection Point	Lesson Type	Cost	TotalCost: [Length of lesson]*[Cost]	
Lesson	Lesson	Lesson Type		
☑	☑	☑	☑	

Figure 8.15

12 Save the query again (by closing the window) as **Lesson Cost Query**.

13 Run the query to test the calculations are correct (see Figure 8.16).

Lesson Cost Query : Select Query

Length of Lesson	Collection Point	Lesson Type	Cost	TotalCost
1	Home Address	Standard	£15.00	£15.00
2	Derby Station	Standard	£15.00	£30.00
1	Home Address	Introductory	£12.00	£12.00
2	John Port School	Standard	£15.00	£30.00
1	Home Address	Test	£25.00	£25.00
1	Home Address	Introductory	£12.00	£12.00
1	Home Address	Standard	£15.00	£15.00
1	Home Address	Standard	£15.00	£15.00
3	Home Address	Standard	£15.00	£45.00
1	Home Address	Standard	£15.00	£15.00
1	Home Address	Standard	£15.00	£15.00

Record: 1 of 11

Figure 8.16

⊕ Unit 9 Setting up forms using Form Wizard

In this section you will learn how to set up the forms to enter, edit and view data in the Pass-It Driving School database. Forms provide a user-friendly on-screen interface.

Initially we will set up three forms:

○ a Student form;
○ an Instructor form;
○ a Lesson Type form.

Wizards can again be used to set up the forms. It is usually easier and common practice to use the wizard to set up a form but then to use Design View to customise the form to your requirements.

Setting up the Student form using AutoForm

1   In the Database Window select **Forms** and click on **New**.

2   In the **New Form** window select **AutoForm: Columnar** (see Figure 9.1).

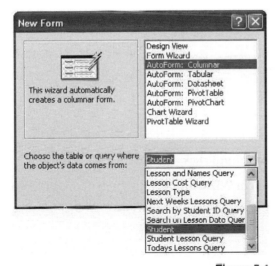

Figure 9.1

3   Select the **Student** table from the drop-down list and click on **OK**.

4   The form is generated automatically. If the form is maximised and uses the full screen, click on the **Restore Window** icon (see Figure 9.2).

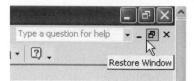

Figure 9.2

5   To ensure that the form is the correct size, click on **Window**, **Size to Fit Form**.

6   Save by closing the form and calling it **Student Form**.

Size to Fit Form is not available if the window is maximised. When you next open the form it will open at its saved size.

The form is shown in Figure 9.3.

Figure 9.3

Setting up the Instructor form using the Form Wizard

1   In the Database Window select **Forms** and click on **New**.

2   In the **New Form** window select **Form Wizard,** select the **Instructor** table from the Tables/Queries drop-down list and click on **OK** (see Figure 9.4).

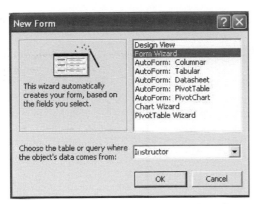

Figure 9.4

3   The **Form Wizard** window opens with the available fields (Figure 9.5). Click the double arrow >> to put all available fields across to the selected fields and click on **Next**.

Note   The single arrow allows you to select one field at a time and the left arrows allow you to deselect fields. Use the single arrow to choose selected fields in a different order from that shown.

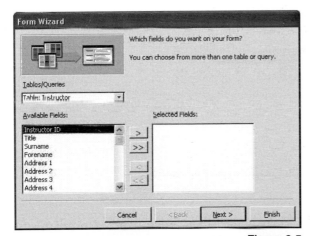

Figure 9.5

4 Select **Columnar** from the range of layouts shown and click on **Next** (see Figure 9.6).

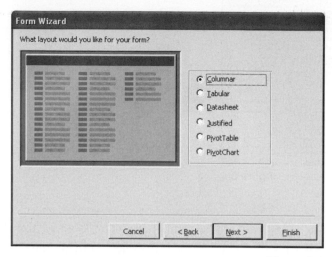

Figure 9.6

5 Select **Standard** style from the next **Form Wizard** window and click on **Next** (see Figure 9.7).

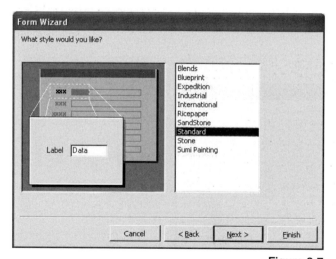

Figure 9.7

6 Save your form as **Instructor Form** and click on **Finish.** The form will open in **Form View** as shown in Figure 9.8.

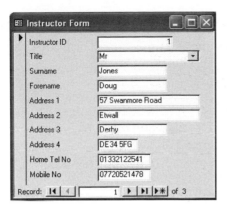

Figure 9.8

Setting up the Lesson Type form using AutoForm: Tabular

1　In the Database Window select **Forms** and click on **New**.

2　In the **New Form** window select **AutoForm: Tabular**.

3　Select the **Lesson Type** table from the drop-down list and click on **OK**.

4　The form is generated automatically and opens in **Form View** as shown below. Save the form in the usual way calling it **Lesson Type Form** (see Figure 9.9).

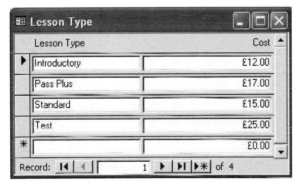

Figure 9.9

The different form views

There are three different views to a form:

○ Form View;
○ Datasheet View;
○ Design View.

Form View

Form View allows you to view and edit records one at a time. Enter Form View from the Database Window by selecting the form and clicking on Open.

Datasheet View

Datasheet View allows you to view and edit the records all on one screen. The Lesson Type Form is shown in Datasheet View (see Figure 9.10).

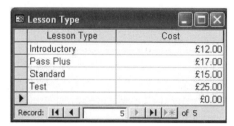

Figure 9.10

Design View

Design View allows you to edit the form and is described in Unit 10. Enter Design View from the Database Window by selecting the form and clicking on **Design**.

Switching between views

There are a number of ways of switching between the Form View, Design View and Datasheet View windows.

The easiest way is to select from one of the first three options on the **View** menu (see Figure 9.11).

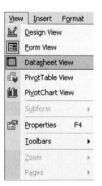

Figure 9.11

Entering Data in Form View

1   Open the **Student Form** in Form View.

2   Use the Record navigation bar shown in Figure 9.12 to scroll through the records.

Figure 9.12

3   Click on the last icon to add a new record.

4   Add the details of some more students to practise entering data into a form.

Alternatively you can use the Page Up and Page Down keys to display Next and Previous records.

⊕ Unit 10 Working in Form Design View

The forms you have produced so far are all standard in layout. Form Design View allows you to customise a form to suit your requirements.

In this section you will learn how to:

○ find your way around a form in Design View;
○ move, align and edit controls;
○ edit the appearance of your form.

Form Design View

You will grasp the concepts more easily by practising and experimenting with the tasks in this section. We will start by working on a copy of a form so that if you make a mistake it will not affect the final system.

1   In the Database Window click on **Forms** and select the **Student Form**. From the menu choose **Edit, Copy**.

2   Click in the Database Window and choose **Edit, Paste**. Name the form **Student Form Copy**.

3   Open the **Student Form Copy** in Design View as shown in Figure 10.1 by selecting **Student Form Copy** and clicking on **Design**.

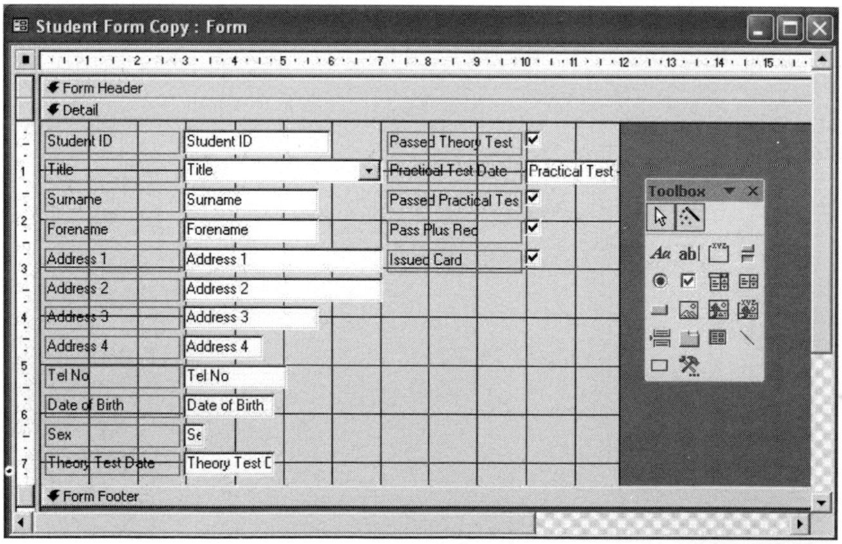

Figure 10.1

The form opens with the following features showing:

○ A **form header** section – this area can contain text, headings, titles and graphics. Toggle the **form header** off and back on by choosing from the menu **View, Form Header/Footer**.

○ A **detail** section – this contains the **controls** that display the data in your tables.

○ A number of **controls** each made up of a **label** containing the field name and a text box which will contain the data in **Form View**.

○ A **toolbox** from which you can add text, lines, shapes, controls, buttons and other features. Toggle the **toolbox** on and off by choosing from the menu **View, Toolbox**.

○ A **form footer** section which can be used in the same way as the Header.

○ A **right margin** which can be dragged wider using the mouse.

○ A **ruler** and **grid** to help you with the layout of your form. Toggle these features on and off by choosing from the menu **View, Ruler** or **View, Grid**.

○ You may also notice the **page header/footer** options which can be added. They will print at the top and bottom of each page in any printout.

Getting a feel for your working area

1   With the **Student Form Copy** open in **Design View** and maximised as shown in Figure 10.1. Move the mouse over the right margin until it turns into a cross and drag the margin wider by about 2 cm. You can use the ruler as a guide.

2   Move the mouse over the border between the **Detail** section and the **Form Header** and drag the **Detail** section down by about 1 cm.

3   In the same way move the **Form Footer** section down towards the foot of the screen.

4   Switch to **Form View** by selecting **View, Form View** from the menu.

5   If the form is maximised, click on the **Restore Window** icon. Click on **Window, Size to Fit Form**. Access will give a best fit to your form as shown in Figure 10.2. It is **NOT** necessary to save this form.

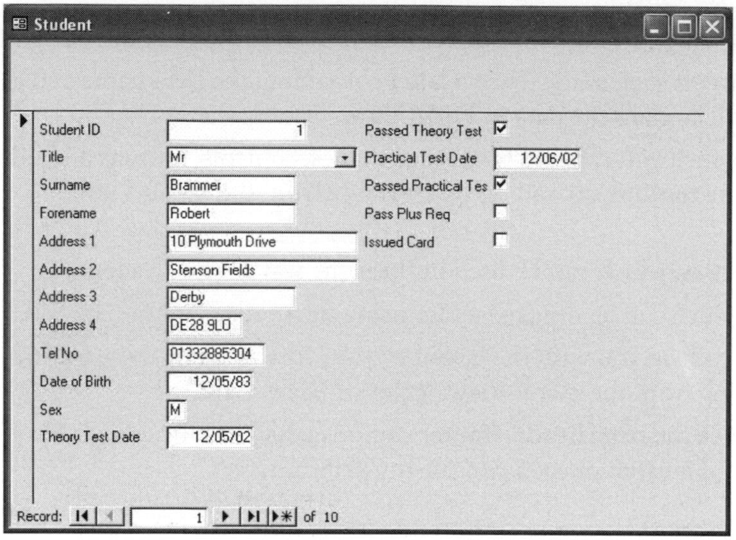

Figure 10.2

Working with controls

The Detail section is initially made up of controls which display the data from your tables. The controls are made up of text boxes and attached labels.

In the Database Window click on **Forms** and select the **Student Form Copy** again. Click on **Design** to open the form in Design View.

It is worth practising all the following steps on the currently opened **Student Form Copy** until you feel confident and competent with handling controls.

Selecting controls

○ To resize, move, delete, copy or change the properties of a control, first you must select it.
○ Simply click anywhere on the control and it will be highlighted with *sizing handles* as shown in Figure 10.3.

○ To select more than one control, simply drag out a rectangle across the controls you wish to select
   or
○ Select the first control and hold down SHIFT while selecting further controls.

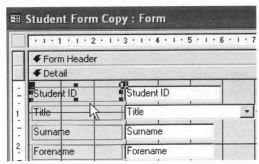

Figure 10.3

Resizing controls

○ Click on the control to select it and then drag the resizing handles in or out to resize it.

Moving controls

○ Click on the control to select it. To move the control and its label, move the pointer to the border of the control. The pointer turns into an open hand as shown in Figure 10.4. Drag the control to a new position.

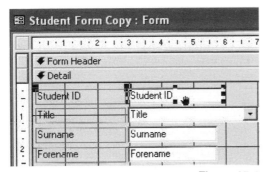

Figure 10.4

○ To move the control without its label, place the pointer over the *move handle* in the top left corner of the control. The pointer changes to pointing finger as shown in Figure 10.5. Drag the control to a new position.

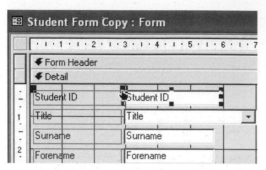

Figure 10.5

You can select more than one control as outlined earlier and move them at the same time.

Deleting controls

○ To delete a control simply select the control and press the DELETE key.

Adding a control

○ If you want to add a control for a field, for example because you have already deleted it, from the menu choose **View**, **Field List** (see Figure 10.6).

Figure 10.6

The Field list will appear on the screen and you can highlight the field and drag and drop it to the required position.

Developing a form

1 Open the **Student Form Copy** in Design View.

2 Drag the Form Footer down and right margin out a little. Move each control in the left column down by about 2 cm to make room for a heading.

3 Select all the controls in the second column and move them down a little further.

4 Select the **Theory Test Date** control at the foot of the first column and move the control to the top of the second column.

Your controls should now be arranged something like Figure 10.7. Do not worry about accuracy. Access provides a number of formatting tools to help you.

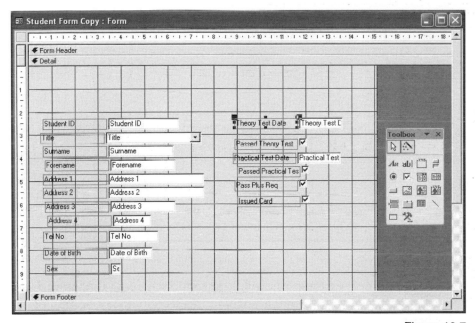

Figure 10.7

It is probable you will have to use the following steps to align all controls correctly. There is no set way but the following steps should ensure accuracy.

1 Highlight the labels in the first column of controls by dragging over them and select **Format, Align, Left**.

2 Highlight the text boxes on the first column of controls by dragging over them and select **Format, Align, Left**.

3 Repeat the same steps for the controls in the right-hand column.

4 Align the control **Student ID** with **Theory Test Date** to establish the uppermost position for each column.

5 Highlight the first column of controls and select **Format, Vertical Spacing, Make Equal.** There are **Increase** and **Decrease** options to help further.

6 Highlight the second column of controls and select **Format, Vertical Spacing, Make Equal**.

7 When you are happy with your design switch to **Form View**, click on the **Restore Window** icon if the form is maximised and select **Window, Size to Fit Form**.

8 Save your form. It should appear as shown in Figure 10.8.

Student			
Student ID	1	Theory Test Date	12/05/02
Title	Mr	Passed Theory Test	☑
Surname	Brammer	Practical Test Date	12/06/02
Forename	Robert	Passed Practical Test	☑
Address 1	10 Plymouth Drive	Pass Plus Req	☐
Address 2	Stenson Fields	Issued Card	☐
Address 3	Derby		
Address 4	DE28 9LO		
Tel No	01332885304		
Date of Birth	12/05/83		
Sex	M		

Record: I◀ ◀ 1 ▶ ▶I ▶✱ of 10

Figure 10.8

During the course of the next exercises you will be introduced to a number of ways of improving the appearance of your form. Throughout this section do not be afraid to practise and experiment – remember you can always delete it and start again or as a last resort get the wizards to do it again!

Fonts, colours and special effects

1 Open the **Student Form Copy** in Design View.

2 Ensure the **Formatting** toolbar is available by clicking on **View, Toolbars, Formatting (Form/Report)**. See Figure 10.9.

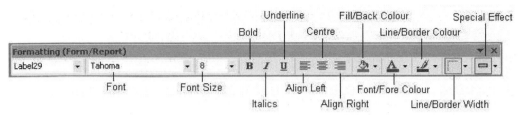

Figure 10.9

Most of the options here will be familiar to students who have a working knowledge of Windows software.

3   Click on the **Detail** area and click the **Fill/Back Colour** drop down on the Formatting toolbar to show the colour palette below. See Figure 10.10.

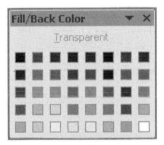

Figure 10.10

4   Select a suitable colour for the background to your form.

5   Select the labels of all the controls and set the font to **Arial Black** (or one of your choice) by clicking the Font Drop down on the **Formatting** toolbar and then clicking on **Bold**.

You will probably have to spend some time resizing the labels or click **Edit, Undo** to try another font.

6   Select all the labels again and click the **Fill/Back Colour** drop-down list on the **Formatting** toolbar.

7   Choose a colour to make your labels stand out from the background colour of the form.

8   With labels still selected click the **Special Effect** drop down and choose **Raised** from the **Special Effect** window shown in Figure 10.11.

Figure 10.11

Note

If you right click in the Detail area or on any control you will get a menu from which a number of toolbar options are offered.

Using the Toolbox to add a text box, rectangle and lines

The toolbox offers a number of features many of which you will meet later in this book (see Figure 10.12).

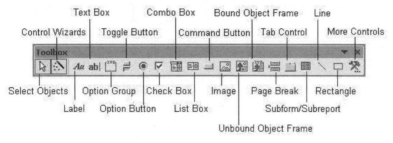

Figure 10.12

1 Click on the **Label** icon and drag out a rectangle near the top of your form.

2 Type in a suitable heading and press return.

3 Set the font, background colour and special effect as required.

4 Select the **Rectangle** tool and drag out a box around the controls.

5 Select the box and choose a style from the **Line/Border Width** drop down on the **Formatting** toolbar (see Figure 10.13).

Figure 10.13

Making a start on the Student Form

We now need to go back to our original Student Form and develop it for later use.

1 Open the **Student Form** in Design View.

2 Move the controls down to make room for a title and move the **Theory Test Date** control to the top of the right column as you did earlier in this unit. Switch to **Form View.** Your form should appear as in Figure 10.14.

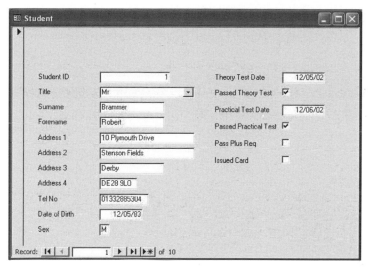

Figure 10.14

3   Switch to **Design View**. Click on the **Label** icon in the Toolbox (see Figure 10.15).

Figure 10.15

4   Drag out a rectangle near the top of the form, type in the text **Students** and press return (see Figure 10.16).

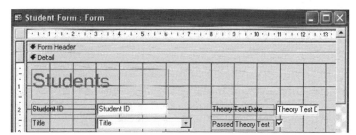

Figure 10.16

5   With the new control selected set the font, font size, foreground colour and border colour as required using the **Formatting** toolbar. We have chosen only to set the font colour to green and font size to 24 point.

6   Save your form.

⊕ Unit 11 Taking form design further

This section describes some of the additional features that you can add to your forms to create a professional feel to your system.

You will learn how to:

○ add graphics;
○ add command buttons;
○ add combo boxes;
○ set form properties;
○ create forms to display data from more than one table.

The Toolbox

Figure 11.1

The toolbox (see Figure 11.1) should appear when you are in Design mode. It allows you to add control objects to your forms. If it is not visible click **View, Toolbox** from the menu.

Note Some of the functions available can be set up using wizards. If you wish to use the wizards you must ensure the Control Wizards icon is selected.

Adding graphics to the form

Graphics can easily be added to your form using copy and paste. The graphic appears in an unbound object frame enabling you to move or size the frame as needed.

Alternatively, follow these steps:

1   Ensure the image is already saved in a format that Access can recognise, e.g. **jpg**, **gif** or **bmp**. Our image is the *Pass-It* logo (see Figure 11.2).

Figure 11.2

2 Open the **Student Form** in **Design View**.

3 Select the **Image** icon in the Toolbox (see Figure 11.3).

Figure 11.3

4 Drag out a rectangle near the bottom right of the form.

5 Select the image you wish to add to the form from the Insert Picture Dialogue Box. If the image does not fit the frame then right click on the image, select **Properties** and set the **Size Mode** to **Zoom**.

6 Save your form as **Student Form**. It should appear as in Figure 11.4.

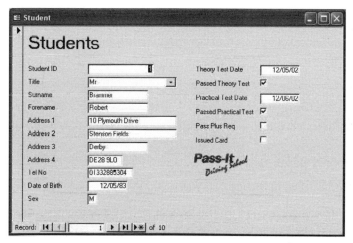

Figure 11.4

The Instructor Form

In exactly the same way as you developed the Student Form, you now need to set up the Instructor Form to look as shown in Figure 11.5.

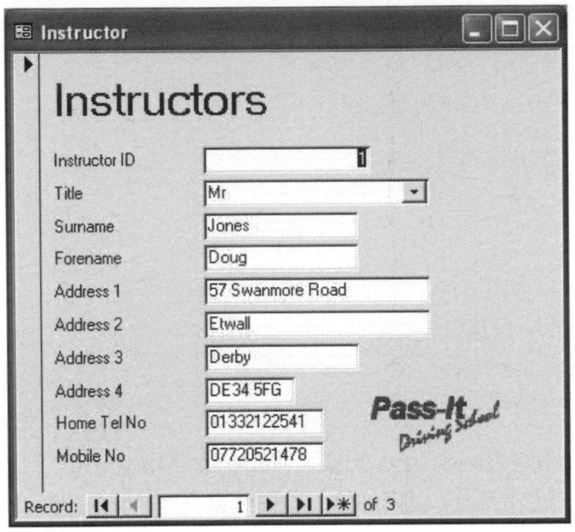

Figure 11.5

Adding command buttons

Access allows you to automate tasks by creating command buttons and placing them on your form.

Command buttons can be added to deal with a number of operations including:

○ record navigation;
○ opening forms and reports;
○ printing;
○ other commonly used operations.

You can set up a command button in one of two ways:

○ Use the Command Button wizard to set up the button and attach the operation.
○ Create the button without the Wizard and attach it to a macro or code.

We will be dealing with macros later. We will start by using the Wizards to set up buttons to move between the records, add a new record and quit the application for our Student Form (see Figure 11.6).

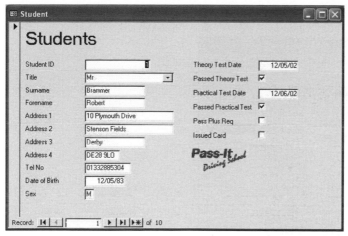

Figure 11.6

1 Open the **Student Form** in Design View.

2 We are going to add the buttons to the lower right of the form. You may have to drag out the detail area to create a little room.

3 Make sure the Toolbox is showing and the **Control Wizards** tool is selected.

Figure 11.7

4 Select the **Command Button** tool (see Figure 11.7) and drag out a button on your form.

This displays the Command Button Wizard dialogue box (see Figure 11.8).

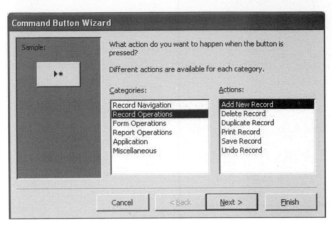

Figure 11.8

5   In the Categories list select **Record Operations**.

6   In the Actions list select **Add New Record** and click on **Next**.

The next window offers you a choice of putting pictures or text on the button. If you choose text you can type in the text you want to go on the button.

If you choose picture you can select from a list or browse the file area to find one of your own (see Figure 11.9).

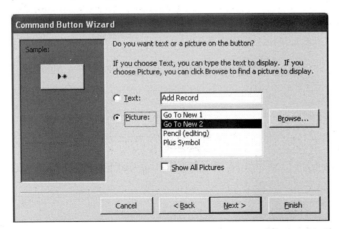

Figure 11.9

7   We are going to use pictures, so choose **Go To New 2** and click on **Next**.

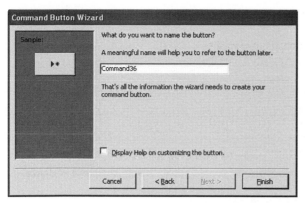

Figure 11.10

8 Give your button a sensible name and click on **Finish** (see Figure 11.10).

The lower half of your form should look something like Figure 11.11 with the **Add New Record** button positioned as shown.

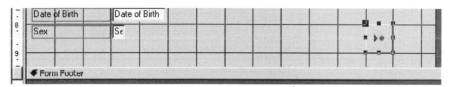

Figure 11.11

9 Add extra buttons from the **Record Navigation Category** using the actions **Go To First Record, Go To Previous Record, Go To Next Record** and **Go To Last Record.** Don't worry about aligning the buttons yet.

10 Add the **Close Form** button from the **Form Operations** category.

You need to arrange the buttons in the order shown in Figure 11.12.

Figure 11.12

11 Select all the buttons and align with **Format, Align, Top**.

12 Distribute the buttons evenly by again selecting all and choosing from the menu **Format, Horizontal Spacing, Make Equal**.

13 You may wish to make the buttons smaller and use the **Format, Size** option to make all buttons the same size.

Adding a control panel

It is common practice to keep user buttons away from data entry areas. We are going to add a background to give a control panel effect.

1   From the toolbox drag out a rectangle big enough to cover the buttons.

2   Select the rectangle and set its **Fill Colour** to **Light Blue**. Set its **Special Effect** to **Sunken**.

3   Select the rectangle and use copy and paste to make a copy of it. Use the resizing handles to make it slightly larger than the first and set its **Special Effect** to **Raised.**

4   Position the smaller rectangle over the larger and centre the buttons on the panel. If the buttons are hidden by the rectangles you may need to use **Format, Bring to Front** (see Figure 11.13).

Figure 11.13

Your form should now appear as in Figure 11.14.

Figure 11.14

You now need to set up buttons in exactly the same way on the **Instructor Form**.

Combo boxes

Combo boxes are drop-down boxes which allow the user to select data from a list of choices or type in a data entry of their own. We will set up a combo box on the Student Form so that user can simply enter M or F in the Sex field from a drop-down box.

Adding a combo box to enter student details

1 Open the **Student Form** in Design View.

2 Select the **Sex** control and press the DELETE key.

3 Click on the **Combo Box** tool in the Toolbox (see Figure 11.15).

Figure 11.15

4 Drag out a small rectangle where the Sex control was.

5 The **Combo Box Wizard** dialogue box is displayed. Check '**I will type in the values that I want**' and click on **Next** (see Figure 11.16).

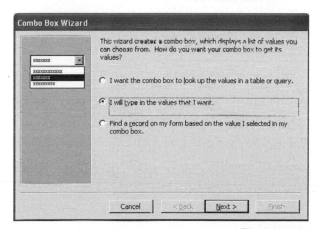

Figure 11.16

6   Enter **M** and the **F** pressing TAB in between entries and click on **Next** (see Figure 11.17).

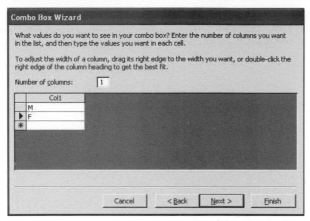

Figure 11.17

7   Check the **'Store that value in this field'** option and select **Sex** from the drop-down box. Click **Next** (see Figure 11.18).

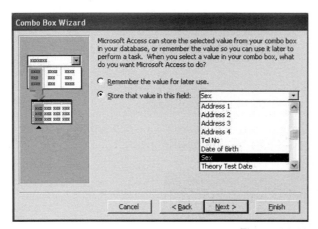

Figure 11.18

8   Set the label to **Sex** and click on **Finish.** You will need to align the control with the others.

9   Save your form as **Student Form**. The combo box should appear as in Figure 11.19.

Figure 11.19

List boxes

List boxes can also be used on forms when a user can only select from a set of predefined choices. They can be added to the form from the Toolbox in the same way as combo boxes. Using Option Buttons and Option Groups are other methods Access offers for entering data on a form. Further information on this can be found in the Tricks and Tips section; 'Using option buttons …' and 'Using option groups'.

Adding a combo box to look up student details

We are going to set up a combo box to display the names of all our students.

When a student is selected in the combo box, their details will appear on the form.

1   Open the **Student Form** in Design View.

2   Click on the **Combo Box** tool in the Toolbox.

3   Drag out a rectangle near the title at the top of the form to start the **Combo Box Wizard**. You will have to group the controls and move them down to create room for the new control (see Figure 11.20).

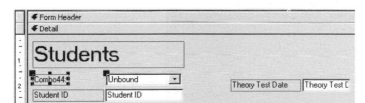

Figure 11.20

4   Click on '**Find a record on my form based on a value I selected in my combo box**'. Click on **Next** (see Figure 11.21).

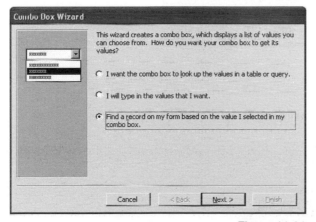

Figure 11.21

5   Click on the **Surname** field and select it with the > icon. Click on **Next** (see Figure 11.22).

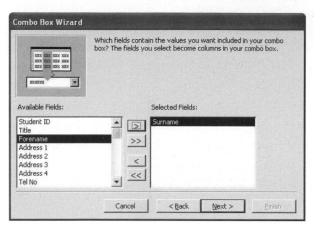

Figure 11.22

6   The **Combo Box Wizard** dialogue box then displays the names. Click on **Next** again (see Figure 11.23).

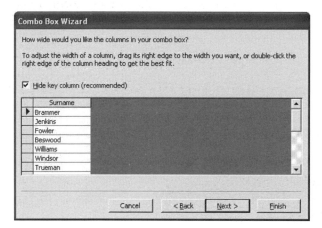

Figure 11.23

7   Give the combo box the name **Find Record** and click on **Finish**.

8   Switch to **Form View**; the **Student Form** should appear as in Figure 11.24.

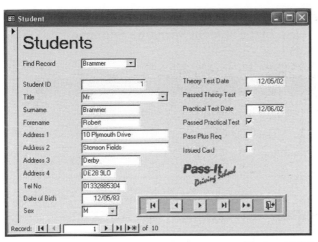

Figure 11.24

Displaying the names in the combo box in alphabetical order

The names in the drop-down list from the combo box on the Student form are in Student ID order and not alphabetical order. To sort these names into alphabetical order:

1   Open the **Student Form** in Design View and select the **Find Record** Combo box.

2   Click on the **Properties** icon or right click the combo box and click on Properties. Click on the **Data** tab.

3   Click on **Row Source** and click on the three dots icon (see Figure 11.25).

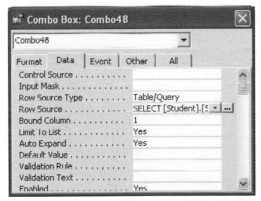

Figure 11.25

4 The SQL Statement Query Builder window opens (see Figure 11.26). It looks similar to Query Design View. In the **Student Surname** column of the QBE grid, select **Ascending** in the Sort row.

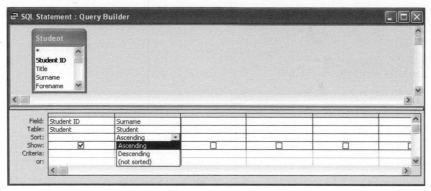

Figure 11.26

5 Close the **Query Builder** window and save the changes.

6 Go into Form View and test that the names are in alphabetical order.

Setting form properties

You can control the behaviour and appearance of your form by setting the form's properties. In the Student Form you have just completed it may look better without a number of features. It still has the Record Selector, the Record Navigation Controls, maximise, minimise and close buttons. These can be removed using the form properties window.

1 In Design View, double click on the **Form Selector** (see Figure 11.27) at the top left of the form in Design View or click on **View**, **Properties**.

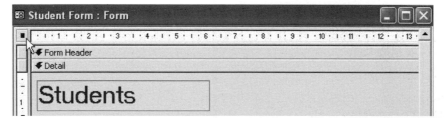

Figure 11.27

2 This displays the **Form Properties** window (see Figure 11.28).

There are far too many properties to cover all the available options here.

You will meet some in later units but Microsoft Help will give details of all the available options.

The properties are grouped for easier access. Clicking on the Format tab will give a range of options covering the appearance of your form.

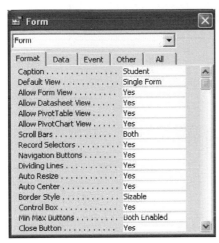

Figure 11.28

3   Change the form caption using the **Caption** property to **Student Details**.

4   Remove the scroll bars at the bottom and right-hand side of the form by setting the **Scroll Bars** property to **Neither**.

5   Remove the record selector on the form by setting the **Record Selectors** property to **No**.

6   Remove the navigation buttons at the bottom of the form by setting the **Navigation Buttons** property to **No**.

7   Remove the dividing lines at the bottom of the form by setting the **Dividing Lines** property to **No**.

8   Make the form appear in the middle of the screen by setting the **Auto Center** property to **Yes.**

9   Remove the maximise and minimise buttons from a form by setting the **Min Max Buttons** property to **None.**

Note

The record selector is a column on the left-hand side of a form used to select a whole record in a form, for example you may use this to delete a record rather than just delete one field.

Your finished form should appear as in Figure 11.29.

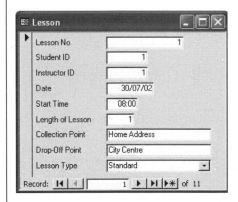

Figure 11.29

Create a form to display data from more than one table

In Unit 9 we used the wizards to design simple Student and Instructor forms. We could also have designed a form to book lessons as shown in Figure 11.30. The form is based on the table Lesson.

Figure 11.30

In the real system it is probable the student would not know their ID number or the operator booking their lesson would like to confirm an ID by seeing the student name on screen.

In this section we will set up the Lesson Booking form. You will find out how to base a form on a query. This will enable us to key in the Student ID on the Booking Form and Access will find the student's name in the student table.

Creating the Lesson Booking form

1   In the Database Window click on **Queries**, select the **Lesson Cost Query** and click **Open** to run the Query.

The output in Figure 11.31 shows the query bringing in the information from all the tables (some of the columns have been hidden to fit the screen). This is the information that will be displayed in your form.

Lesson No	Instructor ID	Instructor	Instructor	Student ID	Student_Sur	Address 2	Collection Point	Cost	Total Cost
1	1	Doug	Jones	1	Brammer	Stenson Fields	Home Address	£15.00	£15.00
2	1	Doug	Jones	2	Jenkins	Etwall	Derby Station	£15.00	£30.00
3	2	Arnold	Batchelor	2	Jenkins	Etwall	Home Address	£12.00	£12.00
4	1	Doug	Jones	3	Fowler	Mickleover	John Port School	£15.00	£30.00
5	3	Andrew	Smith	4	Beswood	Allestree	Home Address	£25.00	£25.00
6	1	Doug	Jones	5	Williams	Littleover	Home Address	£12.00	£12.00
7	2	Arnold	Batchelor	6	Windsor	Allenton	Home Address	£15.00	£15.00
8	1	Doug	Jones	7	Trueman	Allestree	Home Address	£15.00	£15.00
9	1	Doug	Jones	8	Spencer	Stenson Fields	Home Address	£15.00	£45.00
10	1	Doug	Jones	1	Brammer	Stenson Fields	Home Address	£15.00	£15.00
11	2	Arnold	Batchelor	9	Watson	Etwall	Home Address	£15.00	£15.00

Record: 14 4 | 11 | ▶ ▶I ▶*| of 11

Figure 11.31

2   Close the Query, select **Forms** and click on **New**.

3   In the **New Form** window select the **Form Wizard** and choose the **Lesson Cost Query** from the drop-down list. Click on **OK** (see Figure 11.32).

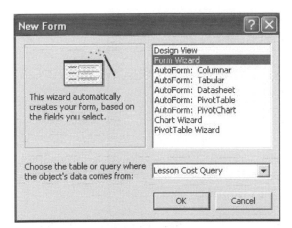

Figure 11.32

4   Click the double arrow >> to select all fields as shown in Figure 11.33 and click
    on **Next**.

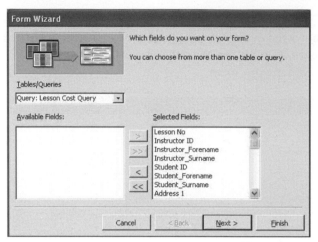

Figure 11.33

5   Select **Columnar** and click on **Next**.

6   Select **Standard** and click on **Next**.

7   Name the form **Lesson Booking Form** and click on **Finish**.

8   Open the form and **Size to Fit.** It should appear as in Figure 11.34.

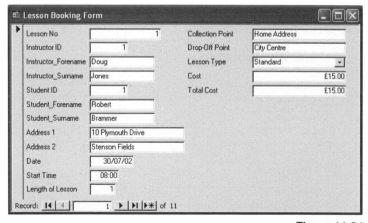

Figure 11.34

We now need to customise the form to give it the same look and feel as the Student and Instructor forms. In Form Design View make the following changes:

○ Move the fields down to make room for a heading.
○ Add the title Lessons in the same font, font size and colour.
○ Edit the labels for the Instructor and Student name control by removing the underscore.
○ Add the Pass-It logo.
○ Add the control panel (not the buttons) by using copy and paste from one of the other forms.
○ Add the buttons using the Wizards as before.
○ Set the form properties to the same as the other forms.

Your finished **Lesson Booking** form should appear as in Figure 11.35.

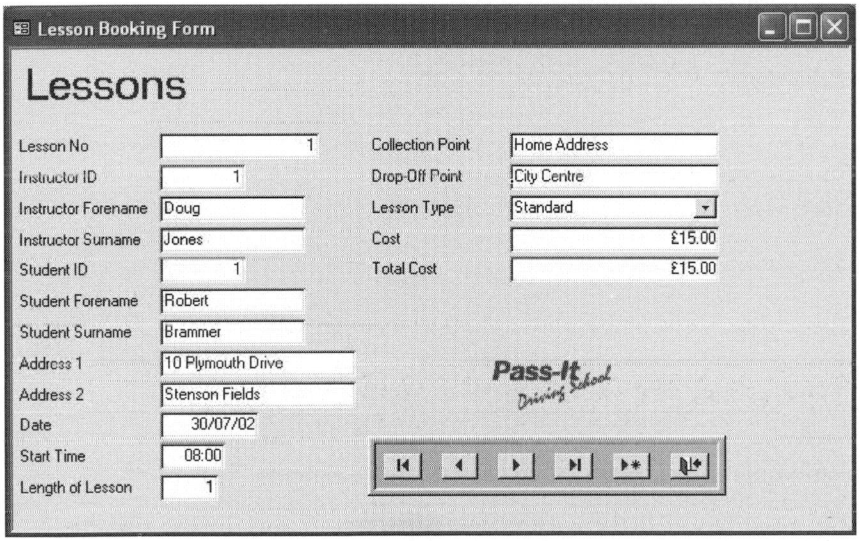

Figure 11.35

When you go to a new record and enter an instructor ID number, click on another control or press the TAB key, the instructor's forename and surname will appear.

Similarly after you enter the student ID, click on another control or press the TAB key; the student's forename, surname and address will appear.

⊕ Unit 12 Setting up reports

In this section you will learn how to set up reports to output information from the Pass-It Driving School database.

A report is a way of presenting data on screen or in printed format. Reports can be based on either a table or a query.

Like a form, a report can be fully customised to suit the user's requirements. Output from a report can include images, text can be positioned where required and the font, size and colour of text can be formatted as shown in Figure 12.1.

Pass-It *Driving School*   ***Instructor Report***

Instructor ID	Name			Address	Phone
1	Mr	Jones	Doug	57 Swanmore Road	01332122541
				Etwall	07720521478
				Derby	
				DE34 5F	
2	Mr	Batchelor	Arnold	13 Gairloch Close	0133255147
				Etwall	0798035145
				Derby	
				DE34 5F	
3	Mr	Smith	Andrew	5b Sunrise Road	01332521452
				Littleover	07980525214
				Derby	
				DE45 4E	

Figure 12.1

As with forms and queries, wizards can be used to create reports.

It will be normal practice to use the wizard to set up a report and then to use the Design View window to customise the report to your requirements.

In this section we will set up two reports both based on tables:

○ a report to show a list of all instructors;
○ a report to show a list of all students.

Report 1: Setting up a report based on a table using AutoReport: Tabular

We want to set up a report to show a list of all instructors and their personal details. This report will be based on the Instructor table.

1 At the Database Window click on **Reports** and click on **New**.

2   Click on **AutoReport: Tabular** and in the drop-down list click on **Instructor**.
     Click on **OK** (see Figure 12.2).

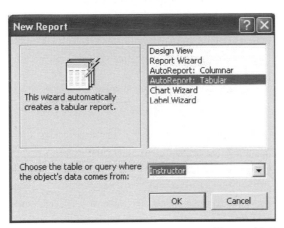

Figure 12.2

3   The wizard generates the report which is shown in Figure 12.3.

Instructor

Instructor ID	Title	Surname	Forename	Address 1	Address 2	Address 3
1	Mr	Jones	Doug	57 Swanmore Road	Etwall	Derby
2	Mr	Batchelor	Arnold	13 Gairloch Close	Etwall	Derby
3	Mr	Smith	Andrew	5b Sunrise Road	Littleover	Derby

Figure 12.3

If you scroll down to the bottom of the report, you will see that the wizard
automatically inserts the date and the page number (see Figure 12.4).

30 July 2002   Page 1 of 1

Figure 12.4

4   Close the report and save it as **Instructor Report**.

The different report views

There are three different views to a report:

○ Print Preview;
○ Design View;
○ Layout Preview.

Print Preview

The Print Preview window allows you to see what the report will look like when you print it out. Figure 12.6 shows the Print Preview window of the Instructor report.

As the cursor moves over the report it turns into a magnifying glass. Click once to zoom out to see the whole page. Click again to zoom in to actual size as shown in Figure 12.5.

Instructor

Instructor ID	Title	Surname	Forename	Address 1	Address 2	Address 3
1	Mr	Jones	Doug	57 Swanmore Road	Etwall	Derby
2	Mr	Batchelor	Arnold	13 Gairloch Close	Etwall	Derby
3	Mr	Smith	Andrew	5b Sunrise Road	Littleover	Derby

Figure 12.5

When you zoom out the Instructor Report will appear as in Figure 12.6.

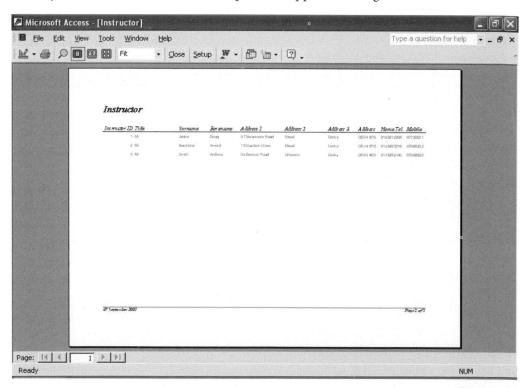

Figure 12.6

There is a Print Preview toolbar (see Figure 12.7).

Figure 12.7

If this toolbar is not displayed, click on **View, Toolbars, Print Preview**.
If there is more than one page in the report you can use the page navigation bar shown
below to scroll through the pages (see Figure 12.8).

Figure 12.8

Printing a report

To print a report, simply open the report at the Database Window in Print Preview
and click on the Print icon.

Design View

The Design View window allows you to customise your report to suit your
requirements. Reports are edited in the same way as editing forms. As with forms it is
possible to:

○ add, edit and remove fields;
○ add text and titles;
○ change the style and layout;
○ change the font format and colours;
○ add controls and command buttons;
○ add images.

Click on **View, Design View** to see the Instructor Report in Design View (see Figure 12.9).

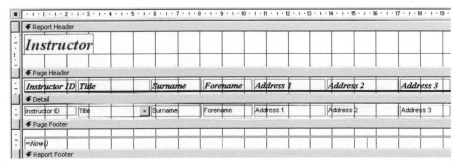

Figure 12.9

The top part of the report is the **Report Header**. Controls in the Report Header appear only once at the beginning of the report. It is suitable for titles.

The second part of the report is the **Page Header**. Controls in the Page Header appear at the top of every page. It is suitable for column headings.

The third part of the report is the **Detail**. This is used for the data in the report.

The fourth part of the report is the **Page Footer**. Controls in the Page Footer appear at the bottom of every page. It is here the wizard has inserted the page number and the date.

The final part of the report is the **Report Footer**. Controls in the Report Footer appear only once at the end of the report.

We will use Design View to customise the appearance of the Instructor Report.

Toolbars

There are two toolbars used in designing reports, the Report Design toolbar (Figure 12.10): and the Formatting (Form/Report) toolbar (Figure 12.11).

Always ensure these toolbars are displayed when in Report Design View by clicking on **View, Toolbars, Report Design** and **View, Toolbars, Formatting (Form/Report)**.

Figure 12.10

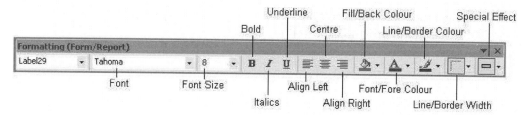

Figure 12.11

Two other useful features of Report Design View are the Field List and the Toolbox. If they are not showing they can be found on the View menu.

Right Click menu

If you right click on an object in Report Design View, you get a shortcut menu. Different options are available depending on the object chosen. From this menu you can control the properties of objects on your report (see Figure 12.12).

Figure 12.12

Orientation of a report

In Design View you can also set a report to be in either portrait or landscape format. Landscape format is often better when the report has many fields in columns.

Click on **File, Page Setup** and click on the **Page** tab to set the orientation of a report to portrait or landscape (see Figure 12.13).

Figure 12.13

Layout preview

The Layout Preview window provides a quick way of seeing the layout of a report when you are in Design View to check that it appears how you want it to. However, if your report is based on a query, layout preview may not include all the data in the report.

Switching between views

There are a number of ways of switching between the Print Preview, Design View and Layout Preview windows. The easiest is to select from one of the first three options on the View menu (Figure 12.14).

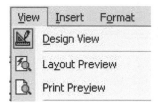

Figure 12.14

Note   You cannot switch from Layout Preview to Print Preview or from Print Preview to Layout Preview. To go between these windows, you must first switch to Design View.

Customising the Instructor Report

We are going to edit the Instructor Report. Some of the columns (e.g. Title) are too wide and some (e.g. Mobile No) are too narrow.

1   Open the report in **Design View**.

2   Click on the title in the **Report Header**, then drag out the resizing handles to increase the size of the control and change the text in the control to **Instructor Report** (see Figure 12.15).

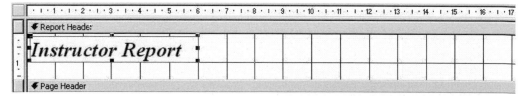

Figure 12.15

3   Select the **Title** control in the **Detail** section and holding the SHIFT key down select the **Title** control in the **Page Header** section (see Figure 12.16).

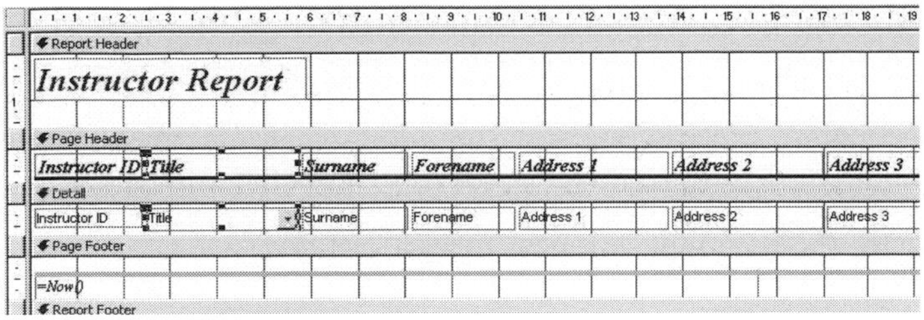

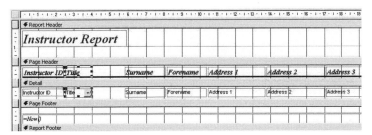

Figure 12.16

4 Drag the resizing handles in to make one of the controls smaller. The other control will also be resized (see Figure 12.17).

Figure 12.17

5 Select all the other controls to the right of **Title** in the **Page Header** and the **Detail** sections. (Click on one, then hold down the SHIFT key and click on each of the others in turn.) With care you may find it easier to drag out a rectangle across the controls.

Note

All the controls on a report can be selected with CTRL+A; then it is sometimes quicker to deselect by simply clicking on the controls not required with the SHIFT key held down.

6 Using the 'open hand', slide all these controls to the left (see Figure 12.18).

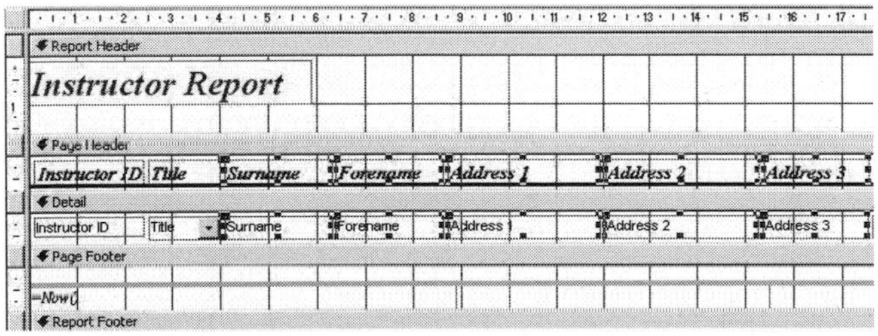

Figure 12.18

7 Select the control for the **Mobile No** and use the resizing handles to enlarge it. You may have to resize other controls.

8 Select the **Instructor Report** control in the **Report Header** and move it 5 cm to the right.

9 Click on the **Image** icon in the Toolbox and drag out a rectangle on the Report Header. Find the image you wish to insert as the logo and click on OK.

If your image is too big for the rectangle you have drawn, either:

- resize the rectangle or
- right click on the image. Click on **Properties.** Click on the **Format** tab and in the **Size Mode** box click on **Zoom.**

Alternatively you can use copy and paste to import an image from another application.

10 Click on **View, Layout Preview** to view your report in Layout Preview mode (see Figure 12.19).

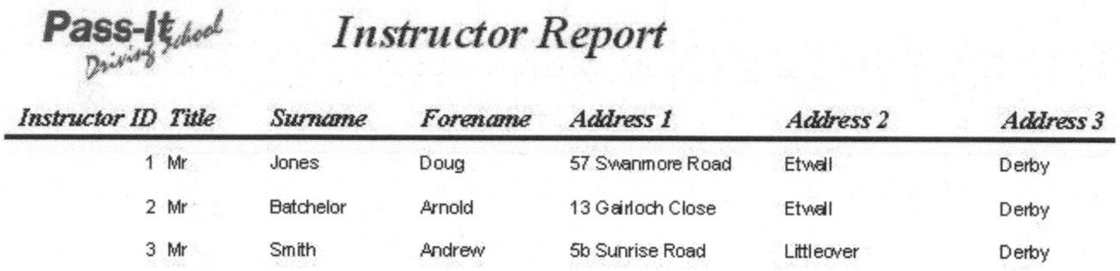
Pass-It Driving School
Instructor Report
Instructor ID Title Surname Forename Address 1 Address 2 Address 3
1 Mr Jones Doug 57 Swanmore Road Etwall Derby
2 Mr Batchelor Arnold 13 Gairloch Close Etwall Derby
3 Mr Smith Andrew 5b Sunrise Road Littleover Derby

Figure 12.19

Further customisation

We can further improve our report as follows:

1 Switch back to Design View and expand the detail area as shown in Figure 12.20.

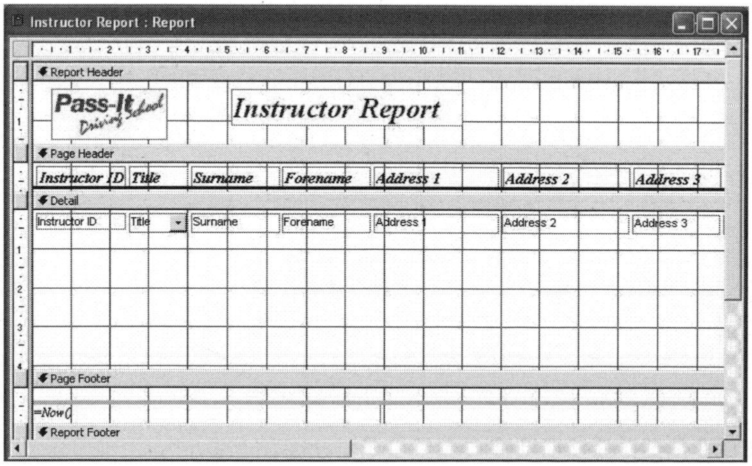
Instructor Report : Report
Report Header
Pass-It Driving School
Instructor Report
Page Header
Instructor ID Title Surname Forename Address 1 Address 2 Address 3
Detail
Instructor ID Title Surname Forename Address 1 Address 2 Address 3
Page Footer
=Now()
Report Footer

Figure 12.20

2 Increase the font size of the data (currently size 8) to size 10 by selecting all the controls in the detail section and choosing size 10 in the formatting toolbar.

3 Delete the labels in the Page Header for **Title**, **Forename**, **Address 2**, **Address 3**, **Address 4** and **Mobile No.** (Select each label in turn and press DELETE.)

4 Edit the remaining labels to read **Instructor ID**, **Name**, **Address** and **Phone** (see Figure 12.21).

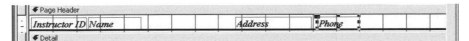

Figure 12.21

5 Move the controls in the Detail section to look like the report below in Figure 12.22.

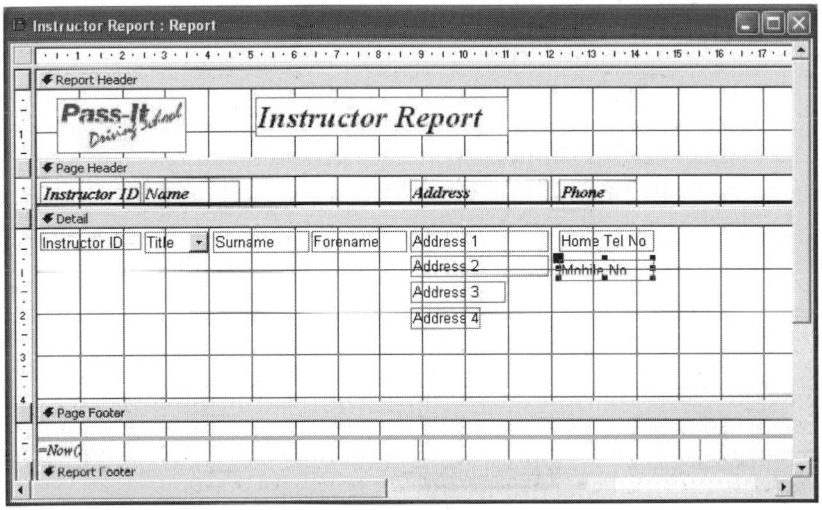

Figure 12.22

6 Move the controls into roughly the right position. Select all the address controls and then click on **Format, Align, Left** to get the controls in a straight line. Click on **Format, Vertical Spacing, Make Equal** to space the controls equally.

7   Switch to **Layout Preview** to see the finished report as in Figure 12.23.

Pass-It *Driving School*   *Instructor Report*

Instructor ID	Name			Address	Phone
1	Mr	Jones	Doug	57 Swanmore Road	01332122541
				Etwall	07720521478
				Derby	
				DE34 5F	
2	Mr	Batchelor	Arnold	13 Gairloch Close	0133255214 7
				Etwall	0798035214 5
				Derby	
				DE34 5F	
3	Mr	Smith	Andrew	5b Sunrise Road	01332521452
				Littleover	07980525214
				Derby	
				DE45 4E	

Figure 12.23

Report 2: Student Report using the Report Wizard

We want to set up a report to show a list of all the students. This report will be based on the Student table.

1   At the **Database Window** click on **Reports** and click on **New**.

2   Click on **Report Wizard** and in the drop-down list click on **Student**. Click on **OK**.

3   Click on the double arrow to choose all the fields for your report and click on **Next**.

4   Click on **Next** to ignore any grouping levels.

5   Click on **Next** to ignore sort options.

6   Select **Tabular** and **Landscape** and click on **Next**.

7   Select **Corporate** and click on **Next**.

8   Call the report **Student Report** and click on **Finish**.

The report will open in Report View. Switch to Design View as below in Figure 12.24. You will need to edit the report. There is no set way to do this.

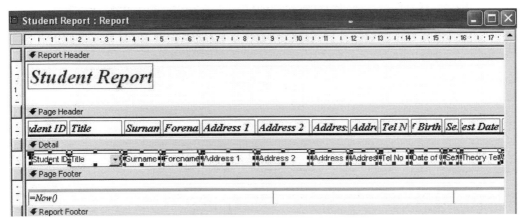

Figure 12.24

Carefully select all the controls in the Detail area by dragging across them and use **Format, Horizontal Spacing, Increase** to create room for editing the controls. You will then need to resize and reposition the labels in the Page Header.

Professional-looking reports

In this unit we have looked at methods of quickly developing a report using the Access wizards and customising the layout using simple formatting techniques. When planning and developing a system ideally the designer would agree on standard layouts and fonts so that all reports are consistent and have a professional look. Access offers a number of facilities to take report design further:

○ the toolbox offers line, rectangle and image tools;
○ colour fill options can be added to Header, Footer and Detail areas;
○ all objects on a report have properties giving you even greater control over the appearance of each.

With a little thought to design the Instructor Report developed earlier in this unit can be presented as in Figure 12.25.

Pass-It *Driving School*

Instructor Report

24 November 2002

Instructor ID	Name			Address	Phone
1	Mr	Jones	Doug	57 Swanmore Road Etwall Derby DE34 5F	01332 22541 07720521478
2	Mr	Batchelor	Arnold	13 Gairloch Close Etwall Derby DE34 5F	01332552147 07980352145
3	Mr	Smith	Andrew	5b Sunrise Road Littleover Derby DE45 4E	01332521452 07980525214

Figure 12.25

Load the Instructor Report in Design View and experiment with the following instructions to achieve a more professional look.

In the Report Header:

1   Right click on the logo to view its properties. Set its **Special Effect** to **Raised**, **Border Style** to **Solid**, **Border Colour** to **Black** and **Border Width** to **1pt**.

2   Move the Instructor Report title to the right. Set its Border properties as above, **Font Name** to **Times New Roman**, **Font Size** to **20**, **Font Weight** to **Bold**, **Fore Colour** to **Black** and **Font Italic** to **No**.

3   Drag the Date control in the Footer to the Header area and align with the Instructor Report title. Leaving its Font Size at 9, set its border and other font properties to those used in step 2.

4   Right Click in the Report Header area and set the **Fill/Back Colour** to **Light Grey**. You will now need to set the **Back Style** property of the **Date** control to **Normal**.

In the Page Header:

5   Select all the Heading controls and select **View, Properties**. Set the **Font Name** to **Times New Roman**, **Font Size** to **11**, **Font Weight** to **Bold**, **Fore Colour** to **Black** and **Font Italic** to **No**.

6   Remove the blue line the Access wizard uses. From the Toolbox select the Line tool and drag out a line the width of the report. View its properties and set its **Border Width** to **3 pt** and **Border Colour** to **Light Grey**.

7   From the Toolbox select the Rectangle tool and drag out a box around the headings. You will need to create a little room. Set its Border properties as above.

In the Page Footer:

8   Drag the grey line in the Page Footer to the bottom of the Detail area.

9   Move the page numbering control to the left of the Page Footer, set its **Text Align** property to **Left** and other **Font** properties to those used above.

10   Align all controls, lines and boxes to the right and left of the page as appropriate.

⊕ Unit 13 Further reports

In this section we are going to design two further reports. Both will be based on Queries.

○ A report to produce a membership card for one student.
○ A report to produce all the instructors' timetables for a particular date.

Report 1: Membership Card Report

We will set up a report to produce a membership card for a single student. When this report is opened, it will ask for the Student ID number and produce a membership card for that student.

The report will be based on the Query called Search by Student ID Query that we set up in Unit 7. We will use AutoReport: Columnar to set the report up.

1   At the Database Window click on **Reports** and click on **New**.

2   Click on **AutoReport: Columnar** and select **Search by Student ID Query** from the list. Click on **OK** (see Figure 13.1).

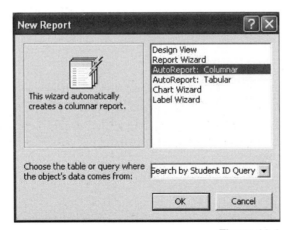

Figure 13.1

3   The report will load. As the report is based on a parameter query, this dialogue box will be displayed (see Figure 13.2).

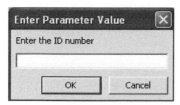

Figure 13.2

4 Enter Student ID **6** and you will see the membership card for student number 6 (see Figure 13.3).

Search by Student ID Query

Student ID	6
Surname	Windsor
Forename	David
Address 1	86 Milford Road
Address 2	Allenton
Address 3	Derby
Address 4	DE57 4PT
Tel No	01332389144
Date of Birth	18/08/84
Sex	M

Figure 13.3

5 Close the window and save the report as **Membership Card Report**.

6 However, the report needs to be customised. The wizard puts all the data in boxes with a border which we don't want. Open the **Membership Card Report** and switch to Design View.

7 Select all the controls in the detail section by dragging a rectangle over all of them or by pressing CTRL+A and deselecting the header and footer controls by clicking the control with SHIFT held down (see Figure 13.4).

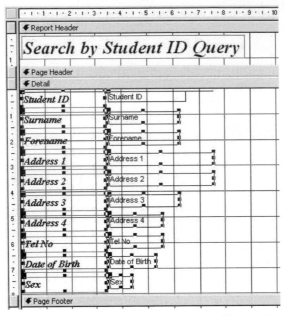

Figure 13.4

8 Click on the toolbar **Properties** icon or click on **View, Properties**.

9 Click on the **Format** tab and click in the **Border Style** box and select **Transparent** (see Figure 13.5).

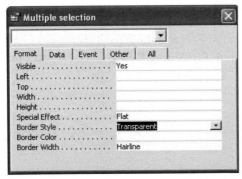

Figure 13.5

10 Switch to Print Preview to check that the boxes have been removed as shown in Figure 13.6.

Search by Student ID Query

Student ID	6
Surname	Windsor
Forename	David
Address 1	86 Milford Road
Address 2	Allenton
Address 3	Derby
Address 4	DE57 4PT
Tel No	01332389144
Date of Birth	18/08/84
Sex	M

Figure 13.6

As you can see, two controls, Student ID and Date of Birth, are not left aligned.

11 Switch back to Design View. Select each of these controls in turn and click on the **Align Left** icon. (You can also align the text by clicking on **View**, **Properties**, clicking on the **Format** tab and set the **Text Align** property to **Left**.)

12 Click on the **Image** icon from the Toolbox and drag out a box in the report header to add the company logo image as before.

13 Change the title in the Report Header to **Membership Card**.

14 Expand the Page Footer by dragging the border down. Delete the date and page number controls. Click on the **Label** icon in the Toolbox. Drag out a rectangle in the Page Footer. Enter the text as shown in Figure 13.7. Use SHIFT+ENTER to force a return and format to centre.

Pass-It *Driving School* *Membership Card*

Student ID	6
Surname	Windsor
Forename	David
Address 1	86 Milford Road
Address 2	Allenton
Address 3	Derby
Address 4	DE57 4PT
Tel No	01332389144
Date of Birth	18/08/84
Sex	M

*Please keep this card safe and
bring it with you to lessons.
Please inform us if any information is incorrect*

Figure 13.7

15 Save the report as **Membership Card Report**. Test the report for different Student IDs.

Note

This report is included purely to demonstrate certain features in Access. To develop further, refer to the Tricks and Tips section and use No. 39 entitled 'Mailing labels and membership cards' to provide a fully customised solution.

Report 2: Instructors' Timetable Report

We are going to set up a report showing all the instructors' timetables for a particular date. We will base this report on the query called **Full Details by Date Query** set up in Unit 8.

This report introduces you to grouping data in reports. We need to group together all the lessons for instructor number 1, then instructor number 2 and so on. If you want to group data, it is easier to use the Report Wizard than AutoReport.

1   At the Database Window, click on **Reports** and click on **New**.

2   Click on **Report Wizard** and select **Full Details by Date Query** from the list. Click
     on **OK** (see Figure 13.8).

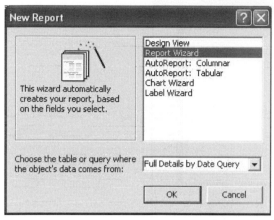

Figure 13.8

3   In the next dialogue box, click on the field **Student_Forename**, then click on the
     single arrow (>) to add to the selected fields. In the same way add
     Student_Surname, Instructor ID, Start Time, Length of Lesson and click on
     Next.

4   The next dialogue box asks how you want to view your data. Click on **by Lesson**.
     Click on **Next** (see Figure 13.9).

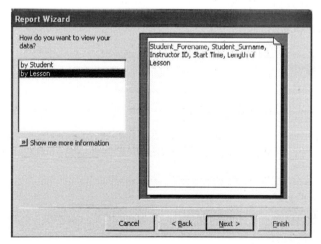

Figure 13.9

5   When asked '**Do you want to add any grouping levels?**' click on **Instructor ID** to group by instructor and click on the arrow icon (>). Click on **Next** (see Figure 13.10).

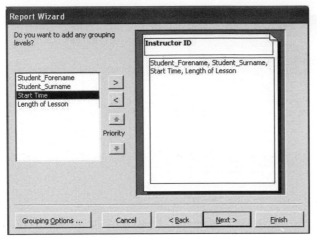

Figure 13.10

6   Sort by **Start Time**. Click on **Next**.

7   Click on **Align Left 1** and click on **Next**.

8   Click on **Corporate** and click on **Next**.

9   Call it **Instructors' Timetable Report** and click on **Finish**.

10 Enter the date **30/07/02** when prompted.

The report should look like the one in Figure 13.11.

Instructors' Timetable Report

Instructor ID			1	
	Start Time	Student_Forename	Student_Surname	Length of Lesson
	08:00	Robert	Brammer	1
	09:00	Steven	Jenkins	2
	11:00	Mary	Trueman	1
	12:00	Victoria	Spencer	3

Instructor ID			2	
	Start Time	Student_Forename	Student_Surname	Length of Lesson
	12:00	David	Windsor	1

Figure 13.11

We can see that the output is grouped by instructor, but it is rather unsatisfactory because:

○ the instructors' names are not on the report;
○ the date is not on the report;
○ the column headings are Student_Forename and Student_Surname.

Switch to Design View and:

1 Alter the **Student_Forename** column heading in the **Instructor ID Header** to read **Name**.

2 Delete the **Student_Surname** column heading by selecting it and pressing the DELETE key.

3 If the Field List is not displayed, click on the **Field List** icon or click on **View, Field List**.

4 Drag **Date** from the Field List on to the Report Header.

5 Select the new **Date** control (not the label). Click on the **Properties** icon and click on the **Format** tab. Set the first (**Format**) property to **Long Date** (see Figure 13.12).

Text Box: Date

Date

| Format | Data | Event | Other | All |

Format . . . . Long Date
Decimal Places . . . . Auto
Visible . . . . Yes
Hide Duplicates . . . . No
Can Grow . . . . No
Can Shrink . . . . No
Left 13.198cm
Top 0.399cm
Width 3cm
Height 0.423cm
Back Style . . . . Transparent

Figure 13.12

6 Select the label for the **Date** field and delete it by pressing the DELETE key.

7 Drag both the **Instructor_Forename** and **Instructor_Surname** from the Field List on to the **Instructor ID Header**.

8 Select the labels for these fields and delete them.

9 Move the title and add a company logo as before.

The report looks like this in Design View (Figure 13.13).

Figure 13.13

10   Switch to Print Preview mode. Enter the date **30/07/02**. The report should look similar to Figure 13.14.

Pass-It *Driving School* **Instructors' Timetable Report**   30 July 2002

Instructor ID		1 Doug	Jones

Start Time	Name		Length of Lesson
08:00	Robert	Brammer	1
09:00	Steven	Jenkins	2
11:00	Mary	Trueman	1
12:00	Victoria	Spencer	3

Instructor ID		2 Arnold	Batchelor

Start Time	Name		Length of Lesson
12:00	David	Windsor	1

Figure 13.14

Putting each instructor on a new page

Sometimes you might want each section of a report on a new page. For example, in the above report, you may want the timetable for each instructor printed on a separate page, one to give to each instructor.

To force a new page in a report:

1   Load the report in Design View. We need an **Instructor ID Footer**. Make sure the Report Design toolbar is showing (see Figure 13.15). Click on the **Sorting and Grouping Icon** or click on **View, Sorting and Grouping**.

Figure 13.15

2   In the dialogue box that appears (see Figure 13.16), click on **Instructor ID** and change **Group Footer** to **Yes**.

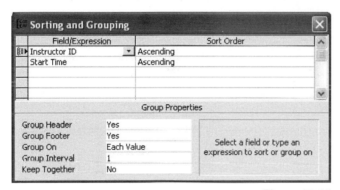

Figure 13.16

A blank **Instructor ID Footer** has now appeared below the Detail section (see Figure 13.17).

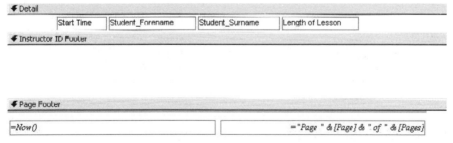

Figure 13.17

3   Click in the **Instructor ID** Footer.

4   Click on the **Properties** icon or click on **View, Properties.**

5   Click on the **Format** tab and set **Force New Page** to **After Section** (see Figure 13.18).

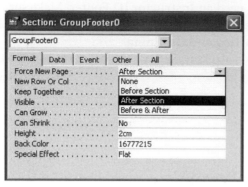

Figure 13.18

6   Switch to **Print Preview** mode to check that each instructor is on a new page.

Note   The driving school logo and details should be in the Page Header and not the Report Header so that they appear on every page. Enlarge the Page Header, then select the contents of the Report Header and drag them into the Page Header.

⊕ Unit 14 Macros

A **macro** combines a series of Access instructions into a single command. Macros can be run by clicking a button, e.g. on a form or switchboard or can be triggered by an event, such as closing a form.

The Pass-It system consists so far of the three forms to manage information about the Students, Instructors and Lesson Bookings together with a number of reports.

In this section you will learn how to use a few simple macros to begin to automate the system. Macros will be dealt with in more detail later.

Macro 1: A macro to open the Student Form

1   At the Database Window click on **Macros** and click on **New**.

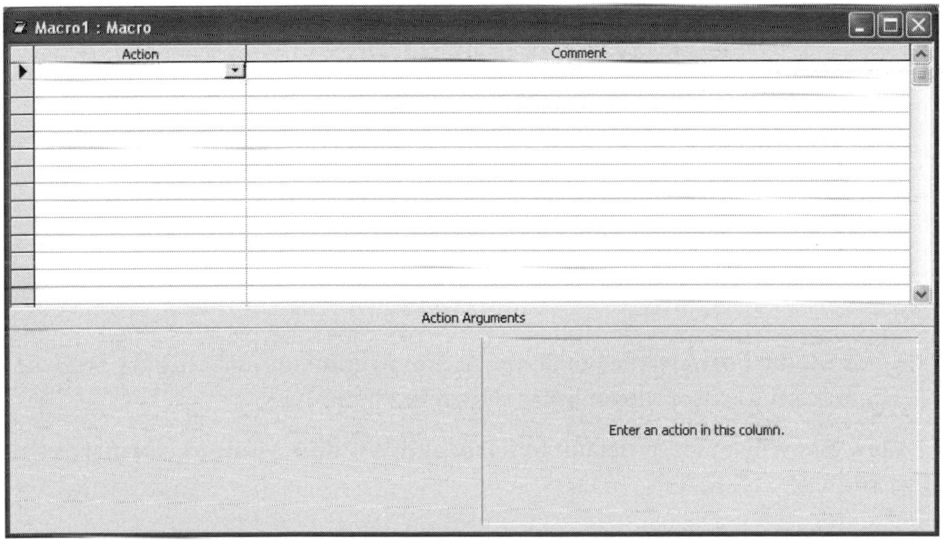

Figure 14.1

The Macro window opens as shown in Figure 14.1. It consists of an Action column from which you choose the actions and a Comments column where you can add comments to remind you of each function.

2 Click on the drop-down arrow in the **Action** column and click on **OpenForm** (see Figure 14.2).

Figure 14.2

You now need to choose which form to open in the Action Arguments section (see Figure 14.3).

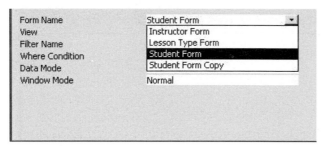

Figure 14.3

3 Click on the **Form Name** box in the Action Arguments and click on **Student Form** from the drop-down list as shown in Figure 14.3.

The **View** box will be set by default to **Form** and **Window Mode** to **Normal** as shown in Figure 14.4.

Form Name	Student Form
View	Form
Filter Name	
Where Condition	
Data Mode	
Window Mode	Normal

Figure 14.4

4   Close the Macro window and save as **Student Macro**.

5   At the Database Window, test the macro by clicking on the Run icon.

Macros can have more than one action. When you open a form, you may want to add a new student. We can edit the macro to open the form with a new blank record.

6   Open the **Student** macro in Design View. In the second row of the Actions column select **GotoRecord** from the drop-down list (see Figure 14.5).

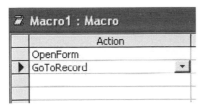

Figure 14.5

7   In the arguments section set **Record** to **New** (see Figure 14.6).

Figure 14.6

8   Save the macro. Go back to the Database Window and test it works.

Macro 2: Set up another macro called **Instructor Macro** to open the **Instructor Form** in the same way.

Macro 3: Set up another macro called **Lesson Macro** to open the **Lesson Booking Form** in the same way.

Macro 4: Setting up a message box

Most software packages have an About message box giving details of the company or developer. This can be set up using a macro.

1   At the Database Window click on **Macros** and click on **New**.

2   Select **MsgBox** in the Action column.

3   In the Action Arguments, click on the **Message** box and type **System by B Clough © 2001**.

4   In the **Beep** box select **Yes**.

5   In the **Type** box select **Information**.

6   In the **Title** box type **Pass-It Driving School** (see Figure 14.7).

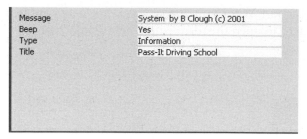

Message	System by B Clough (c) 2001
Beep	Yes
Type	Information
Title	Pass-It Driving School

Figure 14.7

7   Save the macro as **About** and test it (see Figure 14.8).

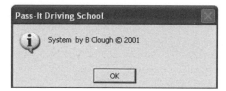

Figure 14.8

Hint

To get the copyright symbol, type (c) in Microsoft Word. AutoCorrect changes it into © and you can use copy and paste to take it into Access.

Using macros to customise a front end

You can use macros to pull your system together and produce an automated front end (see Figure 14.9). You may use this as an alternative to the switchboard shown in Chapter 15.

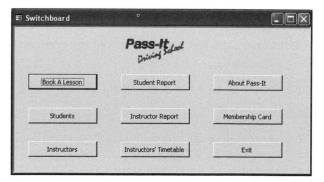

Figure 14.9

1   To set up a front end, at the database window, click on **Forms**. Click on **New**. Click on **Design View** and click on **OK**. This produces a blank form. You will need to enlarge it.

2   Use the **CommandButton** icon in the Toolbox to add command buttons to run the macros to open the **Student, Instructor** and **Lesson Booking** forms. You will have to click on **Miscellaneous** and select **Run Macro**. Set the text for the buttons as shown in Figure 14.9.

3   Add another button to run the **About** macro. Set the text to **About Pass-It**.

4   Set up another command button. Click on **Application.** Click on **Quit Application** and set the text to **Exit**.

5   Using the OpenReport macro command set up macros to run the following reports: **Instructor Report, Student Report, Membership Card Report** and **Instructors' Timetable Report**. Complete the form as shown in Figure 14.9.

6   Double click on the **Form Selector** to display the Form properties. Change the form caption using the **Caption** property to **Switchboard**. Make the form appear in the middle of the screen by setting the **Auto Center** property to **Yes**.

7   Remove the scroll bars, the navigation buttons, the record selector and the dividing lines.

8   Save the form as **Switchboard**. Refer to the tricks and tips section, tip number 42, to set up a macro called **AutoExec** to load this form automatically when the file is opened.

⊕ Unit 15 Adding a switchboard

In the previous units you have designed the tables, queries, forms and reports that go to make up the Pass-It system.

All these options need to be available from a menu that loads when you start up your system. This is sometimes known as the front end or in Access as the switchboard (see Figure 15.1).

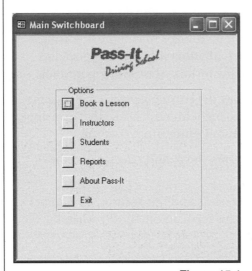

Figure 15.1

In this section we look at creating the switchboard shown above.
The switchboard will need to be able to:

○ open the Lesson Booking Form to find out lesson details or to book a lesson;
○ open the Student Form to find out student details;
○ open the Instructor Form to find out instructor details;
○ produce a list of instructors (Instructor Report);
○ produce a list of students (Student Report);
○ produce a membership card (Membership Card Report);
○ produce a timetable for an instructor (Instructors' Timetable Report);
○ run the About (message box) macro;
○ exit from the system.

To fit on all these options, it is best to use two switchboards. One switchboard will link to the reports; the main switchboard will link to the other options. The switchboards will link as shown in Figure 15.2.

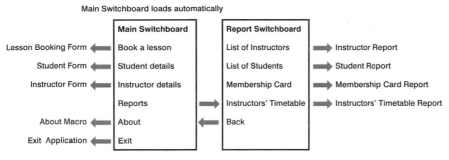

Figure 15.2

There is a Switchboard Manager wizard to help you set up a switchboard.

Creating a switchboard with the Switchboard Manager

First you will need to delete or rename the switchboard set up in Unit 14. To set up a new switchboard go to the Database Window.

1   In Access 2000 and Access 2002, click on **Tools, Database Utilities, Switchboard Manager.** In Access 97, click on **Tools, Add-Ins, Switchboard Manager**.

It will ask if you want to create a switchboard (see Figure 15.3). Click on **Yes**.

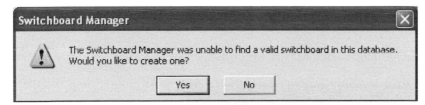

Figure 15.3

This sets up a default switchboard called the Main Switchboard (see Figure 15.4). From here we need to set up another switchboard for the reports.

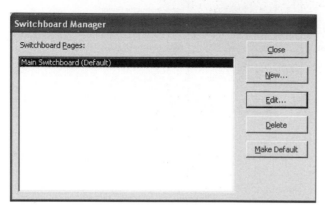

Figure 15.4

2   At the **Switchboard Manager** dialogue box click on **New** (see Figure 15.4). Enter the name of the second switchboard, **Report Switchboard**, and click on **OK** (see Figure 15.5).

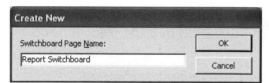

Figure 15.5

3   Select the **Main Switchboard** and click on **Edit** (see Figure 15.6).

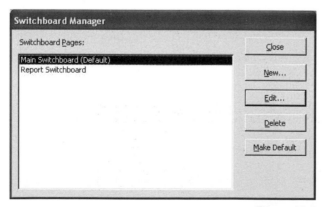

Figure 15.6

4   At the **Edit Switchboard Page**, click on **New** (see Figure 15.7).

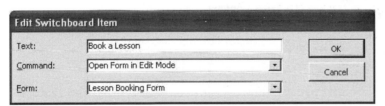

Figure 15.7

5   Edit the Text in the **Edit Switchboard Item** dialogue box so that it reads **Book a Lesson** (see Figure 15.8).

6   Click on **Open Form in Edit Mode** from the drop-down text in the **Command** box.

7   Click on **Lesson Booking Form** in the **Form** box. Click on **OK**.

Figure 15.8

These steps set up the first button on our switchboard with the text Book A Lesson. When you click the button it will open the Lesson Booking Form.

There are many options at this stage (see Figure 15.9). It is worth exploring the different options.

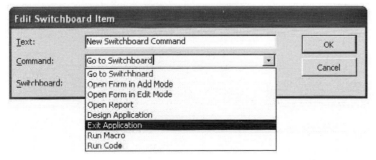

Figure 15.9

The development of a system

We will now continue to set up the other buttons on the switchboard.

8   Click on **New** to set up another Switchboard item. The text should be **Instructors**. Click on **Open Form in Edit Mode** in the **Command** box. Select **Instructor Form**. Click on **OK**.

9   Click on **New** to set up another Switchboard item. The text should be **Students**. Click on **Open Form in Edit Mode** in the **Command** box. Select **Student Form**. Click on **OK**.

10   Click on **New** to set up another Switchboard item. The text should be **Reports**. Click on **Go to Switchboard** in the **Command** box. Select **Report Switchboard**. Click on **OK**.

11   Click on **New** to set up another Switchboard item. The text should be **About Pass-It**. Click on **Run Macro** in the **Command** box. Select **About**. Click on **OK**.

12   Click on **New** to set up another Switchboard item. The text should be **Exit**. Click on **Exit Application** in the **Command** box (see Figure 15.10). Click on **OK**.

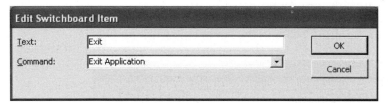

Figure 15.10

13   The **Edit Switchboard Page** will now appear as in Figure 15.11. You can use this page to edit the switchboard, delete or add new items. You can also move items up or down the switchboard list.

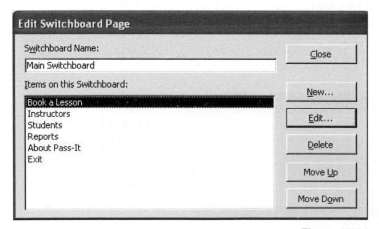

Figure 15.11

14 You have now set up a switchboard with six options. Click on **Close** twice to go back to the Database Window. There will now be a new form listed called **Switchboard** (see Figure 15.12).

Figure 15.12

15 Open the **Switchboard** form. It will look something like Figure 15.13.

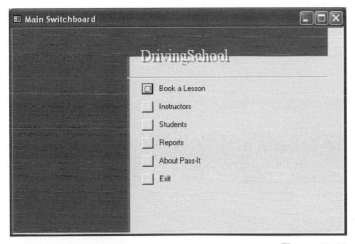

Figure 15.13

Test that each of the buttons works. The Book a Lesson button will create a new record in the Lesson Booking Form. The Report Switchboard will not yet be available.

Customising the switchboard

1   Open the switchboard in Design View so that it can be edited like any other form. You will notice that there are eight buttons even though we only set up six of them. (Do not delete the bottom two buttons.) You will also notice that the label for each button is not shown.

2   Select the title and delete it.

3   There are two green rectangles, one dark grey rectangle and a sunken line. Select them and delete them.

4   Insert your logo near the top of the form in the usual way (see Figure 15.14).

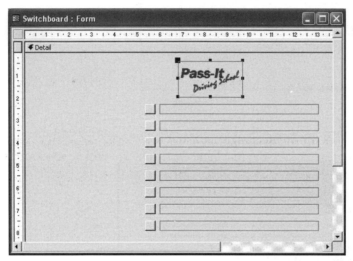

Figure 15.14

5   Highlight all the controls by pressing CTRL+A. Move all the controls to the left of the form and then make the form narrower as shown in Figure 15.15. It will help to reduce the size of the button labels.

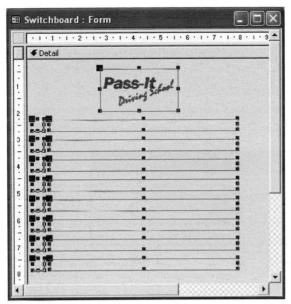

Figure 15.15

6   From the Toolbox click on the Rectangle icon and draw a rectangle around the six
options as shown in Figure 15.16. Add a label **Options**. You will nccd to set its
Back Style property to **Normal** and its **Back Colour** to XP background
(14215660). Position the label over the border of the rectangle.

The completed switchboard is shown in Figure 15.16.

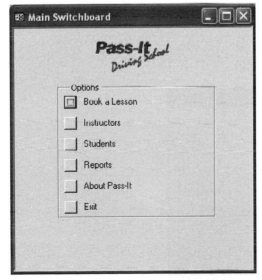

Figure 15.16

Adding the Report Switchboard

1 At the database window, load the **Switchboard Manager** again. Click on **Report Switchboard** and click on **Edit**.

2 Click on **New** to set up another Switchboard item. The text should be **List of Instructors.** Select **Open Report** in the **Command** box. Select **Instructor Report.** Click on **OK** (see Figure 15.17).

Figure 15.17

3 Click on **New** to set up another Switchboard item. The text should be **List of Students.** Select **Open Report** in the **Command** box. Select **Student Report.** Click on **OK**.

4 Click on **New** to set up another Switchboard item. The text should be **Membership Card.** Select **Open Report** in the **Command** box. Select **Membership Card Report.** Click on **OK**.

5 Click on **New** to set up another Switchboard item. The text should be **Instructors' Timetable**. Select **Open Report** in the **Command** box. Select **Instructors' Timetable Report.** Click on **OK**.

6 Click on **New** to set up the final Switchboard item. The text should be **Back.** Click on **Go to Switchboard** in the **Command** box. Select **Main Switchboard**.

The Edit Switchboard Page is now shown in Figure 15.18.

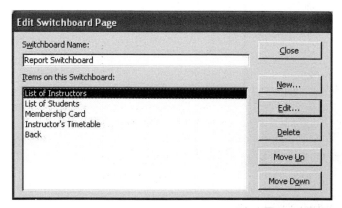

Figure 15.18

7   Click on **Close** twice to exit from the Switchboard Manager.

8   At the Database Window, click on Forms to open the Switchboard and test that all the buttons on both switchboards work. The Report Switchboard will look like the one shown in Figure 15.19.

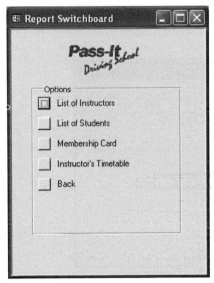

Figure 15.19

If you go back to the Database Window and click on **Tables**, you will see that an additional table called **Switchboard Items** has been set up. If you open the table (see Figure 15.20), you can see that it controls the switchboard.

SwitchboardID	ItemNumber	ItemText	Command	Argument
1	0	Main Switchboa		Default
1	1	Book a Lesson	3	Lesson Booking Form
1	2	Instructors	3	Instructor Form
1	3	Students	3	Student Form
1	4	Reports	1	2
1	5	About Pass-It	7	About
1	6	Exit	6	
2	0	Report Switchbo	0	
2	1	List of Instructor	4	Instructor Report
2	2	List of Students	4	Student Report
2	3	Membership Ca	4	Membership Card Report
2	4	Instructor's Time	4	Instructors' Timetable Report
2	5	Back	1	1
	0			

Record: 14 4 | 1 | ▶ ▶I ▶* of 13

Figure 15.20

This table can be used to edit the switchboard text.

Setting the Startup options

We want the switchboard to load automatically when the file is opened. One way of doing this is to use **Tools, Startup** from the main menu.

Set it up as follows:

1   At the Database Window, click on **Tools, Startup** to load the **Startup** dialogue box (see Figure 15.21).

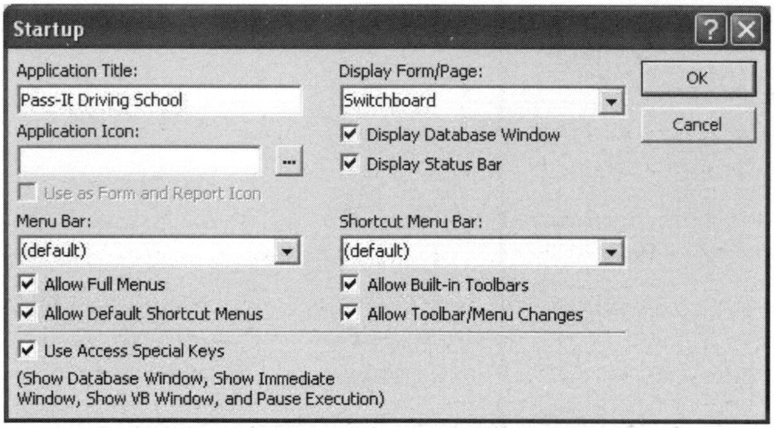

Figure 15.21

2   Click on the **Display Form/Page** drop-down arrow and select **Switchboard.** This is the name of the form you want to load on start-up.

3   In the **Application Title** box enter **Pass-It Driving School.** This is the text that appears at the top of the Access screen.

This dialogue box can also be used to disable the right click, hide the database window and customise the menu bars. **Be careful.** While developing your system you need access to most of these options.

4   Close your system and reload it. Test that the switchboard opens when the system loads and that the application title is displayed.

⊕ Unit 16 Using SubForms

In this section you will learn how to use SubForms.

In Access systems there will be many instances when it is necessary to see data from related tables on one screen. Using a SubForm is one of a number of ways of doing this.

For example:

In a video loans system you may wish to have membership details on screen alongside details of videos loaned by that member.

In a customer ordering system when a customer phones up with an order enquiry it would be useful to have the customer details and details of their orders on screen.

In the Pass-It Driving School you may wish to view instructor details alongside their lessons as shown in Figure 16.1. The Instructor Form is set just to show details of name and ID. A SubForm is added showing details of the lessons for that instructor.

Instructor Main Form

Instructor ID	1
Surname	Jones
Forename	Doug

Lesson

Student ID	Date	Start Time	Collection Point
1	30/07/02	08:00	Home Address
2	30/07/02	09:00	Derby Station
3	31/07/02	13:00	John Port School

Record: ◄◄ ◄ 1 ► ►► ►✱ of 7

Record: ◄◄ ◄ 1 ► ►► ►✱ of 3

Figure 16.1

Typically in this sort of scenario a main form is set up based on the primary table Instructor with a SubForm based on the Lesson table. This is the simplest way forward but you will see later how to have greater control over the SubForm by basing it on a query.

The following three examples take you through setting up similar uses of SubForms but in slightly different ways. It is worthwhile practising the different methods to grasp the concepts involved here.

Worked Example 1

The following steps show you how to set up the SubForm as shown above. We will use the wizard to make a start.

1 At the Database Window select **Forms** and click on **New** to bring up the New Form dialogue box.

2 Choose **Form Wizard** and select the **Instructor** table from the drop-down. Click **OK** (see Figure 16.2).

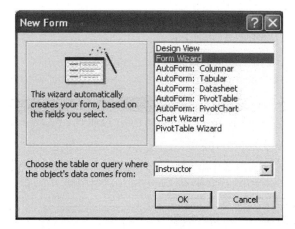

Figure 16.2

3 Select the **Instructor** table and choose the fields **Instructor ID, Surname** and **Forename** from the available fields. Remember you can select the fields one by one by clicking the single arrow. Do not click **Next** yet.

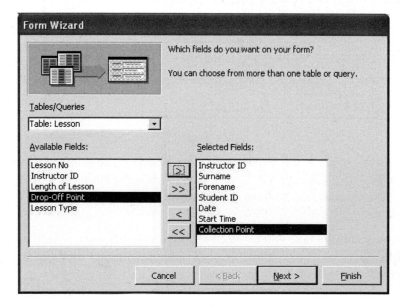

Figure 16.3

4   We now want to select the fields for the SubForm. Select the **Lesson** table from the drop-down and add **Student ID, Date, Start Time** and **Collection Point** from the available fields. Click on **Next** (see Figure 16.3).

5   The Form Wizard then asks you 'How do you want to view your data?' Make sure **by Instructor** is selected and **Form with subforms(s)** is checked and click on **Next** (see Figure 16.4).

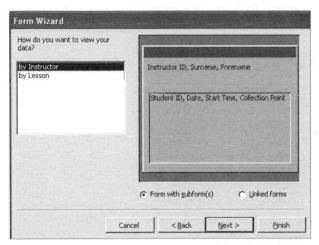

Figure 16.4

6   Select a **Tabular** layout and click on **Next**. Select a **Standard** style and click on **Next.**

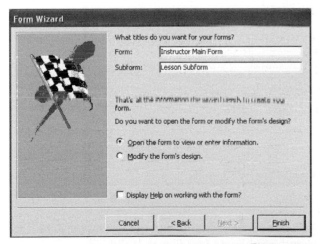

Figure 16.5

7   Name the form **Instructor Main Form** and the SubForm **Lesson Subform.** Click on **Finish** (see Figure 16.5).

Your Main form/SubForm should appear as at the start of the unit. See Figure 16.1. Its appearance will need a little fine tuning.

8 Go into Design View and double click on the **Form Selector** on the main form to bring up the Properties. Remove the **Scroll Bars**, **Record Selectors** and **Dividing Lines**.

9 At the Database Window open the **Lesson Subform** in Design View as shown in Figure 16.6. From here you can edit the labels, adjust the size of the form and call up the properties of each control by right clicking on the control and selecting properties.

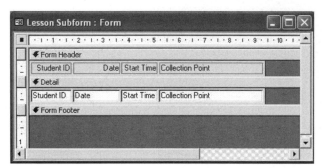

Figure 16.6

10 Format, (we have left-aligned the controls), resize and reposition the form as required and double click on the **Form Selector** and remove the **Navigation buttons.** Save your work.

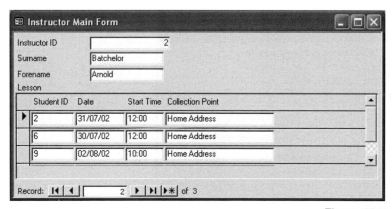

Figure 16.7

11 With the **Instructor Main Form** open scroll through the instructor details to view the details of their lessons in the SubForm (see Figure 16.7).

There are a number of ways of setting up SubForms in Access. As ever you choose the method that suits you best. The next example will take you through setting up a SubForm in a slightly different way.

Worked Example 2

We are going to set up a SubForm on the Student Form giving details of each student's lessons.

1 At the Database Window select **Forms** and click on **New**.

2 Set up a student form by choosing **AutoForm: Columnar** and selecting the **Student** table from the drop-down.

3 Go into Design View to remove the fields just leaving the name and address. Rearrange as shown in Figure 16.8.

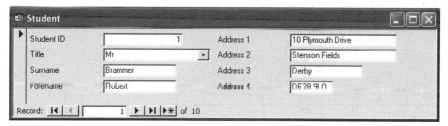

Figure 16.8

4 Go into Design View and from the toolbox click on the **Subform/Subreport** icon and drag out a rectangle about 13 cm by 2 cm across the foot of the form.

5 The SubForm Wizard is displayed. Check **Use existing Tables and Queries** and click on **Next** (see Figure 16.9).

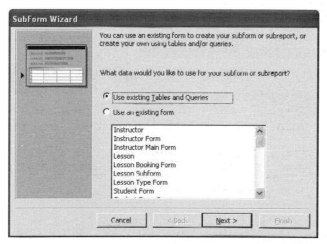

Figure 16.9

6   From the next SubForm Wizard dialogue box, select the **Lesson** table from the drop-down and select the fields as shown below. Click on **Next** (see Figure 16.10).

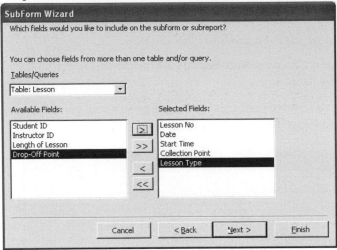

Figure 16.10

7   In the next SubForm Wizard dialogue box the wizard detects the linking fields for you so just click on **Next** (see Figure 16.11).

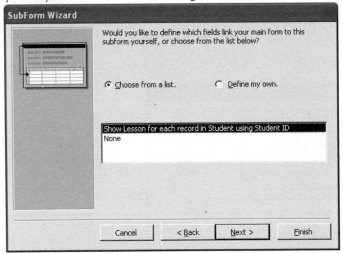

Figure 16.11

8   Call your SubForm **Lesson Details** and click on **Finish**.

9   Save your form as **Student Lesson Details**.

10 Open **Student Lesson Details** form in Form View. You will see that it needs some editing to improve its appearance.

11 Select Design View, double click on the Form Selector of the main form and remove the **Record Selector**, **Scroll Bars** and **Dividing Lines**.

12 Switch back to Form View. The SubForm appears by default in Datasheet View from which you can easily change the widths of the columns by dragging in/out the columns as required.

13 At the Database Window open the **Lesson Details** SubForm in Design View. Edit the labels and align the text as required.

Your form should look something like Figure 16.12.

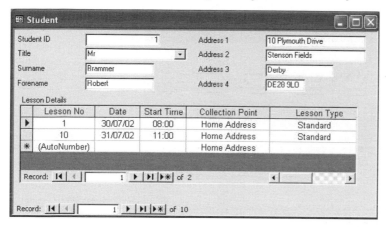

Figure 16.12

Note

None of the forms developed in this section so far is part of the Pass-It system. To avoid confusion it is recommended that you go into the Database Window and delete the forms **Instructor Main Form**, **Lesson Subform** and **Student Lesson Details** by selecting each in turn and pressing DELETE.

Worked Example 3

In the next example we will set up our forms without using the wizards. Very simply the main form and the SubForm are set up separately and then the SubForm is dragged and dropped onto the main form.

1 At the Database Window select **Forms** and click on **New**.

2 Set up a Student form by choosing **AutoForm: Columnar** and selecting the **Student** table from the drop-down list.

3 Go into Design View to remove the fields just leaving the name and address. Rearrange as shown in Figure 16.13.

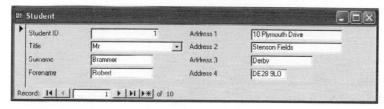

Figure 16.13

4   Save the form as **Student Main Form**.

5   Use the Form Wizard to set up a form based on the **Lesson** table. Select the fields **Lesson No, Date, Start Time, Collection Point** and **Lesson Type**.

6   Select a **Tabular** layout, **Standard** style and name the form **Lesson Details** (you may decide to call it by a different name if you don't want to delete your previous work) (see Figure 16.14).

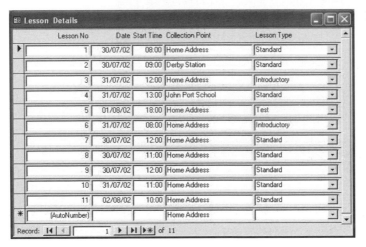

Figure 16.14

7   Open the **Student Main Form** in Design View.

8   Press F11 to view the Database Window and drag and drop the icon for the **Lesson Details** form on to the lower area of the **Student Main Form** (see Figure 16.15).

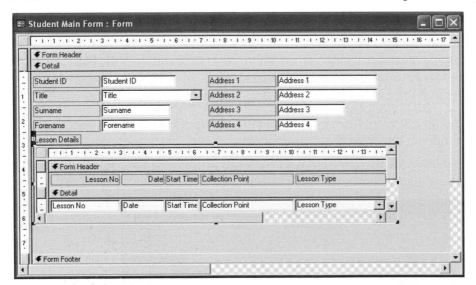

Figure 16.15

9   Click on Form Properties for the **Student Main Form** and remove the Scroll Bars, Record Selectors and Dividing Lines.

10 Position and resize the form as shown in Figure 16.16.

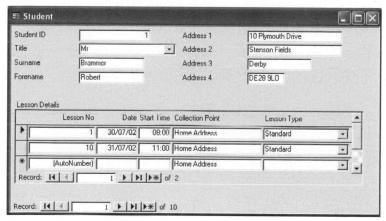

Figure 16.16

Note

Neither of these forms are needed in the Pass-It system and you may decide to delete them.

Setting up the SubForms in the Pass-It Driving School system

We are going to set up two SubForms in the Pass-It system. Both will be based on queries and both will be accessed and displayed from the main Lesson Booking Form at the heart of the system.

When a student rings up to book a lesson the driving school will want to be able to view quickly lesson availability for that day and perhaps for the week for their attached instructor.

This section will also introduce you to using Tab Controls. The Tab Control is selected from the Toolbox as shown in Figure 16.17.

Figure 16.17

These are particularly useful when the information you wish to view is too much for one form.

1   Load the **Lesson Booking Form** in Design View.

2   Drag out the right margin and Form Footer to fill the screen.

3   Select the left-hand controls and drag them toward the top of the screen.

4   Select the right-hand controls and drag to a position below the left-hand controls as shown in Figure 16.18. This creates room for our Tab Controls.

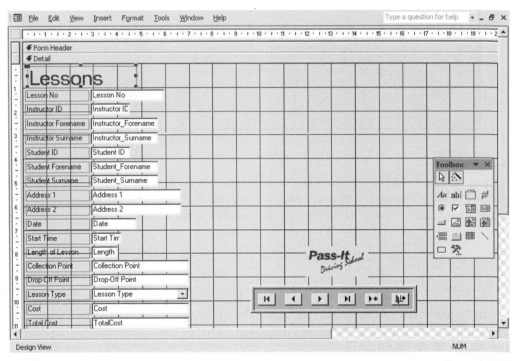

Figure 16.18

5   From the toolbox choose the **Tab Control** and drag out a rectangle across the screen about 12 cm by 7 cm.

Figure 16.19

The Tab Control will be headed by some page numbers as shown in Figure 16.19. Double click on the left one and set its caption property to **Daily Timetable** (see Figure 16.20).

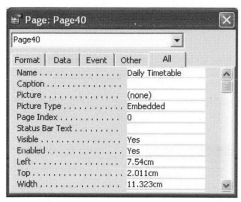

Figure 16.20

6 Double click on the other one and set its caption property to **Weekly Timetable**.

7 We are now going to try and create a little more space. Delete the labels for Instructor Surname and Student Surname.

8 Move the Text boxes for Instructor Surname and Student Surname as shown in Figure 16.21. Rename the labels Instructor and Student respectively.

9 You will need to align the controls, format the vertical spacing and edit the labels but your form should appear as below after a little tinkering.

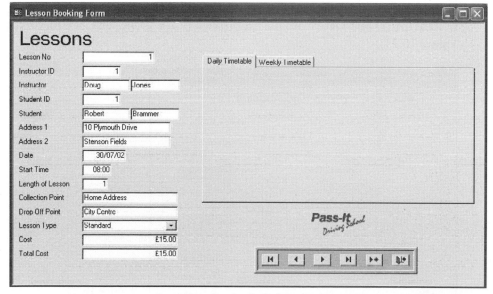

Figure 16.21

Adding the SubForm

1   Load the above form in Design View.

2   From the toolbox click on the **SubForm/SubReport** icon and drag out a rectangle in the Tab control area.

3   The SubForm Wizard opens. Click on **Use existing Tables and Queries** and click on **Next**.

4   In the next window choose the **Full Details Query** and select the available fields as shown in Figure 16.22. Click on **Next.**

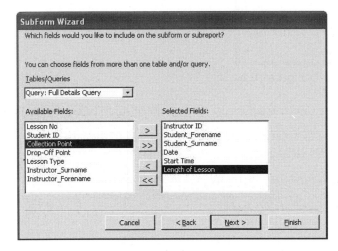

Figure 16.22

5   You then have to define your linking fields. Check **Define my own** and select **Instructor ID** and **Date** from the drop-down boxes as shown. Click on **Next** (see Figure 16.23).

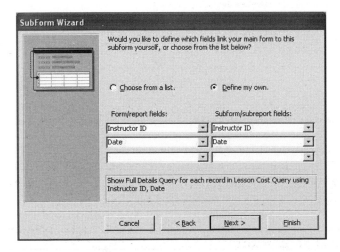

Figure 16.23

6   Call your SubForm **Daily Timetable** (see Figure 16.24). Click on **Finish**.

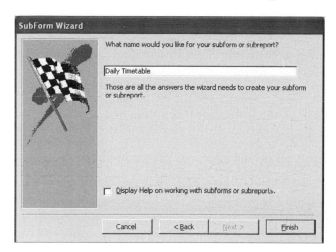

Figure 16.24

If you now open the Lesson Booking Form in Form View you will see it needs resizing and re-positioning. This can be tricky and can take a lot of patience. There are a number of general steps you can take.

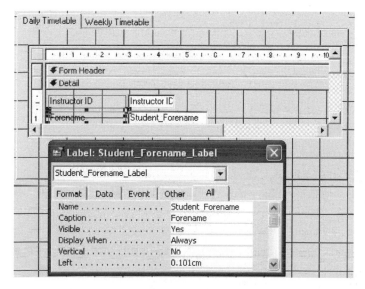

Figure 16.25

1   To change the column headings: In Design View select in turn each label in the **Detail** area of the SubForm. Right click and choose **Properties**. Click on the **All** tab and edit the **Caption**. Change Student_Forename, Student_Surname, Start Time and Length of Lesson to **Forename, Surname, Start** and **Length**.

2   Using the same technique select in turn each Text Box in the **Detail** area of the SubForm and set the **Text Align** property for **Student_Forename** and

Student_Surname to **Left**. Set the **Text Align** property for **Length of Lesson, Start** and **Date** to **Center**.

3   Delete the SubForm label **Daily Timetable.**

4   In Design View, use the ruler to ensure the Tab Control does not go more than 19 cm from the left margin of the form.

5   Go into Form View and adjust the column widths by dragging out or in the column dividers. Right click on the Instructor ID column and select **Hide Columns**.

It will take a little time but your form should appear as shown in Figure 16.26 eventually!

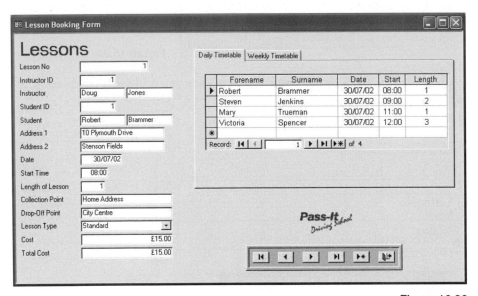

Figure 16.26

Adding the SubForm to display the Weekly Timetable

The process is nearly exactly the same as for the Daily Timetable but you need to base the form on a different query.

You will need to work on the second Tab Control called Weekly Timetable. Drag out a SubForm as before and base it on the **Next Week's Lessons Query** set up in Unit 8.

Use the fields **Instructor ID, Student_Forename, Student_Surname, Date, Start Time** and **Length of Lesson** as before.

When you link the fields in the SubForm, only link the **Instructor ID** and *not* the **Date**. Again you will need to format, resize and reposition the SubForm (see Figure 16.27).

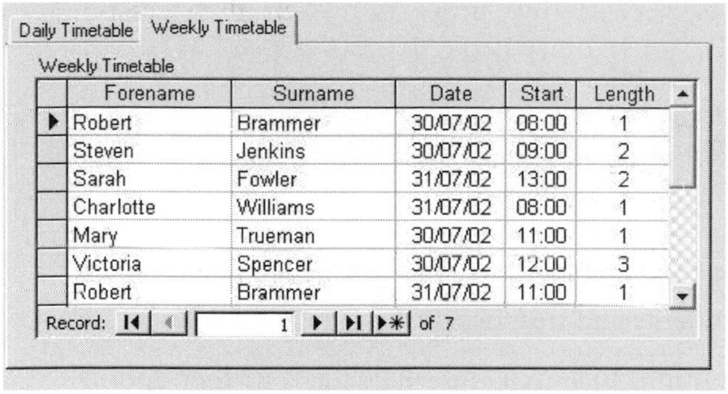

Daily Timetable | Weekly Timetable |

Weekly Timetable

	Forename	Surname	Date	Start	Length
▶	Robert	Brammer	30/07/02	08:00	1
	Steven	Jenkins	30/07/02	09:00	2
	Sarah	Fowler	31/07/02	13:00	2
	Charlotte	Williams	31/07/02	08:00	1
	Mary	Trueman	30/07/02	11:00	1
	Victoria	Spencer	30/07/02	12:00	3
	Robert	Brammer	31/07/02	11:00	1

Record: |◄| ◄ | 1 | ► | ►| | ►* | of 7

Figure 16.27

To test the new SubForm you will need to adjust the dates in your table or adjust the
time clock on your PC.

⊕ Unit 17 Setting up search and sort options

The user of the Pass-It Driving School will often need to quickly search and sort through records of Bookings, Students and Instructors.

In this section we will add user options to search and sort data. A further option will be added to cancel a lesson. The section also includes an option to deal with the scenario when a student phones to book a lesson and cannot remember their ID.

To add these options we will need to add a further Tab Control.

Setting up a New Tab Control

1 Open the **Lesson Booking Form** in Design View.
2 Select the **Tab Control Page** and from the menu choose **Insert, Tab Control Page.** Access adds another Tab Control with a Page Number.
3 Double click on the new Tab Control and in the Property sheet set the **Name** property to **Search Options**. Save your new **Lesson Booking Form**. It should appear as in Figure 17.1.

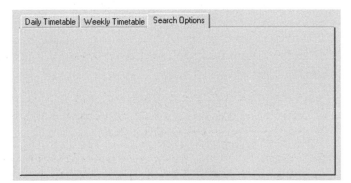

Figure 17.1

Adding filters

It is possible to filter data displayed in a form to display only the lessons with a particular student or only the lessons on a certain date.

We will set up a Command Button on the new Tab Control Page to run a macro to run a filter.

1   Create a new query based on the Lesson Table. Add all the fields from the table.

2   Type [**Enter the ID number**] into the Criteria row of the Student ID column of the QBE grid.

3   Save the query as **Student Lesson Query**.

4   Create a new macro. In the action column select **ApplyFilter**. In the Action Arguments set the **Filter Name** to **Student Lesson Query**.

5   Save the macro as **Search by Student**.

6   Open the **Lesson Booking Form** in **Design View**. Click on the **Search Options** Tab. From the Toolbox add a Command Button to the Tab.

7   In the Command Button Wizard window choose the **Miscellaneous** category, select **Run Macro** and click on **Next**.

8   In the next window choose the **Search by Student** macro and click on **Next**.

9   Select the Text option in the next window and set it to read **Filter by Student**. Click on **Next** and click **Finish** (see Figure 17.2).

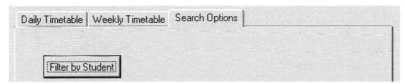

Figure 17.2

10 Go into **Form View** and test the button. You will be asked the Student ID. Scroll through the records to view this student's lessons.

11 Set up another Command Button to add a **Filter by Date** option. You will first need to set up a macro as before using the **Apply Filter** action based on the **Search on Lesson Date Query.** Call the macro **Search by Date**.

When you use the option to filter data into a sub-group of records it is important to restore all records before the next search. We will add a button to the Tab Control to remove the filter.

1   Create a new macro called **Show All Records**. It has just one action, **ShowAllRecords**.

2   Add a Command Button to the Tab Control Page to run this macro. The text on
     the button should read **Show All Records**. Your Tab Control Page should appear
     as in Figure 17.3. You will need to use the **Format, Align** and **Format, Size** menu
     options to position and size the buttons.

Figure 17.3

Adding sort options

You can sort the data displayed in a form into different orders. For example, you may
want to cycle through the records in order of Student ID, Lesson Number or by Date.

We will set up a macro to sort the records and then use a Command Button to run the
macro. The following steps take you through setting up the **Sort by Lesson** option.

1   Create a new macro. In the Action column select **GoToControl**. In the Action
     Arguments set the **Control Name** to **Lesson No.**

2   In the Action column select **RunCommand.** In the Action arguments select
     SortAscending from the drop-down arrow.

3   Save the macro as **Sort Lesson**.

4   Open **Lesson Booking Form** in **Design View**. Click on the **Search Options** Tab.
     Use the Command Button wizard to add a button to run the macro **Sort Lesson**
     and add the text **Sort by Lesson**.

5   Add further buttons to **Sort by Instructor** and **Sort by Student** (see Figure 17.4).

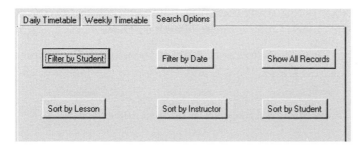

Figure 17.4

6   Go into Form View and test that the buttons work.

Adding further options

When a student phones the Pass-It Driving School to book a lesson they quite often forget their Student ID.

The procedure is:

○ A student phones the school to book a lesson, the operator opens the booking form and clicks on Book a Lesson.
○ The student cannot remember their ID so the operator opens the student form and uses the drop-down to find the student's surname and hence their ID.
○ The operator will then be able to click a button and Access will place the ID number into the Booking Form.

1 Open the **Lesson Booking Form** in Design View. Click on the **Search Options** Tab and use the Command Button Wizard to add a button to open the **Student Form**. Set the text on the button to **Find Student**.

2 Save the form and test the button opens the **Student Form**.

3 The Student Form is already set up with a combo box to select the student. We need to create a macro to paste these details into the **Lesson Booking Form**.

4 Create a new macro. The Actions are as follows:

GoToControl.	Control Name **Student ID**	
RunCommand	Command **Copy**	
Close	Object Type **Form**	Object Name **Student Form**
OpenForm	Form **Lesson Booking Form**	View **Form**
GoToControl	Control Name **Student ID**	
RunCommand	Command **Paste**	

5 Save the macro as **Select Student**.

6   Load the Student Form in Design View and add a button to run this macro. Label the button **Select Student** (see Figure 17.5).

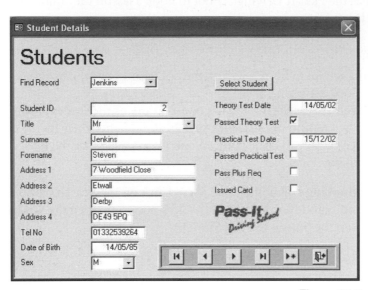

Figure 17.5

When you test this procedure you will find that the system places the ID into the Booking Form but you then have to press return to activate the form. This can be avoided by these simple steps.

1   Create a new macro called **Update** with the single action **RunCommand** and argument **RefreshPage**.

2   Open the **Lesson Booking Form** in Design View and right click on the Student ID field to display its properties.

3   Click on the **Event Tab** and set its **On Change** property to run the macro called **Update**.

The Cancel Booking option

Often students will phone up to cancel a lesson. We need to add an option for the user to be able to cancel bookings.

Use the Command Button Wizard to set up a button based on the Category: **Record Operations** and the Action: **Delete Record**. Set the text on the button to **Cancel Booking**.

Save the **Lesson Booking** Form. Your finished Tab Control for the Search Options should appear as in Figure 17.6.

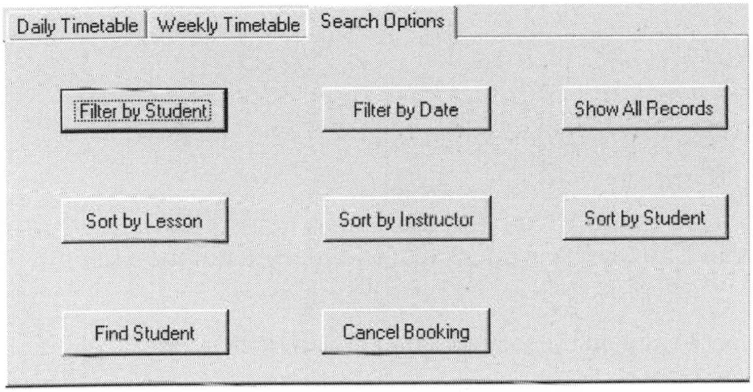

| Daily Timetable | Weekly Timetable | Search Options |

| Filter by Student | Filter by Date | Show All Records |

| Sort by Lesson | Sort by Instructor | Sort by Student |

| Find Student | Cancel Booking |

Figure 17.6

Unit 18 Calculations in reports

Adding data in a report

The **Lesson Cost Query** in Unit 8 set up a calculated field to work out the cost of each lesson.

We want to set up a report to add up the total income for each instructor.

1 Create a new report based on the **Lesson Cost Query** using the **Report Wizard.**

2 Use the arrow icon (>) to select these fields in this order: **Instructor ID, Instructor_Forename, Instructor_Surname, Student_Forename, Student_Surname, Date and TotalCost** (see Figure 18.1). Click on **Next.**

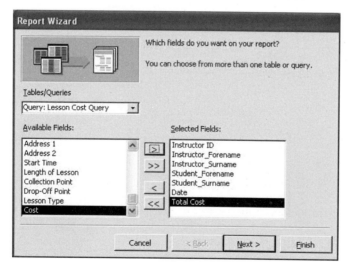

Figure 18.1

3 If the records are not grouped by **Instructor ID** by default, click on Instructor ID and click on the right arrow (see Figure 18.2). Click on **Next.**

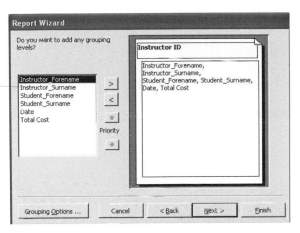

Figure 18.2

4   Sort by **Date** and click on **Next** (see Figure 18.3).

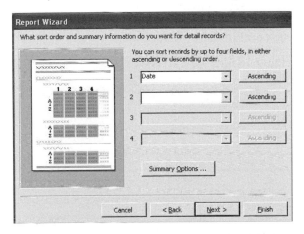

Figure 18.3

5   Click on **Align Left 1** and click on **Next** (see Figure 18.4).

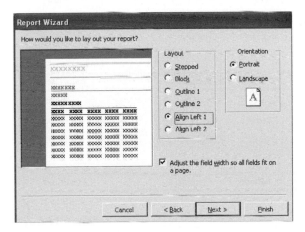

Figure 18.4

6 Click on **Corporate** and click on **Next** (see Figure 18.5).

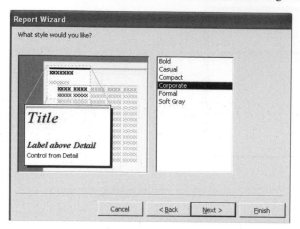

Figure 18.5

7 Name it **Income Report** and click on **Finish**.

The report opens and is shown in Figure 18.6.

Income Report

Instructor ID   *1*

Date	Instructor_F	Instructor_	Student_Fo	Student_S	TotalCost
30/07/02	Doug	Jones	Victoria	Spencer	£45.00
30/07/02	Doug	Jones	Mary	Trueman	£15.00
30/07/02	Doug	Jones	Steven	Jenkins	£30.00
30/07/02	Doug	Jones	Robert	Brammer	£15.00
31/07/02	Doug	Jones	Sarah	Fowler	£15.00
31/07/02	Doug	Jones	Sarah	Fowler	£30.00
31/07/02	Doug	Jones	Charlotte	Williams	£12.00

Instructor ID   *2*

Date	Instructor_F	Instructor_	Student_Fo	Student_S	TotalCost
30/07/02	Arnold	Batchelor	David	Windsor	£15.00
31/07/02	Arnold	Batchelor	Steven	Jenkins	£12.00
02/08/02	Arnold	Batchelor	Greg	Watson	£15.00

Instructor ID   *3*

Date	Instructor_F	Instructor_	Student_Fo	Student_S	TotalCost
01/08/02	Andrew	Smith	Michael	Beswood	£25.00

Figure 18.6

We want to add up the total cost for each instructor.

8 Click on the **Design View** icon or click on **View, Design View** to switch to **Design View**.

9 Click on the **Sorting and Grouping** icon or click on **View, Sorting and Grouping** (see Figure 18.7).

Figure 18.7

10 Add an **Instructor ID Group Footer** by selecting **Instructor ID** and setting **Group Footer** to **Yes**. Close the dialogue box (see Figure 18.8).

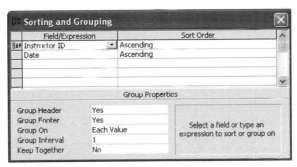

Figure 18.8

11 Click on the **Text Box icon** in the Toolbox and drag out a Text Box in the Instructor ID Group Footer. It will say something like **Text28** and **Unbound** (see Figure 18.9).

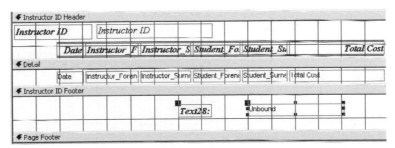

Figure 18.9

12 With the new text box selected, click on the **Properties** icon. Click on the **Data** tab. In the **Control Source** row type in =**Sum([TotalCost])**.

Note

The fieldname in the square brackets must be exactly the same as the calculated field name set up in Unit 8. There is no space between Total and Cost (see Figure 18.10).

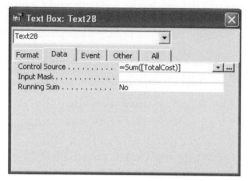

Figure 18.10

13   Still in the Properties window, click on the **Format** tab. In the Format row choose **Currency**. Set the **Font Weight** Property to **Bold** (see Figure 18.11).

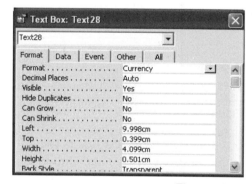

Figure 18.11

14   Close the Properties window.

15   Edit the text in the label of the new text box (Text28) to read **Total** (see Figure 18.12).

✦ Instructor ID Footer												
									Total		=Sum([TotalCost])	
✦ Page Footer												

Figure 18.12

16   Drag **Instructor Forename** and **Instructor Surname** from the Detail into the Instructor ID Header.

17 Delete the **Instructor Forename** and **Instructor Surname** column headings.

18 Change the Student_Forename column heading to Student. Delete the Student_Surname column heading.

19 Add the company logo as before.

20 Go into Print Preview mode and test the report (see Figure 18.13). You may wish to format the layout of column headings and data.

Pass-It *Driving School* *Income Report*

| Instructor ID | | *1* Doug | Jones | |

Date	Student		Total Cost
30.07.02	Victoria	Spencer	£45.00
30.07.02	Mary	Trueman	£15.00
30.07.02	Steven	Jenkins	£30.00
30.07.02	Robert	Brammer	£15.00
31.07.02	Sarah	Fowler	£15.00
31.07.02	Sarah	Fowler	£30.00
31.07.02	Charlotte	Williams	£12.00
		Total	**£162.00**

| Instructor ID | | *2* Arnold | Batchelor | |

Date	Student		Total Cost
30.07.02	David	Windsor	£15.00
31.07.02	Steven	Jenkins	£12.00
02.08.02	Greg	Watson	£15.00
		Total	**£42.00**

Figure 18.13

How to count records in a report

Sometimes you may want to count the number of records in a report. For example, in the above report, you may want to know the number of lessons for each instructor.

1 Open the report in Design View.

2   Click on the Text Box icon and add a small text box to the Instructor ID Footer section (see Figure 18.14).

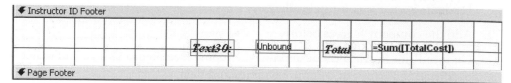

Figure 18.14

3   Select the new text box and click on the Properties icon.

4   Click on the **Data** tab and set the Control Source to **=Count([TotalCost])** (see Figure 18.15).

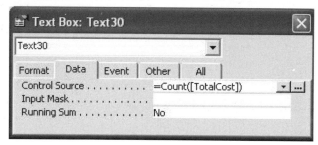

Figure 18.15

5   Edit the text box label so that it says **Count** (see Figure 18.16).

Figure 18.16

6   Switch the Print Preview to check that the count is correct (see Figure 18.17).

Income Report

Instructor ID		1 Doug	Jones	
Date		**Student**		**TotalCost**
30/07/02		Victoria	Spencer	£45.00
30/07/02		Mary	Trueman	£15.00
30/07/02		Steven	Jenkins	£30.00
30/07/02		Robert	Brammer	£15.00
31/07/02		Sarah	Fowler	£15.00
31/07/02		Sarah	Fowler	£30.00
31/07/02		Charlotte	Williams	£12.00
	Count	7	*Total*	**£162.00**

Figure 18.17

How to get a running total in a report

Sometimes you may want a running total in a report. For example in the above report, you may want the Total to be a running total and give the income for all instructors.

To set the total to be a running total:

1   Load the **Income Report** in **Design View**.

2   Select the **Total** control.

3   Click on the **Properties** icon or click on **View, Properties**.

4   Click on the **Data** tab and set the **Running Sum** row to **Over All** (see Figure 18.18).

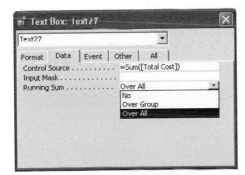

Figure 18.18

5   Close the Properties window and change the label **Total** to **Running Total**.

6 Switch to Print Preview mode and check that the running total is correct (see Figure 18.19).

Instructor ID		2 Arnold	Batchelor	

Date		Student		Total Cost
30/07/02		David	Windsor	£15.00
31/07/02		Steven	Jenkins	£12.00
02/08/02		Greg	Watson	£15.00
	Count		3 Running Total	£204.00

Instructor ID		3 Andrew	Smith	

Date		Student		Total Cost
01/08/02		Michael	Beswood	£25.00
	Count		1 Running Total	£229.00

Figure 18.19

Reports with no records

Some reports have no data in them. For example you might be searching for lessons on a day when none has been booked. It is possible to check if there is no data in a report and give a warning to the user.

1 Set up a macro called **No Data** that displays this message box (see Figure 18.20).

Pass-It Driving School

ⓘ There is no data in this report

OK

Figure 18.20

The action is **MsgBox.** The arguments are as shown (see Figure 18.21).

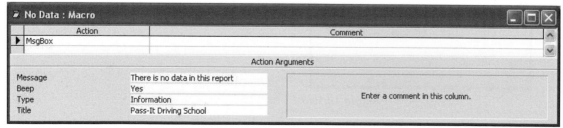

No Data : Macro	
Action	Comment
▶ MsgBox	

Action Arguments	
Message	There is no data in this report
Beep	Yes
Type	Information
Title	Pass-It Driving School

Enter a comment in this column.

Figure 18.21

2 Save the macro and test it.

Attaching a macro to a form or a report

We want to run this macro when we open the Instructors' Timetable Report. We can set this up using the report properties.

3   At the Database Window, click on **Reports**.

4   Select the **Instructors' Timetable Report** and click on **Design**.

5   Click on the **Properties** icon or click on **View, Properties**.

The Report properties will be displayed.

6   Click on the **Event** tab (see Figure 18.22).

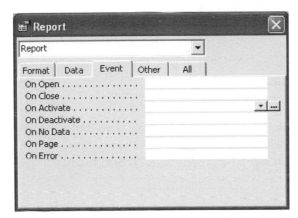

Figure 18.22

You can now select macros to run when:

the report opens	**On Open**
the report closes	**On Close**
the report becomes the active window	**On Activate**
the report stops being the active window	**On Deactivate**
the report has no data	**On No Data**
a page of a report is formatted for printing	**On Page**
there is an error	**On Error**

7   We want the **No Data** macro to run when there is no data in the report so set
the **On No Data** property to **No Data** using the drop-down list as shown in
Figure 18.23.

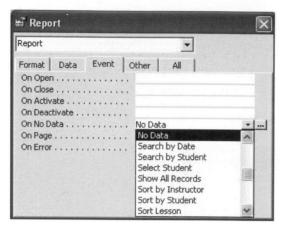

Figure 18.23

8   Save the report and test that the macro works when there is no data by opening
the report and entering a date when you know that there are no lessons. (The
message box actually will appear twice before the blank report loads.)

⊕ Unit 19 Using action queries

In Units 6, 7 and 8 you learned how to use a range of queries to view your data.

In this section you will learn how to use action queries. Action queries actually do something to the data in your system by moving it, changing it or deleting it.

At the end of the unit we will update the switchboard to include these features.

There are four types of action query:

○ Append query
○ Delete query
○ Update query
○ Make Table Query (not used in the Pass-It Driving School).

Append queries

An append query will take data from one table and add it to another.

In a club membership system you may decide to keep details of members who have not renewed their subscriptions rather than delete their records immediately. An append query will enable you to remove their details from the main membership table and transfer them to a table of, for example, expired memberships.

Similarly in a school or college, at the end of each year you could delete all leavers from the system but it is likely you will need to keep records for a period of time. An append query could be set up to transfer leaver details to a table of leavers.

Delete queries

A delete query will remove records from one or more tables according to set criteria.

In the school or college system above you may decide to keep records of ex-students for three years. At the end of each college year you would remove details of all students who left three or more years ago.

Similarly in a Video Hire/Library Loans system details of loans will build up. After a period of time you will need to clear old details from the system.

A delete query can be used to carry out these operations.

Update queries

An update query will make changes to data in one or more tables.

In an ordering system you may decide to reduce the prices of all products by 7.5 per cent. At the end of each year in our school system all students will move up a year from Year 7 to Year 8 and so on.

Update queries allow you to make these changes to the data in your tables automatically.

Managing lesson details

In the Pass-It Driving School we need our system to handle information about old lessons.

○ After a lesson has taken place, we want to move details to a table of old lessons. (**Append query**)
○ The details also need removing from the Lesson table. (**Delete query**)
○ After a period of a year we will remove them from the Old Lesson table altogether. (**Delete query**)

When working with action queries it is a good idea to make a copy of your lesson table because you are going to be moving and changing the data. Making a copy will save you re-entering data at a later stage.

1   At the Database Window, click on **Tables.** Click on the **Lesson** table and click on **Edit, Copy** or click on the **Copy** icon.

2   At the Database Window, click on **Edit, Paste** or click on the **Paste** icon.

3   Call the new table **Lesson Copy** and click on **Structure and Data.** Click on **OK** (see Figure 19.1). We will work on the **Lesson** table.

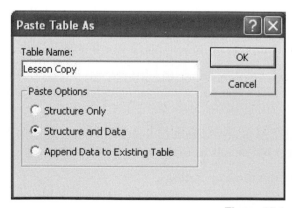

Figure 19.1

As action queries are often based on dates that clearly change you will have to edit the lesson dates before you start.

4   Open the **Lesson** table and change the dates as follows.
   ○ Change the 01/08/02 lesson to today's date.
   ○ Change the 02/08/02 lesson to tomorrow's date.
   ○ Change all the 31/07/02 lessons to yesterday's date.
   ○ Change all the 30/07/02 lessons to the date exactly one year ago today.

Hint

Use **Edit, Replace** to change all the lessons for one day at once.

Append Query to transfer lesson details

We are going to move details of all old lessons from the Lesson table to a table called Old Lesson.

1   At the Database Window, click on **Tables.** Click on the **Lesson** table and click on **Edit, Copy** or click on the **Copy** icon.

2   At the Database Window, click **on Edit, Paste** or click on the **Paste** icon.

3   Name the new table **Old Lesson** and click on **Structure Only.** Click on **OK.**

4   This has created a new empty table called **Old Lesson.** Open this table in **Design View.**

5   Set the **Data Type** of the **Lesson No** to **Number.** (This is vital. It will not work if you don't do this.)

6   Save the table and close it.

7   At the Database Window, click on **Queries.** Click on **New.** Click on **Simple Query Wizard.** Click on **OK.**

8   Select the **Table: Lesson** from the drop-down. Click on the double arrow to choose all the fields and then click on **Next.**

9   In the Simple Query Wizard window click on **Next** again.

10   Name the query **Old Lesson Append Query** and click on **Finish.**

11   Open the query in **Design View** and set the Criteria row in the **Date** column to <**Date().**

12 If the Query design toolbar is showing click on the **Query Type** icon and click on **Append Query** or click on **Query, Append Query** (see Figure 19.2).

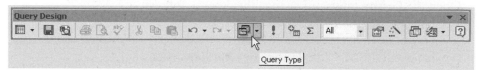

Figure 19.2

13 The Append dialogue box is displayed. Choose the **Old Lesson** table from the drop-down and click on **OK** (see Figure 19.3).

Append

Append To

Table Name: Old Lesson

⊙ Current Database

○ Another Database:

File Name:

Browse...

OK

Cancel

Figure 19.3

Details of the query are then displayed as shown in Figure 19.4.

Field:	Lesson No	Student ID	Instructor ID	Date	Start Time	Length of Lesson	Collection Point	Drop-Off Po	Lesson Type
Table:	Lesson	Lesson	Lesson	Lesson	Lesson	Lesson	Lesson	Lesson	Lesson
Sort:									
Append To:	Lesson No	Student ID	Instructor ID	Date	Start Time	Length of Lesson	Collection Point	Drop-Off Po	Lesson Type
Criteria:				<Date()>					
or:									

Figure 19.4

14 Save the query and close it.

15 At the Database Window, click on **Open** to run the **Old Lesson Append Query**.

16 You will be prompted with two warning messages. Click on **Yes** (see Figure 19.5).

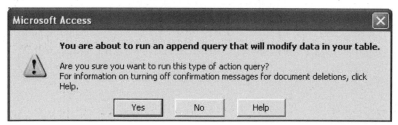

Microsoft Access

You are about to run an append query that will modify data in your table.

Are you sure you want to run this type of action query?
For information on turning off confirmation messages for document deletions, click Help.

Yes   No   Help

Figure 19.5

17 Click on **Yes** at the second message (see Figure 19.6).

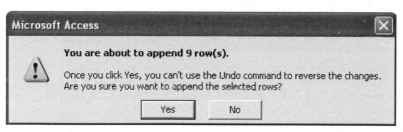

Microsoft Access

You are about to append 9 row(s).

Once you click Yes, you can't use the Undo command to reverse the changes. Are you sure you want to append the selected rows?

[Yes] [No]

Figure 19.6

18 At the Database Window, open the Old Lesson table. Nine records should have been added.

Delete query to remove lesson details from the Lesson table

We now need to clear out the details of all the old lessons which are still stored in the Lesson table. These should be the same nine records.

1 At the Database Window, click on **Queries.** Click on **New.** Click on **Simple Query Wizard.** Click on **OK.**

2 Select the **Table: Lesson** from the drop-down. Click on the double arrow to choose all the fields and then click on **Next.**

3 In the Simple Query Wizard window click on **Next** again.

4 Name the query **Old Lesson Delete Query** and click **Finish.**

5 Open the query in **Design View.** If the Query design toolbar is showing click on the **Query Type** icon and click on **Delete Query** or click on **Query, Delete Query.**

6 Set the Criteria row in the **Date** column to <**Date()** (see Figure 19.7).

Field:	Lesson No	Student ID	Instructor ID	Date	Start Time	Length of Lesson	Collection Point	Drop-C
Table:	Lesson	Lesson	Lesson	Lesson	Lesson	Lesson	Lesson	Lessor
Delete:	Where	Where	Where	Where	Where	Where	Where	Where
Criteria:				<Date()				
or:								

Figure 19.7

7 Save the query and close it.

8 At the Database Window, click on **Open** to run the **Old Lesson Delete Query.**

9 On running the query you will get the following warning prompts. Just click on **Yes** (see Figure 19.8 and Figure 19.9).

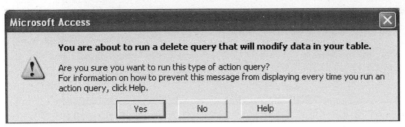

Microsoft Access

You are about to run a delete query that will modify data in your table.

Are you sure you want to run this type of action query?
For information on how to prevent this message from displaying every time you run an action query, click Help.

[Yes] [No] [Help]

Figure 19.8

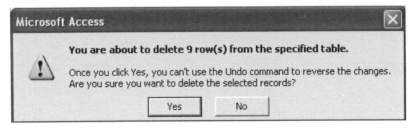

Microsoft Access

You are about to delete 9 row(s) from the specified table.

Once you click Yes, you can't use the Undo command to reverse the changes.
Are you sure you want to delete the selected records?

[Yes] [No]

Figure 19.9

10 At the Database Window, click on **Tables**. Open the **Lesson** table and see that all but two lessons have been deleted.

Delete query to clear out lesson details after a year

We wish to delete details of all lessons over a year old.

1 At the Database Window, click on **Queries.** Click on **New.** Click on **Simple Query Wizard**. Click on **OK**.

2 Select the **Table: Old Lesson** from the drop-down. Click on the double arrow to choose all the fields and then click on **Next.**

3 In the Simple Query Wizard window click on **Next** again.

4 Name the query **Over One Year Delete Query** and click **Finish**.

5 Open the query in **Design View.** If the Query design toolbar is showing click on the **Query Type** icon and click on **Delete Query** or click on **Query, Delete Query**.

6   Set the Criteria row in the **Date** column to <=**Date()-365** (see Figure 19.10).

Field:	Lesson No	Student ID	Instructor ID	Date	Start Time	Length of Lesson
Table:	Old Lesson	Old Lesson	Old Lesson	Old Lesson	Old Lesson	Old Lesson
Delete:	Where	Where	Where	Where	Where	Where
Criteria:				<=Date()-365		
or:						

Figure 19.10

7   Save the query and close it.

8   At the Database Window, click on **Open** to run the **Over One Year Delete Query**.

9   Click on **Yes** to accept the warning prompts.

10   Open the **Old Lesson** table to check that the year old lessons have been deleted.

Setting a macro to automate this task

To have to do this every day or every week is an awkward job. We want the user to be able to do it at the click of a button. We will design a macro to do this task and later attach it to a button on the menu.

1   In the Database Window click on **Macros** and select **New**.

2   Click on the drop-down arrow in the Action column and click on **SetWarnings**. When you do this the Action Arguments section appears in the lower half of the screen. Set the argument to **No** (this will turn off the warning prompts when running the macro).

3   In the Action Column select **OpenQuery** and in the arguments section choose **Old Lesson Append Query** from the drop-down box.

4   In the Action Column select **OpenQuery** and in the arguments section choose **Old Lesson Delete Query** from the drop-down box.

5   In the Action Column select **OpenQuery** and in the arguments section choose **Over One Year Delete Query** from the drop-down box (the queries must be run in this order) (see Figure 19.11).

6   In the Action Column select **MsgBox** and in the arguments section enter the details as shown in Figure 19.11.

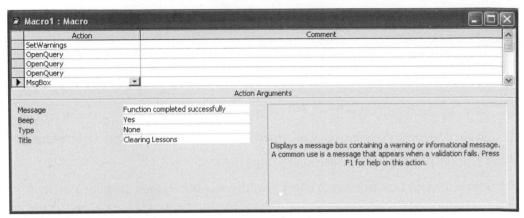

Figure 19.11

7   Save the macro as **Lesson Archive Macro**.

8   Set your data back to the original state and test that the macro moves all the data correctly.

Managing lesson prices

The driving school might occasionally want to increase or decrease its prices. We will use an update query to automate this process.

1   At the database window, click on **Queries**. Click on New. Click on **Simple Query Wizard** and then **OK**.

2   Select **Table: Lesson Type** from the drop-down. Choose **Cost** from the available fields by clicking on the single arrow and clicking on **Next**.

3   In the next Simple Query Wizard window, ensure that **Detail** is checked and click on **Next** again.

4   Call the query **Price Update Query** and click **Finish**.

5   In **Design View,** click on the **Query Type** icon and then click on **Update Query** or click on **Query, Update Query** (see Figure 19.12).

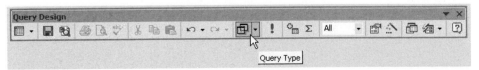

Figure 19.12

6 In the **Update To** row of the **Cost** column of the QBE grid, enter **[Cost]*1.05**.

This increases the value by 5 per cent (see Figure 19.13).
To increase by 25 per cent, use the formula **[Cost]*1.25**
To increase by £1, use the formula **[Cost]+1**, etc.

Field:	Cost					
Table:	Lesson Type					
Update To:	[Cost]*1.05					
Criteria:						
or:						

Figure 19.13

7 Click on the **Run** icon on the Query Design toolbar or from the menu select **Query, Run** to update the records (see Figure 19.14).

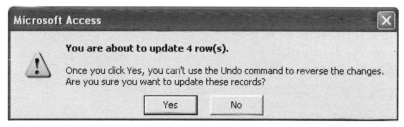

Figure 19.14

8 You will get a warning message. Click on **Yes** (see Figure 19.15).

Microsoft Access

⚠ **You are about to update 4 row(s).**

Once you click Yes, you can't use the Undo command to reverse the changes. Are you sure you want to update these records?

[Yes]   [No]

Figure 19.15

9 The original prices were £12.00, £17.00, £15.00 and £25.00. Click on the View icon to check that the prices have been updated to £12.60, £17.85, £15.75 and £26.25, respectively.

10 Set up a macro called **Adjust Prices** to remove the warnings and run this query.

Note

To stop a query after you start it, press CTRL + BREAK.

Further development

Using an append query and two delete queries, set up a macro called **Student Archive Macro** that will:

○ Search for students who have passed both theory and practical tests and do not require the Pass Plus Course and transfer their details to an Old Student table.
○ Delete students from the Old Student table if at least 30 days have elapsed since they passed their tests.

Make-Table queries

In this unit you have been introduced to Action Queries and shown how to move data with Append and Delete Queries. A **Make-Table** query can be used to create a new table from the results of a query. Refer to Tips and Tricks No. 19 for further information.

⊕ Unit 20 Finishing touches

In this section we will put on the finishing touches to our system including updating the switchboard, tidying up our forms, adding a splashscreen, adding a clock to the switchboard and customising the menu.

Updating the switchboard

After completing the additions to the system in Units 16 to 19, it is necessary to edit the switchboard to include the new options.

1 Open the **Switchboard Manager** and click on **New**. Enter the name of the third switchboard, **System Switchboard** and click on **OK** (see Figure 20.1).

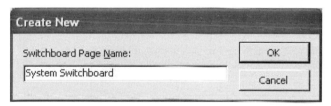

Figure 20.1

2 Select the Main Switchboard and click on **Edit**. Click on **New**. Enter the text **System Functions**. Select the command **Go to Switchboard**. Select the **System Switchboard** (see Figure 20.2).

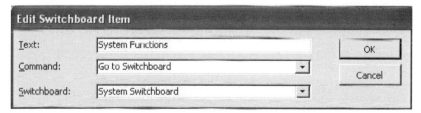

Figure 20.2

3 Use the Move Up button so that this option is below the Reports option (see Figure 20.3).

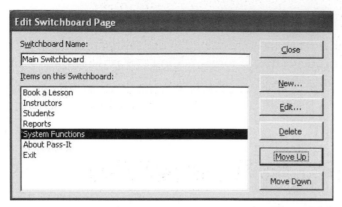

Figure 20.3

4 Click on **Close** and then select the **Report Switchboard**. Click on **Edit**.

5 Add a new option to open the **Income Report** (see Figure 20.4).

Figure 20.4

6 Use the Move Up and Move Down button so that the **Income Report** option is above the Back option.

7 Click on **Close** and then select the **System Switchboard**. Click on **Edit**.

8 Add a new option to run the **Lesson Archive Macro** (see Figure 20.5).

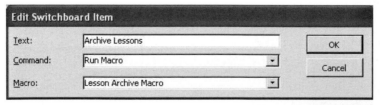

Figure 20.5

9 If you set up the **Student Archive Macro** at the end of Unit 19, add an option to run it.

10 Add a new option run the **Adjust Prices** macro (see Figure 20.6).

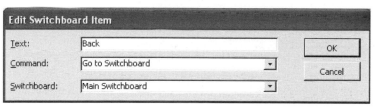

Edit Switchboard Item

Text:	Update Prices
Command:	Run Macro
Macro:	Adjust Prices

OK

Cancel

Figure 20.6

11 Add a new option named **Back** to return to the **Main Switchboard** (see Figure 20.7).

Edit Switchboard Item

Text:	Back
Command:	Go to Switchboard
Switchboard:	Main Switchboard

OK

Cancel

Figure 20.7

12 Close the Switchboard Manager.

13 At the database Window click on **Forms** and open the **Switchboard**. The new Main Switchboard should now look like that shown in Figure 20.8. Test all the buttons to see that they work.

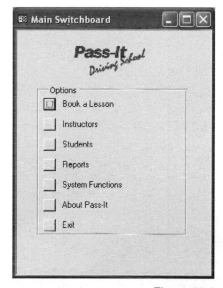

Figure 20.8

Tidying up forms

The form in Figure 20.9 works as expected but is a little untidy. The Student ID control is much too long for a small number. The title control is much too big for a title that is only a few letters long. You can probably see other improvements that could be made.

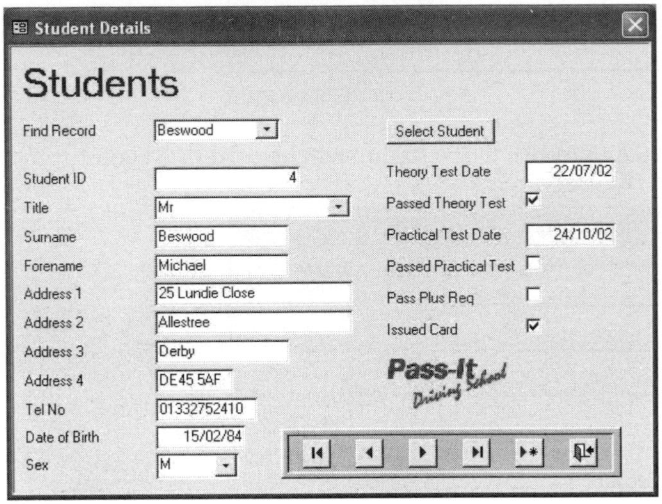

Figure 20.9

Open all your forms in turn and edit them so that controls are aligned, evenly spaced and the right size as shown in Figure 20.10.

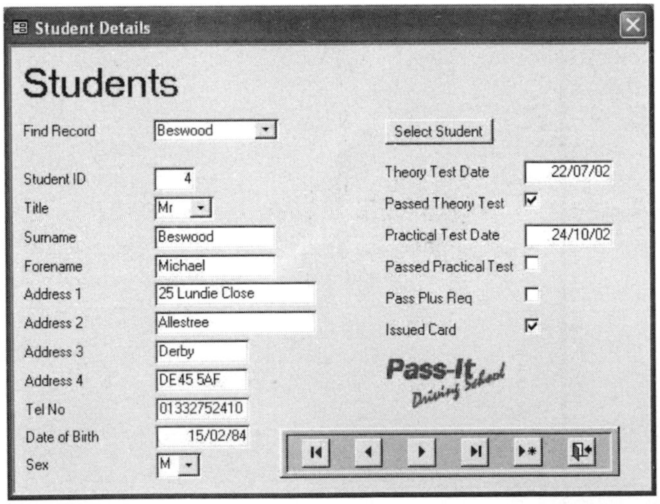

Figure 20.10

Setting up a splashscreen

A 'splashscreen', like the one shown in Figure 20.11, loads when the system loads. It appears for a few seconds before the switchboard loads.

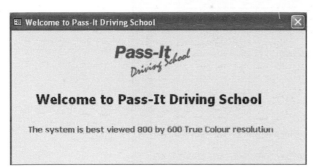

Figure 20.11

Set up a splashscreen as follows:

1   At the Database Window click on **Forms**. Click on **New**. Click on **Design View**. Do *not* select a table or query and click on **OK**.

2   A blank form appears. Enlarge it so that it is roughly 12 cm by 5 cm (see Figure 20.12).

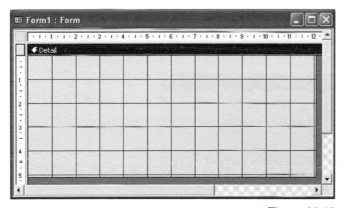

Figure 20.12

3 Use the Toolbox to add the image and to add two labels to display the text as shown in Figure 20.13.

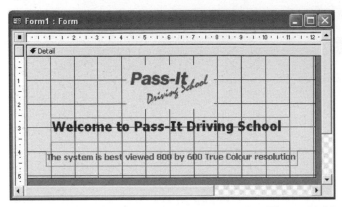

Figure 20.13

4 Double click on the Form Selector and set the Form properties to remove the **Scroll Bars, Record Selector, Navigation Buttons, Dividing Lines** and **Max Min** buttons. Set the Border Style to **Dialog**. Set the Caption to **Welcome to Pass-It Driving School**.

5 Save the form as **Splashscreen.**

6 Go into Form View. Click on **Window, Size to Fit Form**. Your form should look like the one shown in Figure 20.14.

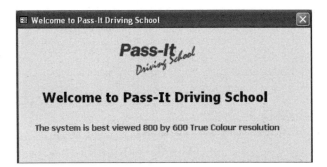

Figure 20.14

7 Close the form. At the Database Window click on Macros and create a new macro to close the splashscreen form.
   ○ The first **Action** is **Close**. The **Object Type** is **Form**. The **Object Name** is **Splashscreen** (see Figure 20.15).
   ○ The second action is to open another form – the **Switchboard** (see Figure 20.16).

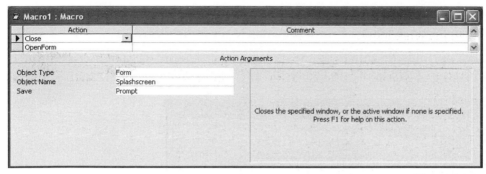

Figure 20.15

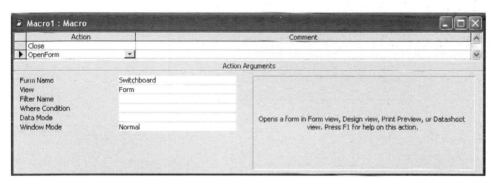

Figure 20.16

8   Save the macro as **Splash**.

9   Load the Splashscreen form in Design View and double click on the Form Selector to view the Form properties. Click on the **Event** tab and set the **TimerInterval** property to **3000**. This is in milliseconds, so this would mean three seconds.

10 Click on the **OnTimer** property and select the **Splash** macro. You may need to go back to the TimerInterval property to adjust your timing a little to get it just right (see Figure 20.17).

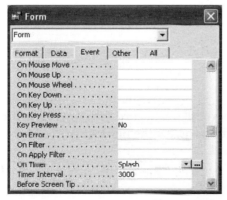

Figure 20.17

11 Save the form. Load the form in Form View mode and test that it stays on the screen for three seconds before switching to the Switchboard.

12 Click on **Tools, Startup** to set the startup options to load the splashscreen form when the system loads (see Figure 20.18).

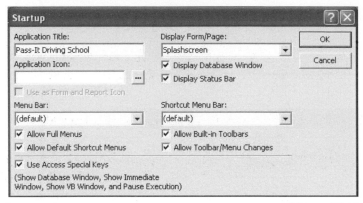

Figure 20.18

Are you sure?

This is an option on the switchboard to exit from the application. It is a good idea to have an 'Are you sure?' box in case this button is pressed by mistake (see Figure 20.19).

Figure 20.19

To set this up:

1 Open another blank form in Design View.

2 Set the Form properties to remove the **Scroll Bars, Record Selector, Navigation Buttons, Dividing Lines** and **Max Min buttons.** Set the Border Style to **Dialog**. Set the Caption to **Pass-It Driving School**.

3 Save the form as **Finish**.

4   Create a macro called **Exit**. The only action is **Quit** with Options set to **Exit** (see Figure 20.20).

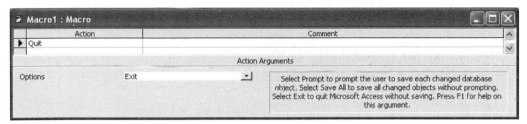

Figure 20.20

5   Create another macro called **NoExit** to close the **Finish** form (see Figure 20.21).

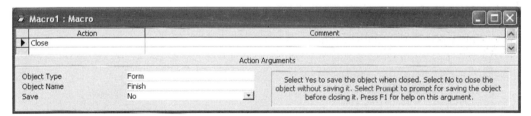

Figure 20.21

6   Open the **Finish** form in Design View. Use the Label icon in the Toolbox to add text similar to the form shown above.

7   Add an image as shown.

8   Add a command button to run the **Exit** macro. Set the text on this button to **Yes**.

9   Add a command button to run the **NoExit** macro. Set the text on this button to **No**.

10 Save the form and close it.

11 Use the Switchboard manager to edit the Exit Application button so that it opens the Finish form in edit mode (see Figure 20.22).

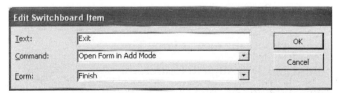

Figure 20.22

12 Open the Switchboard and test the buttons.

Adding a real-time clock to a form

It is possible to add a clock, which updates every second, to an Access form such as the switchboard.

1   Open the switchboard in **Design View** mode.

2   Choose the **Text Box** icon in the Toolbox and drag out a text box at the bottom of the switchboard. The text box will be called something like Text26 (see Figure 20.23).

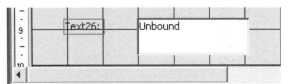

Figure 20.23

3   Click on the label that says the name (Text26) and delete it (see Figure 20.24).

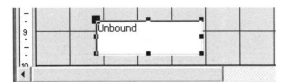

Figure 20.24

4   Click on the text box and click on the **Properties** icon or right click on the text box and choose **Properties**. Click on the **Other** tab and edit the name to **Timer1** (see Figure 20.25).

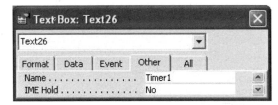

Figure 20.25

5   Click on the **Format** tab and choose the format **Long Time**.

6   Set the **Font Weight** to **Bold** and **Text Align** to **Center**.

7   With the properties window still displayed, click on the Form Selector.

8   This will display the properties for the form. Click on the **Event** tab and set the **Timer Interval** to 1000 (this is one second) (see Figure 20.26).

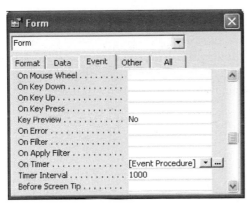

Figure 20.26

9 Choose the **On Timer** property above Timer Interval. Click on the three dots icon and choose **Code Builder.** The Visual Basic Editor loads displaying:

```
Private Sub Form_Timer()
End Sub
```

In the middle line type in: **[Timer1]=Now**

10 Close the Visual Basic Editor and go into Form View mode to test it (see Figure 20.27).

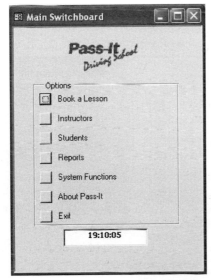

Figure 20.27

Customising menus and toolbars

A fully customised Access system is likely to have customised menus and toolbars. In this section you will learn how to set up a macro to remove or display toolbars, add icons to and remove icons from a toolbar and set up your own toolbar.

Customising toolbars

You can set up the AutoExec macro to remove all toolbars. The AutoExec macro runs automatically when a system loads. For more on the AutoExec macro see Tip 42, p. 282.

Removing toolbars means that you can then devote more of the screen to the forms and reports you have set up.

Use the **ShowToolbar** action. Select the toolbar from the list and set Show to **No**. You need to use this action several times to remove all the toolbars (see Figure 20.28).

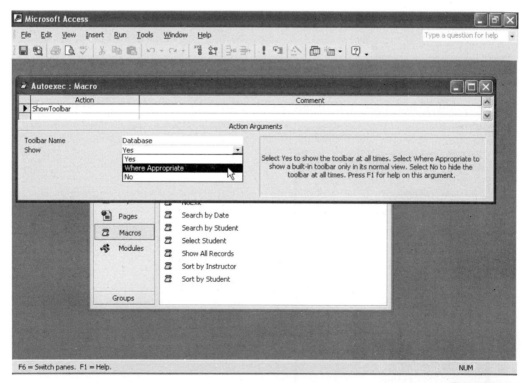

Figure 20.28

Howeve, before you remove all the toolbars, make sure that your system is fully working. It is very annoying to have to edit the system without any icons.

> # Note
>
> You can set up a macro to show toolbars only where they are appropriate as shown in Figure 20.28.

Removing or adding single icons

It is possible to add or remove icons from the toolbars. The method is exactly the same as in Microsoft Word and Microsoft Excel, so you may have seen it before.

1   Click on **Tools, Customize** or right click on the toolbars and click on **Customize**

The Customize Dialogue box appears.

2   Click on the **Commands** tab (see Figure 20.29).

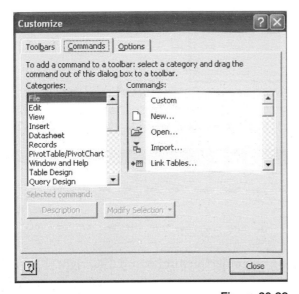

Figure 20.29

3   To remove an icon from a toolbar simply drag it onto the dialogue box.

4   To add an icon, select the menu in the **Categories** box. Find the icon in the **Commands** box and drag it onto the toolbar.

For example, to add an icon to run the **About** macro:

1   Click on the **Commands** tab and scroll down in the **Categories** box until you find **All Macros**.

2 Find **About** in the **Commands** box (see Figure 20.30).

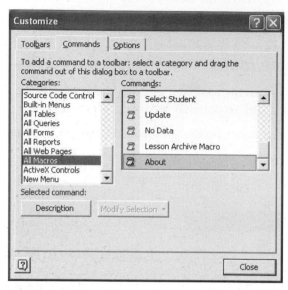

Figure 20.30

3 Drag the **About** icon on to the toolbar (see Figure 20.31).

Figure 20.31

4 Close the dialogue box.

5 You can edit this icon by clicking on **Tools, Customize** and then right clicking on the icon (see Figure 20.32).

6 Select **Edit Button Image** to load a simple painting program to edit the icon or click on **Change Button Image** to show a menu of alternative icons.

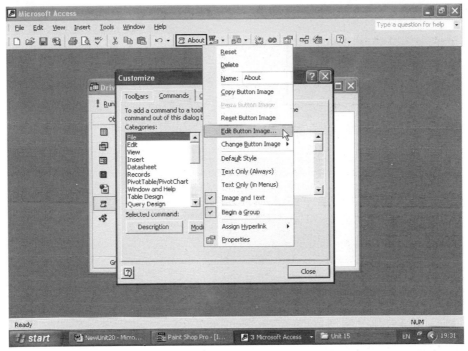

Figure 20.32

Customising menus

Customised menus make finishing touches to a system, bringing a professional feel to it.

1   Click on **Tools, Customize**. Click on the **Toolbars** tab and click on **New** (see Figure 20.33).

Figure 20.33

2   Call the new toolbar **Pass-It Driving School** (see Figure 20.34).

Figure 20.34

A small new blank toolbar has appeared on the screen (see Figure 20.35).

Figure 20.35

3   Drag the toolbar to the toolbar area at the top of the screen (see Figure 20.36).

Figure 20.36

4   Scroll down in the **Categories** box until you find **New Menu** (it is the last one in the list) (see Figure 20.37).

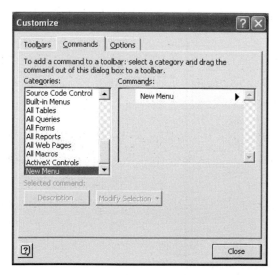

Figure 20.37

5   Drag **New Menu** from the Commands box on to the new toolbar (see Figure 20.38).

Figure 20.38

6   Right click on the words **New Menu** and change the name as shown in Figure 20.38.

7   Click on the word **Navigate** and a small blank menu drops down (see Figure 20.39).

Figure 20.39

8   Click on **All Forms** in the **Categories** list in the dialogue box.

9   Find **Lesson Booking Form** in the Commands list and drag it onto the blank menu (see Figure 20.40).

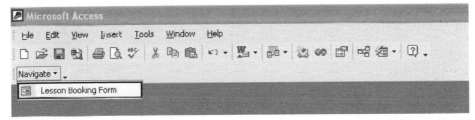

Figure 20.40

10   Click on **Navigate** to make the menu drop down. Right click on **Lesson Booking Form**.

11 Change the name to **Book a Lesson** as shown in Figure 20.41.

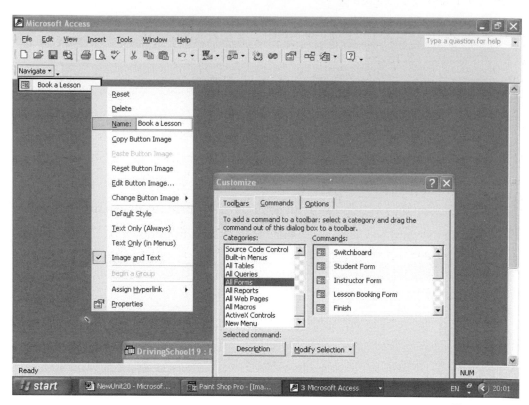

Figure 20.41

12 Close the dialogue box.

13 Test that the new menu loads **Lesson Booking Form**.

You can add more items to your menu and more menus to your toolbar. Include links to your forms and reports.

It is a good idea to include links to the Database Window and have online help in your customised menu.

When your new menu bar is complete, click on **Tools, Startup** and change the startup menu bar as shown in Figure 20.42.

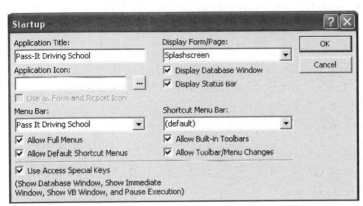

Figure 20.42

Don't forget that to disable the startup options, hold down the SHIFT key as you load the file.

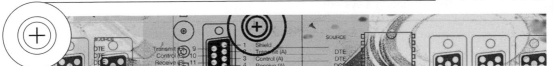

PART TWO

Documenting a system

Unit 21 Documenting a system

An ICT project is much more than just setting up the system using Microsoft Access. You must also include documentation covering the analysis of the system, its design, its implementation, testing, a user guide and evaluation.

The following pages show you how to document your system by looking at some of the documentation provided with the Pass-It system.

Documenting ICT systems has a standard approach which is reflected across exam boards and courses at this level. A quick reference chart is provided in the Appendix.

Examples of courses are:

○ the coursework components for students studying **A/S** and **A levels** in **ICT**;
○ the mandatory unit in Database Design for students studying the **Advanced VCE** in **ICT**;
○ the Computing project component for students studying **A/S** and **A levels** in **Computing.**

Remember

The documentation here is not supposed to be complete but each section offers examples, pointers and hints to what is considered good practice.

The Pass-It Driving School system

Contents

1 Analysis
(a) Problem statement
(b) Interview with the user
(c) The current system
(d) End-user requirements
(e) Data flow diagrams
(f) Input, processing and output requirements
(g) Data dynamics of the problem
(h) Specification
(i) Resources available (including potential and limitations)
(j) Evaluation criteria

2 Design
(a) Possible solutions
(b) Chosen solution
(c) Database design
(d) Implementation plan
(e) Data dictionary
(f) Query designs
(g) Process designs
(h) Screen layouts, forms and reports
(i) Testing plan
(j) Time plan

3 Implementation

4 Testing
(a) Test results
(b) User testing

5 User guide

6 Evaluation

1 Analysis

Analysis involves investigating the current system, establishing what is needed from the new system and detailing a clear specification for the user. This section of the project report would probably include the following headings.

(a) Definition of the problem to be solved.

(b) Details of the initial discussions/fact finding with the end user usually via interview, questionnaire or observation.

(c) A clear and detailed explanation of the current system including where possible:
   ○ looking at the processes involved;
   ○ analysing current documents;
   ○ identifying problems.

(d) The end-user requirements.

(e) Data flow diagrams to illustrate the system.

(f) Input, processing and output requirements.

(g) Data dynamics.

(h) Specification.

(i) Resources available
   ○ Hardware and software, capabilities and limitations
   ○ Human resources, skill levels and training needs

(j) Evaluation criteria for evaluating the success of your system.

Remember

The analysis should provide the designer with all the information necessary to go about his/her work. The output from this section will be used as the input for the next section – the design of the solution.

(a) Problem statement

This should be a clear description of the problem to be solved and briefly outline the purpose of the new computerised system. It would briefly include: details of the user or business, its purpose, the information processing involved, some of the problems it has and some detail as to what you are going to try and solve.

Pass-It Driving School

My user will be Mr Doug Jones, owner of 'Pass-It Driving School', a local driving school which offers driving tuition to learner drivers. He has a number of full-time instructors and around 70 students taking lessons at any one time.

Mr Jones is interested in improving his record-keeping, particularly how he stores details of lessons that have been booked and how he issues information to instructors. At present all these details are stored in a diary which is kept in his office at home.

The system will store many different types of information including:

• details of all the students and instructors;
• details of lessons booked for each day.

It will also improve the image of the driving school.

Mr Jones needs to know which students have lessons each day, with which instructor and at which times. Details of pick-up points and drop-off points will also need to be stored. Data must be able to be entered and retrieved easily.

(b) Interview with the user

The interview with the user is designed to investigate the problem. Its purpose is to:

○ establish how the current system operates and identify the processes involved;
○ identify problems in the current system;
○ analyse existing documents, e.g. appointment cards, pupil record cards, invoices;
○ establish the end-user requirements.

The sort of questions that might be asked are:

Interview Questions

1   How do you store this information at present and what do you store?
2   Could I see how you prepare your timetables/lesson rotas?
3   What are the different categories of lessons and what is the pricing structure?
4   What is the procedure when someone rings up to book a lesson?
5   Do students always have the same instructor?
6   How do you deal with cancellations? Do you keep records?
7   What is the procedure when someone passes their driving test?
8   How long do you keep student details on file?
9   What happens if a student decides to leave the course? Do you keep their records?
10 Have you much experience of using computers and what computer facilities do you have at present (if any)?

Of course there will be many more questions and discussions that arise. It is sometimes easier and more useful to record the interview and document it later. If possible you might be given an opportunity to actually visit and observe the user. It is surprising how useful this can be.

(c) *The current system*

You should now be in a position to describe clearly, and in detail, the current system.

You should be able to list some of the problems in the current system, the solutions to which will clearly lead to some end-user requirements.

In your report, you will find it helpful to include and analyse some of the existing documents. You might find out the paper size, study the layout, consider who fills it in, note the data it contains, look at where it goes and how long it is kept. This will help you establish some of the inputs and outputs needed. It will also lead to end-user requirements and/or help provide detail for the specification for the new system.

For example the page from the booking diary in Figure 21.1 might help establish the detail required and the size and layout of the printed timetables you will include in your system.

Question 4 of the suggested interview investigated the process of booking a lesson. The following suggests how a student might document their findings. This section does need to focus on fact.

Current System

Figure 21.1 is a page from the Pass-It Driving School booking diary. The page is split into rows and columns displaying the instructor initials and available time slots.

Bookings are made by phoning the office and details are entered by hand into available slots.

Cancellations are made in the same way by simply crossing out the bookings. No other record is kept. The column headings show the instructors' initials.

Issuing instructors' timetables is done by photocopying the sheets and giving them to the instructor each day.

This is presenting problems:

- Searching for available time slots can be a lengthy process.
- Issuing timetables is inefficient and, of course, once issued they may still change with late additions and cancellations. At present they have to be rewritten by hand.
- Some instructors like to be able to plan their week ahead.
- The diary is thrown away at the end of the year and there are no historic records.
- It is not easy to view every lesson for a particular student or instructor.

Sunday 19 November							
Time	DJ	AB	AS	AL	SR	BH	JM
0800							Amanda Young
0900							
1000	Robert Brammer						
1100	Mary Trueman				Sam Ellis Cancelled		
1200	Victoria Spencer	David Windsor					Nick Shepherd
1300							
1400							
1500			Wayne Newton		Alison Harris		
1600	Alistair King Introductory						
1700							
1800							
1900							

Figure 21.1

(d) End-user requirements

Having talked to the user and documented current working practices you should be able to identify a set of end-user requirements.

> ### End-user requirements
>
> The main aims of my new system are to:
>
> - reduce the amount of paper work required from the instructor, as the system will create reports and lists of necessary information;
> - have an easy-to-use system;
> - speed up the time it takes to make a lesson booking and remove errors;
> - find information about a student quickly;
> - keep past records of students and lessons;
> - improve the organisation of the driving school by allowing information to be readily available;
> - produce reports on lessons and income;
> - produce a membership card for each student from a link within the system;
> - ....

(e) Data flow diagrams

It is important to be able to illustrate the system using data flow diagrams. They are a diagrammatic way of showing the flow of information through your system, focusing on how incoming data flows (inputs) become outgoing data flows (outputs).

Many texts and some courses take the science of DFD work considerably further than outlined below. The emphasis here is to encourage you to think clearly through the system and present it diagrammatically.

The following symbols are used in data flow diagrams:

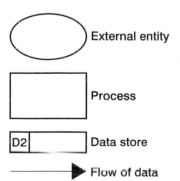

Figure 21.2

External entities

The first step is to identify all the external sources of information and external recipients of information. These are called the *external entities*. These external entities are usually people such as customers, suppliers and users of the system.

In the Pass-It system there are two external identities:

○ the students;
○ the instructors.

Level 0 Context Diagram

The first diagram is the context diagram. This is very much a higher level overview of the system.

Draw a rectangle in the middle of an A4 piece of paper. This rectangle represents the system. Around it draw an oval shape for each of the external entitles (see Figure 21.3).

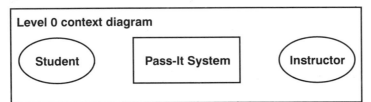

Figure 21.3

You now need to add an arrow for each of the data flows that you have identified. Try to show all the data flowing between these entities and the system.

Start by making a list of all the data flows in the system, who is the external entity and whether they are source or recipient. For example, when a new student joins the driving school, the external entity is the student who is the source.

DATA FLOW	EXTERNAL ENTITY	SOURCE/RECIPIENT
Student joins school	Student	Source
Membership card issued	Student	Recipient
Student details change	Student	Source
Student leaves school	Student	Source
Student books a lesson	Student	Source
Student cancels a lesson	Student	Source
Instructor joins school	Instructor	Source
Instructor details change	Instructor	Source
Instructor leaves school	Instructor	Source
Timetables issued	Instructor	Recipient
Cost of lesson	Instructor	Recipient

For each of the data flows add an arrow to your data flow diagram. The finished Level 0 diagram looks like Figure 21.4.

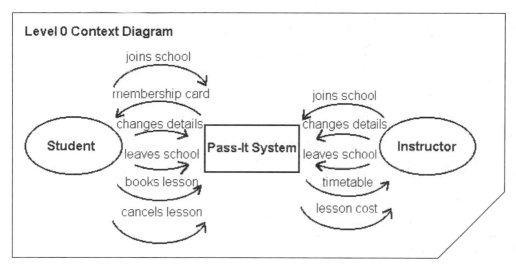

Figure 21.4

The arrows should correspond to the data flows identified.

Level 1 diagrams

At Level 1 the DFD now needs to be broken down by dividing the processes into individual, more detailed, numbered processes. Begin the DFD by identifying each incoming data flow, outgoing data flow and the associated processes.

Each process will refer to a separate part of the finished system. In the case of the Pass-It system, the four processes are student administration, lesson booking, instructor administration and general administration.

These are shown in Figure 21.5. Note that an external entity may appear more than once in a DFD. The diagonal line inside the oval shape shows that the entity appears elsewhere.

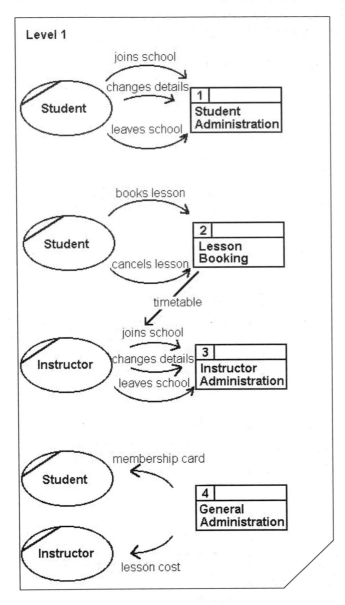

Figure 21.5

Next the data stores need to be shown. Each data store represents a table in the final system. Data stores are numbered D1, D2…

Note

1. As data will be both written to and read from each data store, there must be at least one arrow going into each data store and at least one arrow leading from it.
2. Data cannot flow directly from a data store to an external entity, only via a process.

The completed level 1 diagram is shown in Figure 21.6.

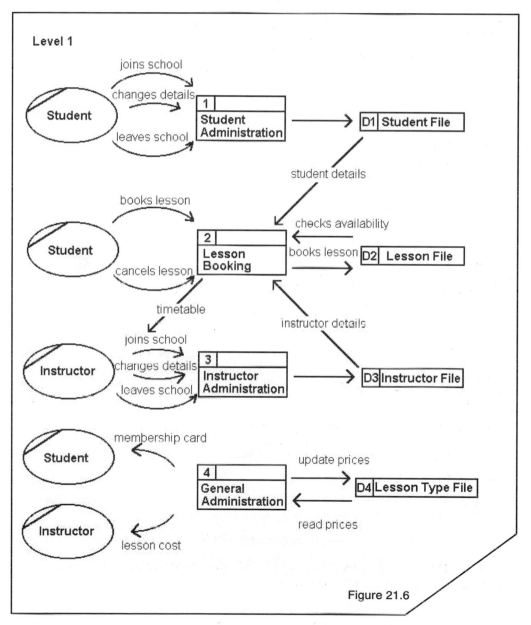

Figure 21.6

Level 2 diagrams

The next stage is to break the system down further into the various processes involved. Each process has its own DFD and is again numbered and the numbering relates to the Level 1 numbers, e.g. Process 1 may be split into three processes 1.1, 1.2 and 1.3.

This is the Level 2 data flow diagram. Examples for the first two processes are shown in Figure 21.7.

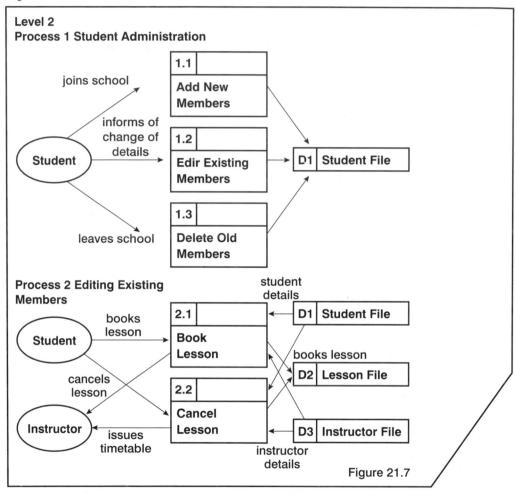

Figure 21.7

Data flow diagrams can be drawn in different ways. However you draw them, it is essential that the way you present your diagrams is consistent.

○ Don't make the DFD too complicated by splitting it into too many processes. The DFD is supposed to help and not hinder the analysis.
○ The external identities and data flows in the Level 2 diagram should correspond to the external identities and data flows in the original Level 0 diagram.
○ Allow a lot of time for redrawing the DFDs to get them correct.

(f) Input, processing and output requirements

From the DFDs it is now possible to establish in more detail what data is to be stored, what data needs to be entered, the information that needs to be output and the processes that the system has to be able to deal with.

Input, processing and output requirements

Data stores

- Student file containing details of students enrolled with the driving school
- Lesson file......
- Instructor file......
- Lesson type file......
- Archive lesson file (to store details of old lessons)......

Inputs

- Student details (name, address, telephone number, test record)
- Instructor details (name, address, telephone number)
- Lesson details (date, time, student, instructor, pick-up and drop-off points)

Processes

- Student joins school, details recorded
- Edit student details when they change address or contact number
- Student leaves school......
- Book a lesson......
- Cancel a lesson......
- Instructor joins school......
- Edit instructor details......
- Instructor leaves school......
- Calculate lesson cost......
- Issue membership cards......
- Update prices......
- Issue timetables......

Outputs

- Timetables for instructors issued daily to each instructor
- Income report......
- Membership cards......

(g) Data dynamics of the problem

This section is about the movement of data after an event such as leaving a club, moving from one school year to the next or passing a driving test. Does the data need to be updated? How long will it be kept? Will it be deleted or stored somewhere else in the system?

Data dynamics

After a user passes the theory and the practical test their details will not be deleted from the system as they may go on to take the Pass Plus course.

However, their data will be transferred from the student data store to a separate data store from where it can easily be retrieved.

Similarly all lessons over one year old will be stored in a separate data store. After another year this information will be deleted altogether.

Instructors are self-employed. They may leave the company and come back at another time, in which case their details will not be deleted completely but sent to a different data store.

(h) Specification

You are now in a position to present a list of detailed sub-tasks that will make up the new system. You need to offer as much detail as possible, as this is a working document for the designer.

Specification

The system will offer some of the following features.

1 Student administration

The user will be able to:
1.1 Add new student details to include Student ID, Surname, Forename......
1.2 Store details of test dates and times......
1.3 Edit existing student details
1.4 Delete student details
1.5 Search for student details by......

2 Lesson bookings

The system will have options to:
2.1 Book lessons by date and time
2.2 Store details of collection point, drop off point......
2.3 Cancel lessons
2.4 Keep records of lessons for a period of time......
2.5 Search and display lessons by student, instructor, date and time

3 Instructor administration

The system will have options to:
3.1 Add new instructors and store details of their name, address and contact.
3.2 Edit and delete instructor details
3.3 Search for instructor details

4 General administration

The user will be able to:
4.1 Print weekly timetables to include details of......
4.2 Update prices as and when necessary
4.3 Produce reports to display lesson prices......
4.4 Calculate lesson prices and print them out
4.5 Issue membership cards to display details of......
4.6 Clear records of lessons which are no longer needed

(i) *Resources available*

The purpose of this section is to look at the hardware and software resources available to the user and make appropriate recommendations. Try and look at this in relation to the problem you are trying to solve. It is not a case of just listing a typical PC specification.

You also need to consider the current skill level of the intended user(s) and identify possible training needs. You might have more than one user of this system. You will need to take this into account when designing your system and writing the user guide.

When looking at the hardware and software you might consider some of the following issues:

○ What PC specification does the user have? Will the user need to buy a new PC?
○ Will it need upgrading? Will it need a faster processor?
○ Will the user need to upgrade the software from Windows 95 to Windows XP?
○ You also need to consider backup and the size of your application.
○ Will a floppy disk suffice as backup or will you need to supply a writeable CD drive?
○ Is printing an issue?
○ What volume of printing does your user need? What quality of printing is needed?
○ What is the potential cost?

Resources available

In the office Doug has a Pentium II with 64Mb of memory. The operating system is Windows 98 and the Office 2000 suite is installed, including Access 2000. He has a six-year-old Canon BJ 200 inkjet printer which came with his previous PC. His only means of backup is to floppy disc.

I think Doug should consider running Windows XP and the latest range of Office software if he is going to learn a new system. He is familiar with Windows and would need little training but the new system will be developed in XP. I would recommend one of the newer standard entry level PCs. He could of course upgrade his current PC to the 128Mb needed for very little money but we have decided that replacing his current PC is more effective.

The size of the application will probably not exceed 2Mb at most and while backup could be maintained in compressed format to floppy disc the newer PC will come with a CD-RW drive which can be used for backup. Printing is limited to: issuing the daily and weekly timetables, membership cards, producing occasional reports and mail merging the occasional letter. This is very low volume printing requiring reasonable print quality. Although the old inkjet is fine it might be time to upgrade to one of the new, low-cost lasers offering more than adequate print speeds and a little better quality. A laser printer offering high quality printing at around 12 ppm can be purchased for around £160.

(j) Evaluation criteria

You must state clearly how you are going to evaluate your solution when it is finished. This involves giving a clear set of performance indicators. These are statements clearly showing how you are going to judge the success or not of your system.

For example they might cover:

- the ease of use of the system;
- the look and feel of the system (user interfaces);
- quality of output from the system (the reports);
- features in the system that will save time;
- the accuracy of output from the system;
- the speed of certain functions in the system.

Evaluation Dos	Evaluation Don'ts
• Only choose criteria that you can back up with evidence.	• List as many criteria as you can in the hope of gaining more marks. • Make vague statements such as it will be quicker, it will be easier to use.

Some performance indicators might be:

PI1 The system will be able to reduce the time taken on the phone when dealing with a booking. It will eliminate the need to search through the booking diary looking for an available slot. I have timed how long it takes to find a booking in the current system. It averages around 15 seconds to see if a time slot is available. I expect the new system to do this in half the time.

PI2 I will ensure that all user interfaces are easy to use with common layouts, icons and styles. During the early development of the system and when the system is complete I will liaise with the user, noting problems and areas for improvement.

PI3 All timetables will be presented with an in-house style and contain no mistakes.

2 Design

The design section should include plans for each sub-task in the specification.

Your design plans should be done away from the computer. Design plans are probably best done by hand.

Good designs will include details of:

○ possible solutions: consider different ways of solving the problem;
○ chosen solution: describe the reasons for the chosen solution;
○ the problem broken down into sub-tasks;
○ entity relationship diagrams;
○ relationship diagrams;
○ data dictionary including validation and input masks;
○ design of data-capture forms if appropriate;
○ query and processing designs;
○ screen layouts, forms and reports;
○ time plan with estimated time allocation for each phase and/or Gantt charts;
○ testing plan.

(a) Possible solutions

In this section you should consider the different possible ways of solving the problem, including the advantages and disadvantages of each. You might consider:

○ improving the existing manual system or parts of it;
○ a Microsoft Access solution;
○ a solution using alternative software providing database facilities;

○ an alternative solution within Microsoft Access using different features or perhaps a different design.

Try always to relate the solution to the problem. Part of two possible solutions is given below.

Possible solutions

Solution using Microsoft Excel

Microsoft Excel is a spreadsheet program for Windows 95/98/2000.

Advantages
- The software is easy to use and easy to learn
- The package is part of the standard Microsoft Office package
- Data can be searched using Auto filter.

Disadvantages
- Every time I book a lesson I will have to enter repeated data which is inefficient.

Solution using Microsoft Access XP

Microsoft Access is a relational database management system for Windows 95/98/2000.

Advantages
- Relationships can be created between tables, linking fields and eliminating redundant data and inconsistency
- The package is fully customisable
- Forms and reports can be created in an appropriate style reflecting the company image.

Disadvantages
- Microsoft Access is not easy to learn.

(b) Chosen solution

You now need to give clear reasons stating exactly why you have opted for the chosen solution.

Chosen solution

I have decided to select Microsoft Access XP as the software in which I will create the new system for the following reasons.

- Relationships between tables will eliminate redundant data.
- The system will be customised to suit the user.
- The system will be fully automated with the use of macros. This means that users do not need to learn how to use Access.

(c) Database design

Having chosen the solution you now need to present design plans for each sub-task in the system.

Database design

From the analysis you can see that there will be four main tables.

- Student table;
- Lesson table;
- Instructor table;
- Lesson type table.

There will also be tables to archive data.

Entity-relationship diagrams

The tables will be related as shown in Figure 21.8.

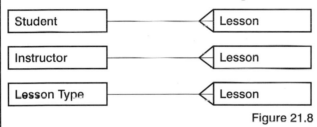

Figure 21.8

All relationships are one-to-many as shown in Figure 21.9.

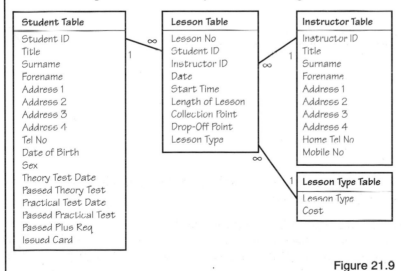

Figure 21.9

(d) Implementation plan

In order to create the system you will need to break it down into smaller tasks, which can be implemented in stages. This will help ensure designs are present for each task. This should also relate to your time plan. The sub-tasks are as follows:

Implementation plan

1   Create a table to store Student details.
2   Create a table to store Instructor details.
3   Create a table to store Lesson Types.
4   Create a table to store Lesson details.
5   Set up the relationships between the tables.
6   Set up a query to search for a student's details.
7   Set up a query to search for a student's lessons.
8   Set up a query to search for an instructor's lessons on any date.
9   Set up a query to search for full lesson details.
10 Set up a query to search for see next week's lessons.
11 Set up a query to calculate income.
12 Create a form to enter new student, edit student details, delete old students.
13 Create a form to enter new instructor, edit instructor details, delete old instructors.
14 Create a form to enter lesson type details.
15 Create a form to book a lesson and cancel a lesson.
16 Create a report to display instructor details.
17 Create a report to display student details.
18 Create a report to issue membership cards.
19 Create a report to display the daily lessons for an instructor.
20 Create an income report.
21 Create a macro to update prices.
22 Create a macro to archive/delete unwanted records.
23 Create a switchboard, which will contain various buttons which will be connected to all the different functions of the system allowing easy control for the end user.

(e) Data dictionary

Student table

FIELD NAME	DATA TYPE	OTHER INFORMATION
Student ID	Autonumber	Primary Key field
Title	Text	Lookup: Mr, Mrs, Miss or Ms Field Size 6
Surname	Text	Field Size 20
Forename	Text	Field Size 20
Address 1	Text	Field Size 30
Address 2	Text	Field Size 30
Address 3	Text	Default 'Derby' Field Size 20
Address 4	Text	Format > Field Size 10
Tel No	Text	Field Size 15
Date of Birth	Date/Time	Format: Short Date
Sex	Text	Lookup table: Must be M or F Field Size 1
Theory Test Date	Date/Time	Format: Short Date
Passed Theory Test	Yes/No	
Practical Test Date	Date/Time	Format: Short Date
Passed Practical Test	Yes/No	
Pass Plus Req	Yes/No	
Issued Card	Yes/No	

Instructor table

FIELD NAME	DATA TYPE	OTHER INFORMATION
Instructor ID	Autonumber	Primary Key field
Title	Text	Lookup Mr, Mrs, Ms, Miss Field Size 6
Surname	Text	Field Size 20
Forename	Text	Field Size 20
Address 1	Text	Field Size 30
Address 2	Text	Field Size 30
Address 3	Text	Default 'Derby' Field Size 20
Address 4	Text	Format > Field Size 10
Home Tel No	Text	Field Size 15
Mobile No	Text	Field Size 15

Lesson Type table

FIELD NAME	DATA TYPE	OTHER INFORMATION
Lesson Type	Text	Primary Key field Field Size 25
Cost	Currency	

Lesson table

FIELD NAME	DATA TYPE	OTHER INFORMATION
Lesson Type	AutoNumber	Primary Key field
Student ID	Number	Long Integer
Instructor ID	Number	Long Integer
Date	Date/Time	Format: Short Date
Start Time	Date/Time	Format: Short Time
Length of Lesson	Number	Integer Set validation between 1 and 8
Collection Point	Text	Default value: Home Address Field Size 30
Drop-Off Point	Text	Default value: Home Address Field Size 30
Lesson Type	Text	Lookup set values as Introductory, Standard, Pass Plus and Test Field Size 25

(f) Query designs

QUERY NAME	UNDERLYING TABLE(S) AND FIELDS	CRITERIA
Search by Student ID Query	Student (Surname, Forename, Address1... Sex)	Parameter Query Student ID = [Enter the ID number]
Full Details Query	Student (Surname, Forename) Instructor (Surname, Forename) Lesson (All fields)	–

(g) Process designs

MACRO NAME	ACTIONS
Archive lessons	Run the Old Lesson Append Query
	Run the Old Lesson Delete Query
	Run the Over One Year Delete Query

(h) Screen layouts, forms and reports

You need to present designs for all important screen layouts such as forms, reports and switchboards. Two examples are shown below.

Screen layouts

The system switchboard must have:

- the company logo;
- links to other forms;
- links to reports;
- links to system functions.

It will look like Figure 21.10.

Main Switchboard Design.

Loads automatically when system is loaded.

Six buttons loading different functions.

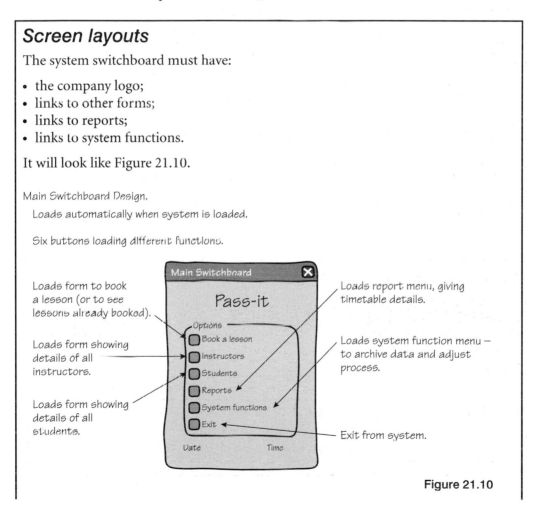

Loads form to book a lesson (or to see lessons already booked).

Loads form showing details of all instructors.

Loads form showing details of all students.

Loads report menu, giving timetable details.

Loads system function menu – to archive data and adjust process.

Exit from system.

Figure 21.10

The lesson booking form will look like Figure 21.11.

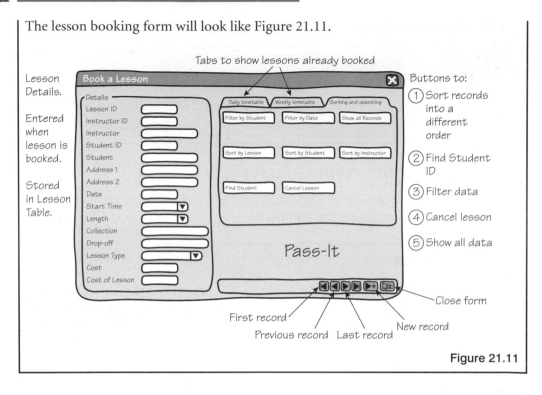

Figure 21.11

Note

Ideally interface designs should be consistent. You would expect all input forms to have a common look and feel. For example, headings and control buttons would be positioned in the same place; colour schemes and fonts used would be consistent.

If your system has many forms you could design one of them in detail showing all the common features. The other forms could be listed, with detail of the features that are different perhaps shown in a tabular format. It really depends how much time you have and how much you enjoy doing hand-drawn designs! You could apply the same principle to your output and processing designs.

Design dos	Design don'ts
• Present your plans in a format such that a reasonably competent person could take them and make a start on setting up your system. You could get another student to try them out. • Make them legible and neat. This person must be able read them.	• Use screen dumps from the actual system as part of your design plans.

(i) Testing plan

Testing is an integral part of developing an IT system and your design should include a test plan, saying exactly what you will test and how. Tests should:

- be numbered;
- state the purpose of the test;
- specify the data to be used, if any;
- outline the expected result;
- cross-reference to clear hard copy usually in the form of a screen dump;
- provide evidence of the actual results plus any comments;
- outline any action needed or taken.

Where appropriate test data should include typical data and, if possible, extreme, invalid or awkward data.

Test plan

TEST	PURPOSE	TEST DATA	EXPECTED OUTCOME	ACTUAL OUTCOME	ACTION TAKEN
...					
4. Search by Student ID Query	To test that the query provides the correct data	7	Details for Mary Trueman appear		
...					
15. Instructors' report	To test that the instructors' report output fits on to a page and is legible	Whole file	Full details of each instructor appear in the report		
...					
17. End-user test, initial Student Instructor and Lesson form	Ease of use for the user	User to run through all options	Comments for future action		
...					
21 Test Student lookup combo box on the student form	To check it returns correct details for a student on file and see how it it handles a student entered not on file	Name of Student Jenkins Name of Student Clough	Details for Jenkins shown Details for Clough not shown		

Test plan dos	Test plan don'ts
• Try to make your system go wrong! To find errors you have to try and provoke failure. • Remember that you are testing whether the data is processed correctly, not just whether a button works or not. • Test that your system meets the end-user requirements and involve the end-user.	• Forget that the purpose of testing is to show your solution works. • Include many similar tests such as testing all the navigation buttons on every form. Find a way of grouping them into one test.

(j) Time plan

Present a detailed time plan for the whole of your project either as a calendar of events or as a Gantt chart.

WEEKS BEGINNING	PROCESS
29 Oct	Decide on project. Write up problem statement. Interview user
05 Nov–19 Nov	Analyse problem – establish requirements, draw data flow diagrams, establish sub-tasks
26 Nov–03 Dec	Start design work, write up possible and chosen solutions, present interface designs to the user
10 Dec	Improve designs on user's comments, produce testing plan
	...
14 Jan	Sub-tasks 1 to 4. Create tables. Enter test data
21 Jan	Sub-tasks 5 to 8. Create relationships. Create queries
	...

3 Implementation

This section should contain clear evidence that you have implemented each part of your system.

The information presented here should reflect your specification and design plans.

Screen dumps and/or fully labelled printouts need to be used to support and provide evidence of work done.

This is your chance to sell yourself and all the techniques you have used in your project. Include:

○ printouts of all tables, queries, forms, reports and macros;
○ screen shots where appropriate, e.g. the relationship window;
○ a concise commentary on how you set up the system.

Task 1 Create a table to store student details

The first task that was required was the creation of the tables to contain the system's data. This involved setting up the fields, setting the validation and input masks and choosing the primary key.

Field Name	Data Type	Description
Student ID	AutoNumber	Student's ID number
Title	Text	
Surname	Text	
Forename	Text	
Address 1	Text	
Address 2	Text	
Address 3	Text	
Address 4	Text	
Tel No	Text	
Date of Birth	Date/Time	
Sex	Text	
Theory Test Date	Date/Time	
Passed Theory Test	Yes/No	
Practical Test Date	Date/Time	
Passed Practical Test	Yes/No	
Pass Plus Req	Yes/No	
Issued Card	Yes/No	

Field Properties

Figure 21.12

I set up the Student table with the fields as shown in Figure 21.12. I set student ID as the Primary Key field.

I used the Lookup Wizard to set my own values for the Title field as shown in Figure 21.13. I chose Mr, Mrs, Ms and Miss. This makes entering data easier.

Figure 21.13

I didn't set any validation rules because they weren't necessary but I did set an Input Mask on all Date/Time fields which again makes entering data easier as shown in Figure 21.14.

	9	Mr	Watson	Greg	☑	21/12/02	☐
	10	Miss	Jones	Lucy	☑	_/_/_	☐
*	(AutoNumber)				▣		▣

Figure 21.14

Task 5   Set up the relationships between the tables

In the Database Window I opened the Relationships window and added the tables Student, Instructor, Lesson and Lesson Type. See Figure 21.15.

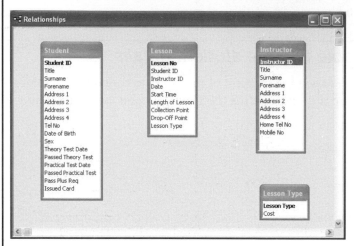

Figure 21.15

To set the links I dragged each key field from the tables Student, Instructor and Lesson Type and dropped them on the same field in the Lesson Table. All relationships were set as one-to-many.

I set Referential Integrity each time to avoid invalid data being entered. When I linked the Student ID fields I also checked Cascade Deletes. This is so that if and when I delete a student record all related lessons taken by that student will be deleted from the lesson table. This is shown below in Figure 21.16.

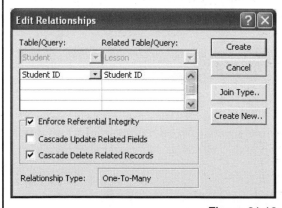

Figure 21.16

The screenshot in Figure 21.17 shows all the relationships set as one-to-many and the layout saved.

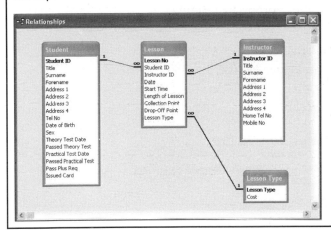

Figure 21.17

Task 16   Create a report to display instructor details

To generate this report I used the wizard and the AutoReport: Tabular option. I based the report on the instructor table (see Figure 21.18).

Instructor

Instructor ID	Title	Surname	Forename	Address 1	Address 2	Address 3	Address	Home Tel	Mobile
1	Mr	Jones	Doug	57 Swanmore Road	Etwall	Derby	DE34 5FG	0133212254	07720521
2	Mr	Batchelor	Arnold	13 Gairloch Close	Etwall	Derby	DE34 5FG	0133255214	07980352
3	Mr	Smith	Andrew	5b Sunrise Road	Littleover	Derby	DE46 4ED	0133252145	07980525

Figure 21.18

The layout wasn't really what I wanted. The report only just fitted the page and a number of headings were not in the right place. So I went into Report Design View and made the changes as shown in Figure 21.19.

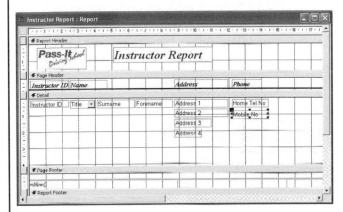

Figure 21.19

- I removed some of the column headings and grouped them as Name, Address and Phone.
- I grouped the text boxes under the appropriate headings.
- I added the Driving School Logo and edited the title to Instructor Report.
- I realigned all labels and data.

The finished report appeared as in Figure 21.20.

Pass-It *Driving School*   *Instructor Report*

Instructor ID	Name			Address	Phone
1	Mr	Jones	Doug	57 Swanmore Road	01332122541
				Etwall	07720521478
				Derby	
				DE34 5F	
2	Mr	Batchelor	Arnold	13 Gairloch Close	01332552147
				Etwall	07980352145
				Derby	
				DE34 5F	
3	Mr	Smith	Andrew	5b Sunrise Road	01332521452
				Littleover	07980525214
				Derby	
				DE45 4E	

Figure 21.20

Implementation dos	Implementation don'ts
• Be clear and concise. • Use screen dumps to record your explanation. • Describe all the steps in setting up your system. • Describe clearly the features of the software you have used. • Ensure screen dumps are readable.	• Undersell the work you have done and remember exam board moderators can only give credit for what they can see. • Submit work set up by the wizards and claim you did it on your own! • Reproduce large tracts of Access manuals; it is not a guide to using the software.

4 Testing

Include:

○ details of test data;
○ actual results of testing with expected results and evidence – printouts or screenshots;
○ actions taken as a result of testing;
○ evidence of full end-user involvement in testing.

(a) Test results

TEST	PURPOSE	TEST DATA	EXPECTED OUTCOME	ACTUAL OUTCOME	ACTION TAKEN
...					
4. Search by Student ID Query	To test that the query provides the correct data	7	Details for Mary Trueman appear	Details for Mary Trueman appear. See Test Result 4	None needed
...					
15. Instructors' report	To test that the instructors' report output fits on to a page and is legible	Whole file	Full details of each instructor appear in the report	Full details of each instructor appear in the report but some columns are not wide enough. See Test Result 15.	Widths of columns adjusted so that all the text fits in. Headings moved also. Added logo. See Test Result 15a.
...					
17. End-user test, initial Student Instructor and Lesson form	Ease of use for the user	User to run through all options	Comments for future action	See user comments under Test Result 17.	Action taken later in finishing touches to the system.
...					
21 Test Student lookup combo box on the student form	To check it returns correct details for a student on file and see how it handles a student entered not on file	Name of Student Jenkins Name of Student Clough	Details for Jenkins shown Details for Clough not shown	Details shown correctly Not accepted. Access gives error message.	None needed Advice given in user guide.

Test result 4

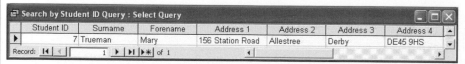

Figure 21.21

Test result 15

Instructor

ructor ID	Title	Surnam	Forena	Address 1	Address 2	Address	Addr	Home	Mob
1	Mr	Jones	Doug	57 Swanmore	Etwall	Derby	DE34	0133212	0772
2	Mr	Batchelor	Arnold	13 Gairloch Cl	Etwall	Derby	DE34	0133255	0798
3	Mr	Smith	Andrew	5b Sunrise Ro	Littleover	Derby	DE45	0133252	0798

Figure 21.22

Test result 15a

 Pass-It *Instructor Report*

Instructor ID	Name		Address	Phone
1	Mr	Jones	Doug	57 Swanmore Road	01332122541
				Etwall	07720521478
				Derby	
				DE34 5F	
2	Mr	Batchelor	Arnold	13 Gairloch Close	01332552147
				Etwall	07980352145
				Derby	
				DE34 5F	
3	Mr	Smith	Andrew	5b Sunrise Road	01332521452
				Littleover	07980525214
				Derby	
				DE45 4E	

Figure 21.23

Test result 17

After designing the initial forms I asked Mr Jones to sit with me and go through the main features on each. I also wanted him to comment on the ease of use, general layout and appearance of the form.

He made the following comments:

- All forms excellent in design and colour schemes used.
- The tool tips over the control buttons were a little unfriendly: First Record, Add a record, etc.
- Some of the boxes for entering data were far larger than was needed, e.g. Student ID, Lesson No, Title. Mr Jones found this a little confusing when entering data.

Action taken:

- Tool tips over all buttons were made more user friendly, e.g. Add a Record changed to Make a Booking.
- Form sizes adjusted accordingly.
- Text boxes for a number of fields made smaller. For example on the student form in Figure 21.24 Student ID and Title reduced to fit typical data.

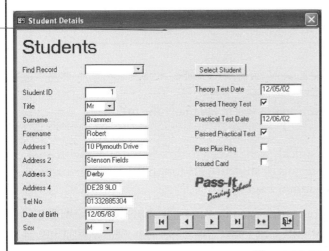

Figure 21.24

Test result 21

The Student form showing details of Jenkins displayed correctly (see Figure 21.25).

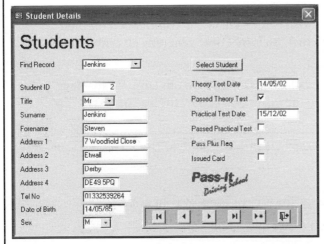

Figure 21.25

When student Clough entered (or any student not on file) Access will not accept name and issues an error message (see Figure 21.26).

Figure 21.26

(b) User testing

Doug Jones used the system a few times to test it. He made the following observations:

He found it easy to book lessons quickly as he needs to do when dealing with phone enquiries and it was easy to find details of students. He found no major errors in the system but commented on some minor issues.

He thought the system was generally user-friendly but he had problems fitting reports to a page. Reports came out on two pages and it was not easy to alter the report to one page.

I will correct this by using landscape format for reports.

Doug said that the system should offer quick information on lessons already booked further ahead than just the day of the call and for the coming week. This is something I will need to investigate improving.

Doug thought the design of all forms was excellent. He commented on their professional look but he noticed that the forms were generally all different sizes. He found this annoying.

He also said that some of the boxes for data entry were too large for the data to be entered. I will need to resize the forms and review the size of text boxes.

5 User guide

A user guide is just that – a guide for the user or users of your system.

It should include details of:

○ the purpose of the system;
○ how to get started;
○ the main menu options;

○ how to perform each of the routine tasks that make up your system;
○ common problems or error messages and possible solutions;
○ technical issues such as the minimum system requirements needed to run your system, installation instructions, security measures, backup procedures and passwords needed.

User Guide to the Pass-It Driving School system

Introduction

The system allows the user to store details of students and instructors and make bookings for lessons. The system also offers a number of reporting features to deal with bookings, student records and instructor timetables.

System requirements

You require a minimum of a Pentium 3 PC with at least 128Mb of memory and Windows 95 or later, preferably Windows XP. Microsoft Office XP needs to be installed including the component Access 2002.

The system initially uses nearly 2 Mb of disc space (see figure 21.27), although this will increase as more records are added.

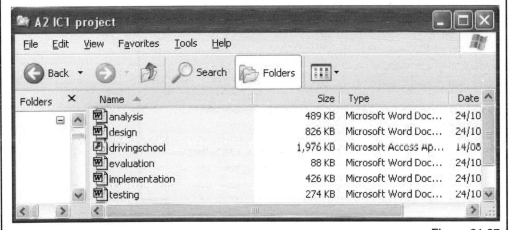

Figure 21.27

A laser printer is recommended to ensure high quality output.

How to install the system

The system is supplied on a 1.44 Mb floppy disc and is in a compressed folder called **drivingschool**.

1 Insert the floppy disc containing the system.
2 Click on the **Start** button and click on **My Computer** icon. Then click on the $3\frac{1}{2}$ **Floppy (A:)** icon. The drivingschool zipped folder will be shown as in Figure 21.28.

Figure 21.28

3 Right click on **drivingschool** and click on **Extract All**, as in Figure 21.29.

Figure 21.29

The Compressed (zipped) Folders Extraction Wizard will extract the drivingschool file for you and ask you where you want to store the extracted file.

You must extract the file to the hard drive of your computer (C:) It is best to make a new folder in which to store the file. The Extraction Wizard allows you to do this.

Getting started

To boot up the system double click the file icon called **drivingschool** (see Figure 21.30).

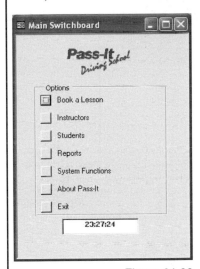

Figure 21.30

The system displays the switchboard giving the user seven options:

1 **Book a Lesson**
2 **Instructors**
3 **Students**
4 **Reports**
5 **System Functions**
6 **About Pass-It**
7 **Exit**

Booking a lesson

1   To book a lesson, click on the **Book a Lesson** button.

The Book a Lesson form loads.

2   Click on the Make a Booking button for a new booking see Figure 21.31.

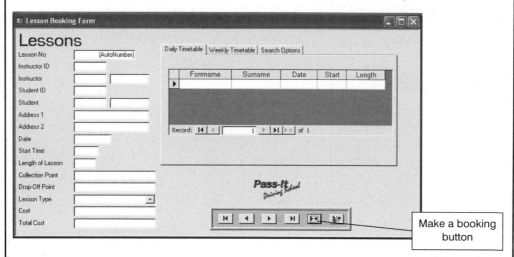

Figure 21.31

3   Enter the Instructor ID in the Instructor ID box.

4   Enter the Student ID in the Student ID box.

5   If you do not know the Student ID number, click on the Search Options tab.

6   Click on Find Student.

The Student form will load, as in Figure 21.32.

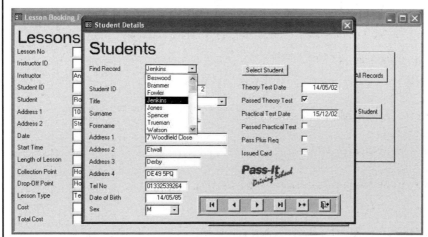

Figure 21.32

7 Click on the Find Record drop-down arrow. The students are in alphabetical order of surname.

8 Select the student's name.

9 Click on Select Student to paste the details into the booking form.

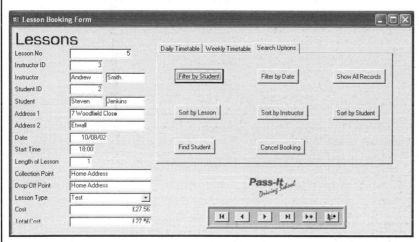

Figure 21.33

10 Enter the date of the lesson.

11 Click on the Daily Timetable tab. Check what times have been booked already with that instructor that day.

12 Enter all the details. Click on the Make a Booking button to confirm the booking.

Further development

It is likely that the user guide for this system would go on to include:

1 Details of the other user options such as:
   - how to cancel a lesson;
   - editing student details;
   - editing instructor details;
   - adjusting prices;
   - producing membership cards;
   - issuing timetables;
   - procedures for archiving student and lesson details.

2 Possible problems and troubleshooting.

3 Instructions for backing up the system during daily operation – both when and how.

User guide dos	User guide don'ts
• Contain simple, clear, step-by-step instructions to using your system. • Be jargon free and well illustrated. • Consider forming or being part of online help built into the system.	• Be a guide to using the software – it is a guide to your system. • Include large tracts of text from user manuals and try to avoid using jargon.

6 Evaluation

This section requires the student to report on the degree of success of their project.

Evaluation dos	Evaluation don'ts
• Go back to the end-user requirements and comment on whether each has been achieved successfully • Return to the evaluation criteria and again comment on each, considering successes, problems and possible solutions. • Involve the end-user in this process, note problems, limitations and recommend action for further development.	• Moan about the lack of time. Time management is your responsibility. • Pretend it is all working when some parts are incomplete. Do not be afraid to tell the truth. • Report on how well you did but focus on how well your system achieved its aims.

Some examples are given below:

End user requirements

UR1   Produce an Instructors' Report to include contact details only.

This option was relatively easy to set up using the wizards in Access. However, there were problems fitting it to the page and on reflection it might have been easier to set all reports to landscape. It took a certain amount of time editing to arrange the headings and data to fit the page. Currently the report offers details of all instructors in a continuous list which was not always needed. **See Action Point 1.**

Performance indicators

PI1 The system will be able to reduce the time taken on the phone when dealing with a booking. It will eliminate the need to search through the booking diary looking for an available slot. I have timed how long it takes to find a booking in the current system. It averages around 15 seconds to see if a time slot is available. I expect the new system to do this in at least half the time.

The system does eliminate the need to search through the daily booking diary looking for an available slot and therefore does save time. Booking availability was offered in about five seconds. The system at present only offers quick access to availability on the day of the call and for the coming week. **See Action Point 2**.

PI2 I will ensure all user interfaces are easy to use with common layouts, icons and styles. During the early development of the system and when the system is complete I will liaise with the user, noting problems and areas for improvement.

The user described the design of all forms as excellent. He liked the professional look but was concerned about a few minor irritations he found when working with them. The forms were generally all different sizes. A number of the boxes for data entry were too large for the data to be entered. The control panel on each form while looking very professional was a little unfriendly and it was not obvious at first what each button did. **See Action Point 3**.

Future development

Action Point 1

I need to investigate designing all reports as landscape. I also need to add an option to the menu which will allow the user to choose the instructor on which they wish to have a report. I will need to base the report on the instructor table using a parameter query.

Action Point 2

When a student makes a booking, lesson availability can only be viewed on the current day and over the next seven days. Clearly a number of students book lessons over a week ahead or indeed block book the same time each week for a number of weeks. I need to investigate this for further development. Currently the user will have to jot down the booking manually and enter the details offline.

Action Point 3

- Design all forms to be the same size. Consider redesigning the system to use the whole screen.
- Add text to the buttons in the control panel or consider adding tool tips for each button.
- Adjust size of all data entry boxes on each form as required.

Presenting your coursework documentation

Documentation should:

- be well written and presented;
- be well organised and illustrated;
- clearly show the development of the system from the initial analysis to design, through to its implementation and testing.

When your project documentation is finished you should:

- produce a front cover; your name, centre and candidate number should be clear;
- get your project in order; page numbering and the use of headers and footers is to be encouraged;
- produce a contents page which clearly cross references to each section in the project;
- bind your project securely; often coursework has to be sent for checking; it needs to be firmly attached but ring binders are not encouraged.

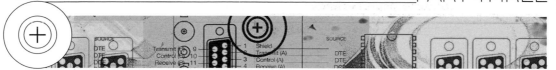

PART THREE

50 Access tips and tricks

Unit 22 Access tips and tricks

Here are 50 tricks and tips that have been found to be more than useful when implementing Access projects.

Tables

1 Forcing text in a field to be in upper case
2 Shortcuts with the CTRL key
3 Preventing duplicate values in a field
4 Preventing duplicate combinations of data
5 Hiding a table
6 Filtering data by selection
7 Filtering data by form
8 Importing data from Excel
9 Using copy and paste to take an Excel worksheet into Access

Queries

10 Wildcard searches
11 Finding all the surnames that begin with a letter or combination of letters
12 Finding all the surnames containing a letter or combination of letters
13 Searching for all records this month
14 Using a query to combine two fields
15 Using the DateDiff function
16 What day of the week is a date?
17 Viewing action queries before running them
18 Searching for records that contain no values
19 Make-Table queries

Forms

20 Adding a calculated field to a form

50 Access tips and tricks

Reports

Macros

Others

1 Forcing text in a field to be in upper case

You can ensure that data entered into a field is in upper case by setting its Format property.

1   Go to Design View for the table.

2   Click on the **Field Name**.

3   In the Field Properties, enter a greater than symbol (>) in the **Format** property to make the field upper case. Do not include the brackets!

Note   To force a field to be in lower case, however it is entered, enter a less than symbol (<) in the Format field property.

2 Shortcuts with the CTRL key

○ When entering data in a table, you often want to copy the data from the previous record. Do this by simply pressing CTRL and '(apostrophe).

○ You can enter the current time into a table by simply pressing CTRL and : (colon).

○ Similarly you can enter the current date into a table by simply pressing CTRL and ; (semi-colon).

3 Preventing duplicate values in a field

Data in the key field cannot be repeated; for example you could not have two cars with the same Reg. No. You can prevent two records in another field having the same value by doing the following:

(a) At the Database Window, select the table and click on **Design.**

(b) Select the Field Name and set the Field Property **Indexed** to **Yes (No Duplicates).**

4 Preventing duplicate combinations of data

A theatre uses an Access database to store details of seats sold. A seat like A1 may be sold many times. Many seats may be sold for a performance on 12 October. But any seat must only be sold once for each performance. How can we prevent seats being sold twice?

The theatre has a sales table. The key field is the **Booking no**. Among the other fields in this table are **Seat No** and **Date**. Once a seat number and date has been entered this combination cannot be entered again.

(a) In the **Design View** for this table click on the Indexes icon or click on **View, Indexes**, as in Figure 22.1.

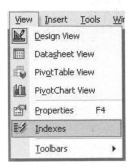

Figure 22.1

The Indexes dialogue box is displayed as in Figure 22.2.

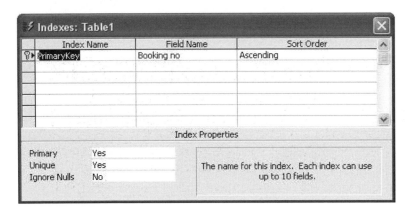

Figure 22.2

(b) Add an index name such as **Norepeats** underneath Primary Key as in Figure 22.3. The name you choose does not matter.

(c) In the next column select the first of the two fields which must not be duplicated. Below it select the second field.

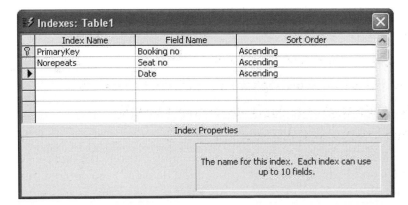

Figure 22.3

(d) Click on **Norepeats** and set the Unique box to **Yes** as in Figure 22.4.

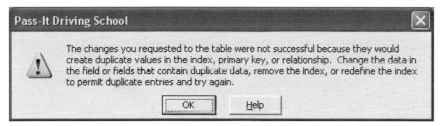

Figure 22.4

(c) Test it to make sure you get the error message in Figure 22.5.

Pass-It Driving School

The changes you requested to the table were not successful because they would create duplicate values in the index, primary key, or relationship. Change the data in the field or fields that contain duplicate data, remove the Index, or redefine the index to permit duplicate entries and try again.

OK   Help

Figure 22.5

5 Hiding a table

You can hide a table from the Database Window.

(a) At the Database Window select the table, then choose **View, Properties**.

(b) In the Properties dialogue box, check **Hidden**.

(c) Click on **Apply** and then click on **OK**.

The table will not appear in the Database Window.

(a) To show the table, click on **Tools, Options** and click on the **View** tab.

(b) Check **Hidden Objects,** click on **Apply** and then click on **OK**.

The Database Window will now display your hidden table.

6 Filtering data by selection

A filter enables you to search quickly for records in a table. For example, you can find all lessons with Instructor ID 1.

(a) From the Database Window, open the **Lesson** table in the Pass-It system.

(b) Click on a number 1 in the Instructor ID column. (It doesn't matter which one you choose.)

(c) Click on the **Filter by Selection** icon (see Figure 22.6) or click on **Records, Filter, Filter by Selection.**

Filter By Selection

Figure 22.6

You will now see only the records for Instructor number 1.

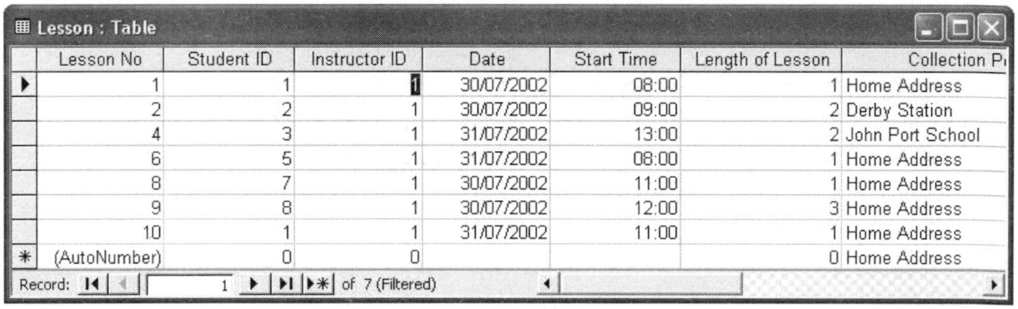

Lesson No	Student ID	Instructor ID	Date	Start Time	Length of Lesson	Collection Pi
1	1	1	30/07/2002	08:00	1	Home Address
2	2	1	30/07/2002	09:00	2	Derby Station
4	3	1	31/07/2002	13:00	2	John Port School
6	5	1	31/07/2002	08:00	1	Home Address
8	7	1	30/07/2002	11:00	1	Home Address
9	8	1	30/07/2002	12:00	3	Home Address
10	1	1	31/07/2002	11:00	1	Home Address
(AutoNumber)	0	0			0	Home Address

Record: 1 of 7 (Filtered)

Figure 22.7

(d) To remove the filter, click on the **Remove Filter** icon or click on **Records, Remove Filter/Sort** as shown in Figure 22.8.

Remove Filter

Figure 22.8

7 Filtering data by form

Filter by form enables you to carry out more complex searches for records in a table. For example you can find all the lessons that are on 30/07/02 AND have Instructor ID 2.

(a) Open the **Lesson** table in the Pass-It system.

(b) Click on the **Filter by Form** icon or click on **Records, Filter, Filter by Form.**

Figure 22.9

(c) Click in the **Date** column. A drop-down box appears. Choose **30/07/02.**

(d) Click in the **Instructor ID** column and choose **2.**

(e) Click on the **Apply Filter** icon or click on **Filter, Apply Filter/Sort.**

Figure 22.10

(f) Click on the same icon to clear the filters.

Note You can find lessons lasting more than one hour by starting a **Filter by Form** and typing >1 in the **Length of Lesson** column.

Blank fields can be found by typing **Is Null** into a filter by form. The opposite is to type **Is Not Null.**

8 Importing data from Excel

Importing data from Excel is easily done in Access using the **Import Spreadsheet Wizard.**

Suppose we wish to import into Access the Excel file of **Names** shown in Figure 22.11.
Note: Row 1 contains the **Field Names** for each column and the names are stored in
Sheet1.

	A	B	C	D	E	F	G
1	Title	Surname	Forename	Address 1	Address 2	Address 3	Address 4
2	Mr	Brammer	Robert	10 Plymouth Drive	Stenson Fields	Derby	DE28 9LO
3	Mr	Jenkins	Steven	7 Woodfield Close	Etwall	Derby	DE49 5PQ
4	Miss	Fowler	Sarah	19 Sea View Road	Mickleover	Derby	DE34 8NT
5	Mr	Beswood	Michael	25 Lundie Close	Allestree	Derby	DE45 5AF
6	Miss	Williams	Charlotte	21 Church Street	Littleover	Derby	DE33 8RD
7	Mr	Windsor	David	86 Milford Road	Allenton	Derby	DE57 4PT
8	Miss	Trueman	Mary	156 Station Road	Allestree	Derby	DE45 9HS
9	Miss	Spencer	Victoria	73 Mayfield Road	Stenson Fields	Derby	DE28 9VB
10	Mr	Watson	Greg	7 Derwent Close	Etwall	Derby	DE49 8HU
11	Miss	Jones	Lucy	183 Uttoxeter Road	Allenton	Derby	DE57 2GN

Sheet1 / Sheet2 / Sheet3 /

Figure 22.11

(a) Open the database into which you wish to import the file called **Names**. Click on
File, Get External Data and select **Import**. The **Import** dialogue box appears.
Select the file **Names** from the **Look in** and click on **Import**.

(b) The **Import Spreadsheet Wizard** loads. Click on **Sheet1** (if it is not already
highlighted) to tell the wizard where the data is stored. Click on **Next**.

(c) In the next **Import Spreadsheet Wizard** dialogue box check **First Row Contains
Column Headings** as shown in Figure 22.12. (Access will use these as field names
in the table.) Click on **Next**.

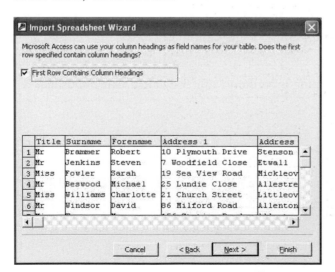

Figure 22.12

(d) Select the **New Table** option as shown in Figure 22.13. Click on **Next**.

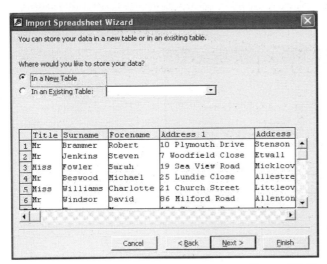

Figure 22.13

(e) The next **Import Spreadsheet Wizard** dialogue box gives you the option to specify information about the data or skip import. Click on **Next**.

(f) In the next dialogue box you are given some **Primary** key options. Select **Let Access add the primary key** (see Figure 22.14). You will notice Access inserts a Primary Key ID. Click on **Next**.

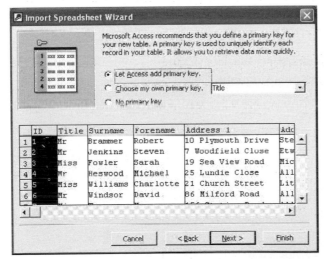

Figure 22.14

(g) In the final dialogue box click in the **Import to Table** box and type **Names** (see Figure 22.15). Click on **Finish**. At the Database Window open the table Names to check the import has been successful.

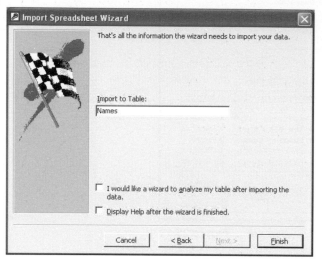

Figure 22.15

9 Using copy and paste to take an Excel worksheet into Access

This method gives you less control than Tip 8 but is quick and easy. It helps to include the field names in the first data row of the Excel worksheet. To try it you will need the Excel file called Names used in Tip 8.

(a) Open the Excel file **Names** and select the data (including column headings) that you want to paste into Access. Click on **Edit, Copy**.

(b) At the Database Window in Access, select the **Tables** tab and click **Edit, Paste**.

(c) Access will ask you if the first row of data contains column headings. Answer **Yes**.

(d) Open the table to view your data. Access calls the table **Sheet1**. Switch to Design View and edit as you need.

10 Wildcard searches

You can use the asterisk (*) as a wildcard in searches and queries.

For example: a query searching on a postcode equal to **DE34*** will find all the postcodes beginning with DE34.

11 Finding all the surnames that begin with a letter or combination of letters

We want to set up a query so that when we enter a letter or combination of letters the query will return all surnames beginning with those letters. For example, if we enter **Ste** the query would return Stebbins, Stephenson and Stevens, etc.

Create a parameter query in the normal way and use the **LIKE** operator and the wildcard symbol (*).Use this statement in the query:
Like [Enter the first letter of the surname:] & "*"

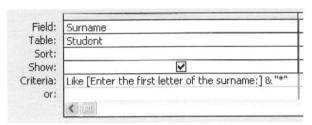

Figure 22.16

12 Finding all the surnames containing a letter or combination of letters

We want to set up a query so that when we enter a letter we get all the surnames containing that letter (or combination of letters). Use this statement in the query:
Like "*" & [Enter the letter in the surname:] & "*"

13 Searching for all records this month

Suppose I want to find all records of driving lessons this month.

(a) Create a new query based on the Lesson table in the Pass-It Driving School.

(b) In the Date column of the QBE Grid, type the following in the Criteria row:
Year([Date])=Year(Now()) and Month([Date])=Month(Now())

14 Using a query to combine two fields

You can join together the text from two fields using &.

For example, use a calculated field in a query to get a person's full name by entering the following in a new column in the QBE grid:
Full Name: [Forename] & " " & [Surname]

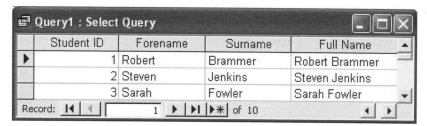

Figure 22.17

When you run the query it combines Surname and Forename as shown in Figure 22.18.

Query1 : Select Query

Student ID	Forename	Surname	Full Name
1	Robert	Brammer	Robert Brammer
2	Steven	Jenkins	Steven Jenkins
3	Sarah	Fowler	Sarah Fowler

Record: 1 of 10

Figure 22.18

15 Using the DateDiff function

Use the DateDiff function in a calculated field in a query or form to work out the difference between two dates. One of those dates could be today's date.

For example it can be used to work out someone's age from their date of birth or how many weeks to someone's driving test, e.g.
=DateDiff("yyyy",[date of birth],now()) gives the age in years.

Use "m" to calculate date differences in months, "ww" to calculate in weeks and "d" to calculate in days.

16 What day of the week is a date?

How can we find out what day of the week a date in a query is? You can use the Lesson table in the Pass-It system to test this.

(a) Open a query based on the Lesson table in **Design View.**

(b) Scroll across to the **Date** field in the QBE grid. Select the next field and click on **Insert, Columns.**

(c) Enter this expression in the Field row of the new column:
Day of the Week: [Date]

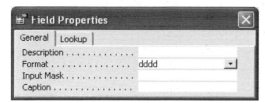

Figure 22.19

(d) Right click on this field and select **Properties.**

(e) In the Format box type **dddd** as in Figure 22.20.

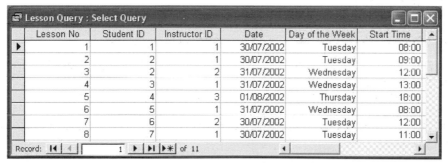

Figure 22.20

(f) Run the query to test it. You should get the results in Figure 22.21.

Lesson No	Student ID	Instructor ID	Date	Day of the Week	Start Time
1	1	1	30/07/2002	Tuesday	08:00
2	2	1	30/07/2002	Tuesday	09:00
3	2	2	31/07/2002	Wednesday	12:00
4	3	1	31/07/2002	Wednesday	13:00
5	4	3	01/08/2002	Thursday	18:00
6	5	1	31/07/2002	Wednesday	08:00
7	6	2	30/07/2002	Tuesday	12:00
8	7	1	30/07/2002	Tuesday	11:00

Record: 14 ◄ 1 ► ►I ►* of 11

Figure 22.21

17 Viewing action queries before running them

You can see the results of an action query before running it. Once you've created your query in the query design grid, you can run the query by clicking on the **Run** icon.

You can't undo any changes made by an action query so, instead of clicking **Run**, click on the **View, Datasheet View** from the menu. This will display a preview of your action query's results without permanently committing those changes.

18 Searching for records that contain no values

In the Pass-It system suppose you wanted a list of instructors who didn't have a mobile phone. You need to set up a query using the **Is Null** operator.

(a) Open a query based on the Instructor table.

(b) In the Criteria cell for the Field Name: Mobile No enter **Is Null**.

Field:	Instructor ID	Title	Forename	Surname	Mobile No
Table:	Instructor	Instructor	Instructor	Instructor	Instructor
Sort:					
Show:	☑	☑	☑	☑	☑
Criteria:					Is Null
or:					

Figure 22.22

The operator **Is Not Null** would return all records containing any value.

19 Make-Table queries

In Unit 19 you were introduced to Action Queries and shown how to move data with Append and Delete Queries. A **Make-Table** query does just that, it creates a new table from the results of a query.

The following example searches the student table and makes a table of students who have received membership cards.

(a) Set up a query in the usual way based on the **Student** table. Select the fields **Forename, Surname, Address 1, Address 2, Address 3** and **Issued Card**.

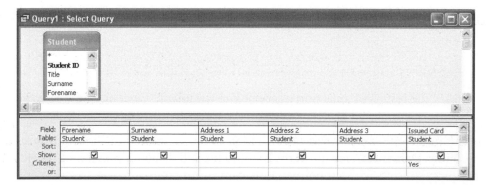

Figure 22.23

(b) In the Field **Issued Card** set the Criteria to **Yes**.

(c) Click on **Query, Make-Table Query**.

(d) You will be prompted for a Table Name. Type **Membership Cards**.

(e) Run the Query. You will receive the warning that a number of rows are to be pasted into a new table. Click on **OK**.

(f) In the Database Window open your new table **Membership Cards** and check the data has transferred correctly.

Forename	Surname	Address 1	Address 2	Address 3	Issued Card
Michael	Beswood	25 Lundie Close	Allestree	Derby	-1
Chalotte	Williams	21 Church Street	Littleover	Derby	-1
David	Windsor	86 Milford Road	Allenton	Derby	-1
Mary	Trueman	156 Station Road	Allestree	Derby	-1
Victoria	Spencer	73 Mayfield Road	Stenson Fields	Derby	-1
Greg	Watson	7 Derwent Close	Etwall	Derby	-1
Lucy	Jones	183 Uttoxeter Road	Allenton	Derby	-1

Membershp Cards : Table — Record: 8 of 8

Figure 22.24

Note

You will notice that the new table does not inherit the field properties or primary key settings from the original table. Go into table Design View and set the Format for the Issued Card field to Yes/No.

In Unit 8 the Lesson Cost Query was used to calculate the cost of lessons. The actual costs are just displayed and not stored. A Make-Table query could be used to store the costs in a new table.

20 Adding a calculated field to a form

In Unit 8 you added a calculated field to a query. The query created a new field based on the data from two other fields, in this case the new field **TotalCost**, which was the result of [**Length of Lesson**] * [**Cost**].

Field:	Length of Lesson	Collection Point	Lesson Type	Cost	TotalCost: [Length of Lesson]*[Cost]
Table:	Lesson	Lesson	Lesson	Lesson Type	
Sort:					
Show:	☑	☑	☑	☑	☑
Criteria:					
or:					

Figure 22.25

Calculated fields are created by using a blank column of the QBE grid and entering the formula in the Field row as shown above (Figure 22.25). Other examples are:

PURPOSE	EXAMPLE
Multiply a field by a number	VAT: [Cost]*17.5/100
Add one field to another	Total: [Cost]+[VAT]
Adding seven days to a date	ReturnDate: [Date]+7
Calculating the number of years since a date	Age:DateDiff('yyyy',[Date of birth],Now())

Note

Field names must be in square brackets.

You can also add a calculated field to a form. Follow these steps to set up a form quickly.

(a) Load the **Lesson Cost Query** in Design View and delete fields to leave those shown in Figure 22.26.

Field:	Lesson No	Instructor ID	Student ID	Date	Start Time	Length of Lesson	Lesson Type	Cost
Table:	Lesson	Lesson	Lesson	Lesson	Lesson	Lesson	Lesson	Lesson Type
Sort:								
Show:	☑	☑	☑	☑	☑	☑	☑	☑
Criteria:								
or:								

Figure 22.26

(b) Use the Form wizards to set up a form based on the above query (Figure 22.27).

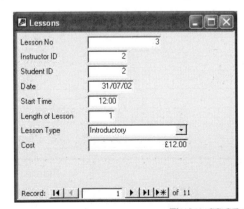

Lessons
Lesson No	3
Instructor ID	2
Student ID	2
Date	31/07/02
Start Time	12:00
Length of Lesson	1
Lesson Type	Introductory
Cost	£12.00

Record: ◄ ◄ 1 ► ►I ►* of 11

Figure 22.27

(c) Switch to Design View and from the Toolbox add a Text Box at the foot of the form as shown in Figure 22.28.

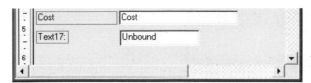

Figure 22.28

(d) Edit the label to read **Total Cost**. In the Text Box type [**Cost**] * [**Length of Lesson**]. See Figure 22.29.

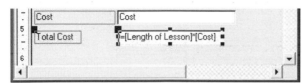

Figure 22.29

(e) Display the **Properties** for the Text Box, click the **Format** tab and set the **Format** to **Currency**. Switch to Form View to see the form as shown. Save your form as Lessons.

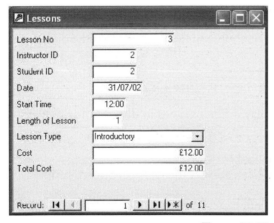

Figure 22.30

Using the expression builder

The expression builder shown in Figure 22.31 helps you set up expressions in Access, for example when setting up calculated fields in a query or calculated controls on a form.

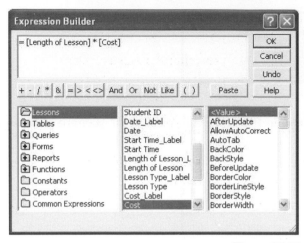

Figure 22.31

(a) Load the form Lessons in Design View.

(b) Highlight the Total Cost text box and delete the formula.

(c) Right click to call up its properties, select the Data tab and in the Control source click the three dots to load the expression builder.

(d) Build your expression by pasting the symbols and field names from the dialogue box.

21 Formatting dates on forms and reports

You can use the Format function to display different dates in different formats or different date components on a form or a report.

For example, suppose you have a field called Date.
Set up a new text box called Day of the Week and set the Control Source property to:
=**Format([date],"d")**

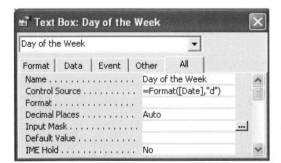

Figure 22.32

This will display the date's day, e.g. 31 if the date was 31/10/03.

=**Format**([**date**],"**m**") displays the month number, e.g. 12.
=**Format**([**date**],"**yy**") displays the abbreviated year number e.g. 01.

=**Format**([**date**],"**mmm**") displays the abbreviated month name e.g. Dec.
=**Format**([**date**],"**mmmm**") displays the full month name e.g. December.
=**Format**([**date**],"**yyyy**") displays the full year number e.g. 2003.

You can also combine the formats to create your own format, e.g.
=**Format**([**date**],"**dmmmyy**")

which would display the day, the abbreviated month, and a two-digit year value, with no spaces in between each component.

You can also display a literal character, such as a comma, and space in a date to make it 17 June, 2003. Just use this format:
=**Format**([**date**], "**d mmmm**" "," "**yyyy**")

22 Removing the menu bar from a form

The Menu Bar is the area across the screen that says File, Edit, View, etc. To remove the menu bar when a form is loaded:

(a) Load the form in Design View and choose the Form Properties.

(b) Click on the **Other** tab and set the **MenuBar** property to =**1** as shown in Figure 22.33.

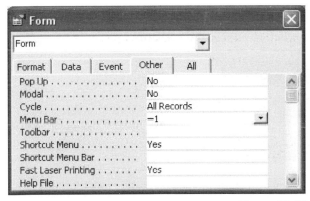

Figure 22.33

23 Making a command button the default button

You can choose a command button by clicking on it or pressing ENTER if no other button has the focus.

(a) Open the form in Design View.

(b) Right click on the button you want to respond to ENTER and choose **Properties.**

(c) Click the **Other** tab and set the **Default** property to **Yes.**

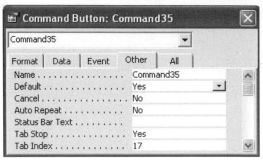

Figure 22.34

When you open the form pressing ENTER will run the command button action.

24 Changing the properties of a group of controls

(a) Open the form in Design View.

(b) Select the first control whose property you wish to change. Hold down SHIFT and select the other controls you wish to change.

(c) Right click on any of the controls and choose Properties.

(d) The Properties window opens with the title **Multiple Selection**. From here any property you select will be applied to all selected controls.

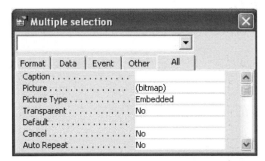

Figure 22.35

25 Preventing users from adding records to a form

(a) Load the form in Design View and choose the Form properties.

(b) Click on the **Data** tab and set the **Allow Additions** property to **No.** When the form is opened the New Record icon is greyed out.

26 Creating read-only fields on a form

Sometimes you may wish to make a field available but not allow it to be changed by the user.

(a) In Design View, select the field and click on the Properties icon. Click on the **Data** tab.

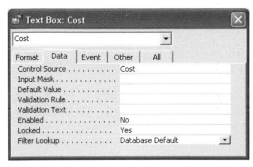

Figure 22.36

(b) Set the **Enabled** property to **No** and the **Locked** property to **Yes**. The field will not be greyed out but the user will not be able to change it.

27 Putting a border around a control

Borders and other effects can be attached to controls using the control's properties.

(a) Right click the control or label in Design View and select **Properties.**

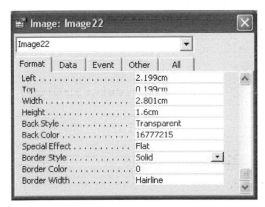

Figure 22.37

(b) Click the **Format** tab and set the **Border Style** to **Solid** instead of **Transparent.**

Figure 22.38

(c) Set the **Border Colour** and **Border Width** as required.

(d) Set the **Special Effect** property to **Raised** (see Figure 22.39).

Figure 22.39

28 Designing your own button images

You can use images as buttons on a form. There are two ways to get started:

○ Use Paint or a similar program to design your image; or
○ Find an image via a clip art library or the internet.

In this example we use the road sign image to turn right as shown in Figure 22.40. The image is taken from the internet.

Figure 22.40

It is important to resize your image to the size of an Access button (about 39 x 39 pixels). This is easily done in an image editor such as Paint or Paint Shop Pro.

(a) Open a form in Design View and use the Command Button Wizard to set up a button choosing picture when asked if you want text or a picture on your button.

(b) Select the button and right click on it to display its properties.

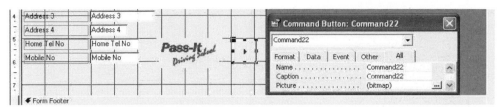

Figure 22.41

(c) Click on the **Format** tab (see Figure 22.41).

(d) In the **Picture** property click on the three dots to display the **Picture Builder** window shown in Figure 22.42.

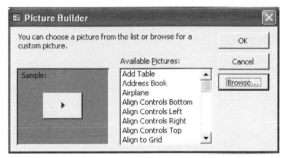

Figure 22.42

(e) Click on **Browse** to find the image.

(f) Resize and position the image as required.

Figure 22.43

29 Positioning and sizing your form automatically

It is easy to position your form using its Form properties. Set the properties as follows. Your form will open centred and sized to display a complete record.

(a) Open the form in Design View.

(b) From the menu choose **View, Properties.**

(c) Click the **Format** tab in the Properties Window.

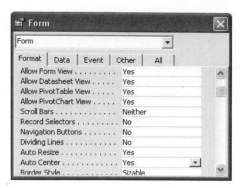

Figure 22.44

(d) Set the **Auto Center** property to **Yes.**

(e) Set the **Auto Resize** property to **Yes.**

30 Controlling the position and size of your form from a macro

(a) Create a new macro and add the Action **Open Form** from the drop-down list. In the Arguments select the Form Name for the form you wish to open.

Figure 22.45

(b) Add the Action **MoveSize** and set the options as required.

Figure 22.46

Right is the distance from the left of the window.
Down is the distance from the top of the window.
Width is the window's width.
Height is the window's height.

31 Starting a form from scratch

Throughout the study units we used the wizards to set up our forms. Of course, as ever, you could choose to ignore the wizards and set up the form manually.

(a) In the Database window, select **Forms** and then click on **New.**

(b) Select Design View and base the form on the Student table as shown in Figure 22.47.

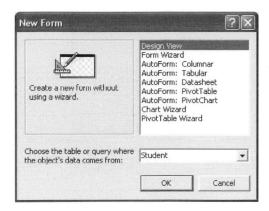

Figure 22.47

(c) The blank form will open in Design View with the **Field List** for the Student table as shown in Figure 22.48.

(d) Drag and drop the fields needed as required.

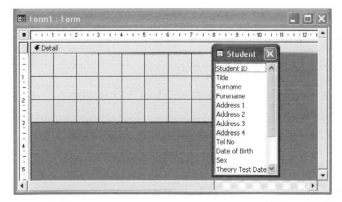

Figure 22.48

Note

If the Field List is not displayed then choose **View, Field List** from the menu.

If you accidentally delete a control during the customisation of your form, display the Field List and drag and drop the field from the Field List onto the form.

32 Using option buttons (sometimes called radio controls)

Option buttons are frequently used to represent Yes/No fields. For example, on the Student form shown in Figure 22.49, an option button could be used for the Issued Card field.

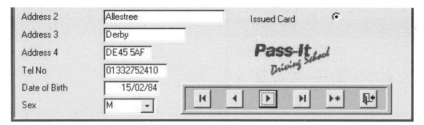

Figure 22.49

(a) Open the Student form in Design View and delete the Issued Card check box.

Figure 22.50

(b) From the Toolbox, click on the **Option Button** icon and drag out a button on the form. Set the label to **Issued Card**.

(c) Select the control and right click to view its properties. Click on the **Data** tab and set the **Control Source** to the **Issued Card** field as shown in Figure 22.51.

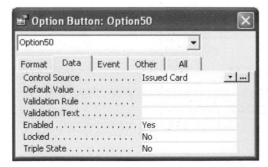

Figure 22.51

Toggle buttons and check boxes can be set up in the same way but it is important when designing forms to be consistent.

33 Using option groups

Option groups let the user choose one option from a list of alternative values. For example, the title field on the Instructor form shown below could be entered using option buttons in a group. It is important to note, that Access stores the data as a number, e.g. 1 = Mr, 2 = Mrs, etc.

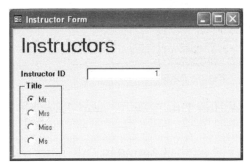

Figure 22.52

(a) Open the **Instructor Form** in Design view, delete the **Title** field and create some room for the Option Group.

(b) From the Toolbox, click on the **Option Group** icon and drag out a rectangle. In the **Option Group** dialog box set the labels as shown in Figure 22.53 and click on **Next**.

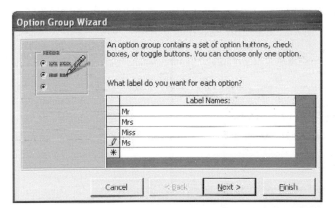

Figure 22.53

(c) Select the default value required and click on **Next**. Click on **Next** again to accept the values as shown in Figure 22.54.

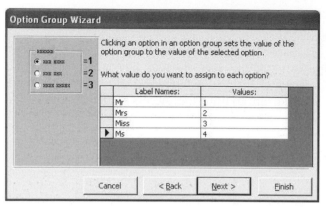

Figure 22.54

(d) Click on **Store the value in this field** and select **Title** from the drop-down list. Click on **Next**.

(e) Choose your control style, click on **Next** and set the **Caption** to **Title**. Click on **Finish**.

34 Printing a form without the buttons

You may wish to print an on-screen form without printing the buttons and other objects such as images. We will use the **Instructor Form** set up in the Driving School as an example.

(a) Open the **Instructor Form** in Design View. Highlight the objects you don't want to print, in this case the Control Panel and Pass-It logo.

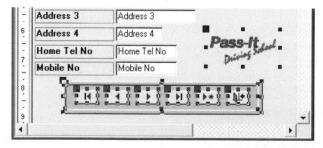

Figure 22.55

(b) Click on **View, Properties** and set the **Display When** property to **Screen Only**. Save the form and return to Form View.

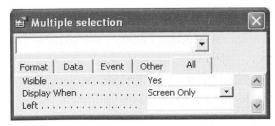

Figure 22.56

If you chose to Print now you would get all the forms printing without the objects. We only want the currently displayed record to print.

(c) At the Database Window select **Macros** and click on **New**.

(d) In the **Action** column select the **PrintOut** command. In the **Action Arguments**, click in the **Print Range** box and choose **Selection**. Name the macro **Print Form**.

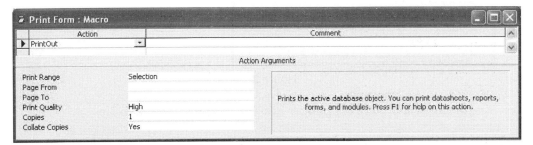

Figure 22.57

(e) Set up a command button on the Instructor Form to run the macro **Print Form**.

35 Adding customised tool tips (screen tips) to your controls

When you move the mouse pointer over a button you get a screen tip explaining what the button does, as shown in Figure 22.58.

Figure 22.58

In Access it is easy to customise these tips and make them more user-friendly.

(a) Open a form in Design View; we have chosen the **Student Form** in the Driving School.

(b) Right click on the button to view its properties. Click on the **Other** tab. Set the **ControlTip Text** property to **Add New Student** or whatever you choose. See Figure 22.59.

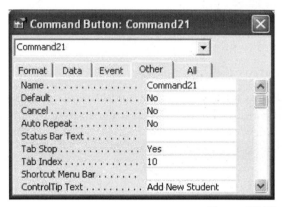

Figure 22.59

(c) Save the form and move the pointer over the button to view your tip.

Figure 22.60

36 Pop Up and Modal forms

When a **Modal** form is open, you cannot move to another object such as another form. This is important if you want data to be entered into the form before moving on.

A **Pop Up** form always remains on top of other Microsoft Access windows when it is open.

When we open the Student Form or the Instructor Form to paste in details, we may want these forms to remain on top and do not want the user to choose any other object. In other words, these forms will be pop-up modal forms.

We can set this up in Form Design View.

(a) Load each form in turn in Design View.

(b) Double-click on the **Form Selector** to show the **Form Properties**.

(c) Click on the **Other** Tab and set the **Modal** and **Pop Up** properties to **Yes**.

Figure 22.61

(d) Switch to Form View and test that you cannot click on objects outside the Form window.

37 Changing the default print margins in reports

At the Database Window, click on **Tools, Options**. Click on the **General** tab to set the print margins.

38 Putting the report name in a report footer

To put the name of your report, add a text box in the footer of your report and enter **=CurrentObjectName**

To put in the filename including the path, enter **=CurrentDb.Name**

39 Mailing labels and membership cards

If you have a list of names and addresses as in the Student table of the Driving School, you can print mailing labels for them as follows. This can then easily be customised into a membership card.

(a) At the Database Window, click on **Reports** and click on **New**.

(b) Select the **Label Wizard** and select the **Student** table. Click on **OK**.

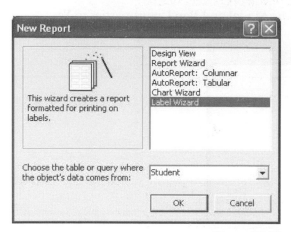

Figure 22.62

(c) Select the label manufacturer, label size and other options as shown in Figure 22.63.

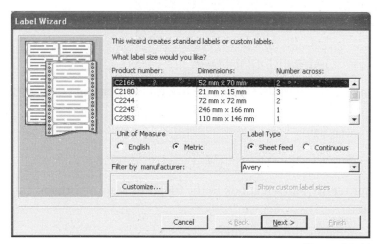

Figure 22.63

(d) Choose the **Font Name**, **Font Weight**, **Font Size** and colour as shown in Figure 22.64 and click on **Next**.

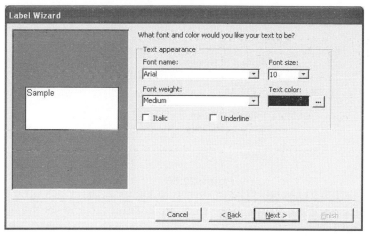

Figure 22.64

The next stage is to position the text and fields on the Prototype label.

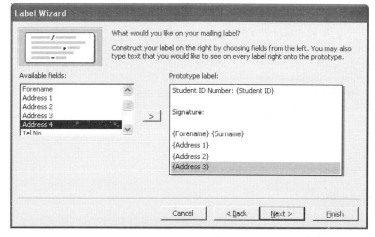

Figure 22.65

(e) Type the text **Student ID Number:**. Select the **Student ID** field from the Available fields and click the right arrow to put the field on to the label next to the text. Press **Return** twice.

(f) Type the text **Signature:** and press **Return** twice.

(g) Transfer across the fields **Forename** and **Surname**, remembering to press the space bar in between them. Press **Return**.

(h) Continue to transfer the fields **Address 1, Address 2** and **Address 3**. Click on **Next**.

(i) Choose to sort by **Surname**. Click on **Next**.

(j) Name the report **Labels** and click on **Finish**. The labels should appear as in

Figure 22.66.

Student ID Number: 4   Student ID Number: 1

Signature: Signature:

Michael Beswood   Robert Brammer
25 Lundie Close   10 Plymouth Drive
Allestree   Stenson Fields
Derby   Derby

Figure 22.66

(k) With the report open, switch to Design View as shown in Figure 22.67. Click on the **Student ID** box, click on **View**, **Properties**, select the **Format** tab and set the **Font Weight** to **Semi-bold**.

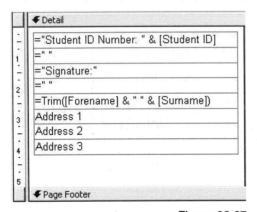

Figure 22.67

(l) Repeat for the **Signature** control.

(m) From the Toolbox select the **Image** icon and import the Pass-It logo (or use Copy, Paste). Position the logo as shown. You will have to set its **Size Mode** property to **Zoom**.

(n) From the Toolbox select the **Rectangle** tool and carefully position a rectangle around the label. Click on **Format, Send to the Back**.

(o) With the rectangle still selected, set its **Special Effect** property to **Shadowed**. See Figure 22.68.

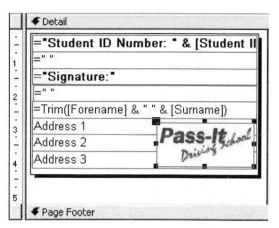

Figure 22.68

(p) Switch to Print Preview to view the Membership Cards as shown in Figure 22.69. Save the report as **Member Cards**.

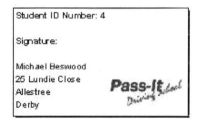

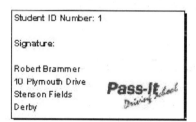

Figure 22.69

40 Formatting text to bold in a message box

You can set text to bold in a message box using the @ symbol.

For example, in the No Data macro used in the Pass-It system set the message as follows:

There is no data in this report@Please close the report and start again@

Figure 22.70

Run the macro and the message box is displayed as in Figure 22.70.

41 Putting hard returns in a message box

You can force Access to put text on the next line in a message box by using the ASCII code for a carriage return: Chr(13).

(a) Set up a new macro and choose the **Action: MsgBox**

(b) In the **Action Arguments**, click in the **Message** box and type
     =**"The Pass-It Driving School"& Chr(13) & "by" & Chr(13) & "Julian Mott and Ian Rendell"**

You can improve the presentation of your message box further by using the code Chr(9) for a tab space.

The message box shown in Figure 22.71 is an information message box using this message:
=**Chr(9) & "The Pass-It Driving School" & Chr(13) & Chr(9) & Chr(9) & "by" & Chr(13) & Chr(9) & "Julian Mott and Ian Rendell"**

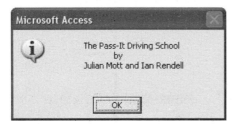

Figure 22.71

Don't forget that by pressing SHIFT and F2 you can zoom and see all the text in a message box.

42 The AutoExec macro

A macro saved as **AutoExec** automatically runs when the database is opened. You can control start-up options from this macro.

(a) Create a new macro with the following Actions and Arguments.

ACTION	ARGUMENT	COMMENT
Echo	No	Hides events
An Hourglass	Yes	Pointer displayed as hourglass
RunCommand	WindowHide	Hides the Database Window
OpenForm	Student Form	Opens the student form
RunCommand	DocMaximise	Maximises the current window

(b) Save the macro and call it **Autoexec**.

Note   Use F11 to display the Database Window again.

If you don't want the AutoExec macro or the Start-up options to run, hold down the SHIFT key when you open the database.

43 Running your system from customised keys

An **AutoKeys** macro allows you to customise keys, typically to run frequently used actions.

In Unit 14 we set up macros to open the **Student, Instructor, Lesson Booking Form** and the **About** message box. Suppose we want to set up hot-keys such as:

○ CTRL + S to run the **Student Macro**
○ CTRL + I to run the **Instructor Macro**
○ CTRL + L to run the **Lesson Booking Form Macro** and
○ CTRL + A to run the **About Macro**

(Choose your hot-keys carefully as CTRL + A is already used for **Select All** and CTRL + S for **Save**. You may wish to use another combination of keys. The key combination you choose replaces that used by Access.)

(a) At the Database Window click on **Macros** and click on **New**.

(b) In the **Action** column select **RunMacro**.

(c) In the **Macro Name** box at the bottom select **Student Macro**.

(d) Click on the **Macro Names** icon or click on **View, Macro Names**.

(e) A new column appears headed **Macro Name**. In the first row of this new column enter the key combination ^S (press CTRL + S).

Figure 22.72

(f) Set up the other key combinations as shown above. The macro design window should appear as in Figure 22.73.

Figure 22.73

(g) Save the macro with the name **AutoKeys**.

The new keys come into effect as soon as you save the macro and each time you open the database. The following table shows the key combinations you can use to set up keys in an **AutoKeys** macro:

SYNTAX	KEY COMBINATIONS
^A	CTRL+A
{F1}	F1
^{F1}	CTRL+F1
+{F1}	SHIFT+F1
{INSERT}	INS
^{INSERT}	CTRL+INS
+{INSERT}	SHIFT+INS
{DELETE} or {DEL}	DEL
^{DELETE} or ^{DEL}	CTRL+DEL
+{DELETE} or +{DEL}	SHIFT+DEL

44 Copy (cut) and paste macro

A macro can be used to cut or copy a record from one table and paste it into another.

Imagine the scenario in the Driving School system when a driving instructor leaves the school. You don't want to delete the record entirely from the Driving School system but just move it into a table called Ex Instructors so that you have a record.

(a) Load the **Driving School** database and at the Database Window highlight the **Instructor** table and click on **Copy**.

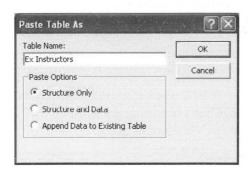

Figure 22.74

(b) Click on **Paste** and in the Paste Table As dialogue box name the table **Ex Instructors** and select **Structure Only**. Click **OK**.

(c) Create a new macro using the following commands:

Action	RunCommand	Command	Select Record		
Action	RunCommand	Command	Cut		
Action	Close	Object Type	Form	Object Name	Instructor Form
Action	Open Table	Table Name	Ex Instructors		
Action	RunCommand	Command	Paste Append		
Action	Close	Object Type	Table	Object Name	Instructor
Action	OpenForm	Form Name	Instructor Form	View	Form

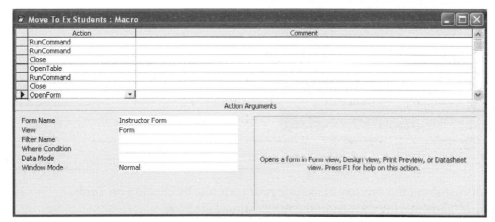

Figure 22.75

(d) Name the macro **File Away**. Open the **Instructor Form** in Design View and place a command button on the form to run the macro.

(e) Open the **Instructor Form** in Form View and test the macro.

45 Using conditions in macros

(a) In the Database Window select the **Macro** tab and click on **New**.

(b) In the Macro window click on **View, Conditions** to insert the **Conditions** column.

It is possible to enter expressions in the **Conditions** column. When the value in the **Conditions** column is true, the action to its right in the **Action** column is performed.

In the example shown in Figure 22.76, the macro will look to see if a student's practical test is on today's date. If it is it will display a message box reminding them. Open the **Student Form** in the Driving School system in Design View and attach the macro to the **On Current** event of the Form.

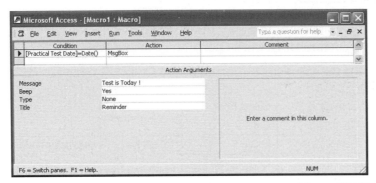

Figure 22.76

Using conditions in macros is an immensely powerful tool. Use Microsoft Help to explore further possibilities.

46 Changing the caption text

The caption appears at the top of the screen. It normally says Microsoft Access.

Figure 22.77

You can customise the caption to include your own text by clicking on **Tools, Startup...** and entering the text in the Application Title box.

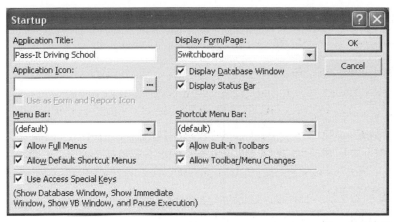

Figure 22.78

Your caption will now appear:

Figure 22.79

47 Changing the application icon

The Microsoft Access icon is normally displayed in the top left of the Access window as shown below.

Figure 22.80

The first stage in replacing this icon is to create your own Icon (*.ico) file.

(a) Open **Paint** and create a new file by clicking **File, New.**

(b) Set the attributes of the file by clicking on **Image, Attributes.** Set the **width** to **32 pixels** and the **height** to **32 pixels,** as shown in Figure 22.81.

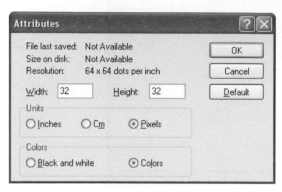

Figure 22.81

(c) You can now create the icon from scratch or cut and paste an image from another source.

(d) When you are happy with the picture click on **File, Save as...** and save the file as **logo.ico**, in the same directory as your Access project.

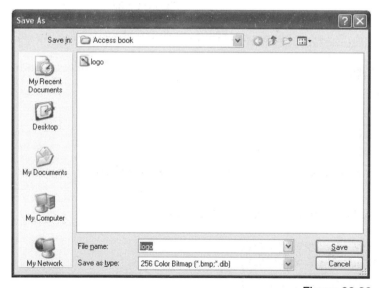

Figure 22.82

Note

It is important that you save the picture as a 256 Color Bitmap, with an 'ico' file extension and that it is in the same directory as your Access file.

(e) To change the logo to your own icon file, go to **Tools, Startup** and click the three dots to the right of "Application icon:". Find the icon file that you have just created and click **OK**, as shown in Figure 22.83.

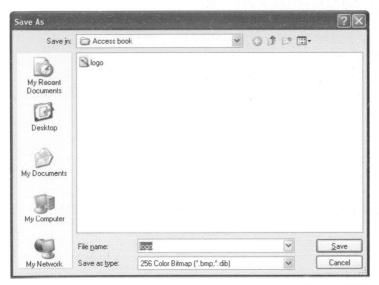

Figure 22.83

(f) Click **OK** again and your icon will be displayed instead of the Access logo:

Figure 22.84

48 Password protecting files

It is easy to add a password to an Access file to prevent unauthorised access, but be careful.

(a) Click on the **Tools, Security, Set Database Password.**

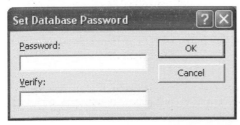

Figuro 22.85

(b) In the **Password** box, type your password.

(c) In the **Verify** box, confirm your password by typing the password again, and then click **OK**.

The password is now set. Passwords are case-sensitive. The next time you open the database, a dialogue box will be displayed requesting the password.

Note You won't be able to set a password in Access XP unless you have opened the database using **Open Exclusive**. Click on **File**, **Open** and choose **Open Exclusive** as shown in Figure 22.86.

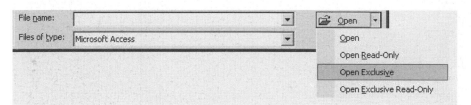

Figure 22.86

To remove a password, click on **Tools, Security, Unset Database Password.**

This command is only available if a password has been set. In the **Unset Database Password** dialogue box, type your password and click on **OK**.

Be very careful. Passwords are annoying if you are still setting up the system and if you forget your password, you won't be able to open your database.

If your password doesn't work, remember that passwords are case sensitive so check that caps lock is turned off.

If this doesn't work, there are companies that produce software to recover such files. You can download them from the internet. They are *not* free. Try sites like www.lostpassword.com/

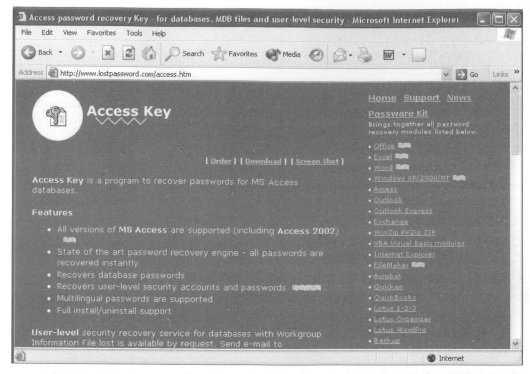

Figure 22.87

This just proves that Access passwords aren't as secure as you might expect.

49 Using help

Online help is available by pressing F1. Type in the keyword and search for advice.

Access 2000 also has an 'Answer wizard' which enables you to type in a question and get help.

50 Useful websites

There are many internet sites offering tips and hints in using Access. As with all internet sites, the quality varies, good sites can be hard to find and sites are appearing and disappearing all the time.

Go to any search engine and search on *Access Hints*. Here are just a few examples:

www.microsoft.com/office/ is full of information tips, tricks, and how-to articles and frequently asked questions for Microsoft Office programs like Access.

50 Access tips and tricks

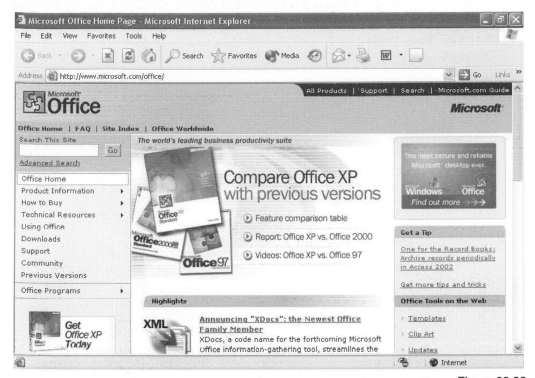

Figure 22.88

support.microsoft.com/ has a knowledge-base search to look for technical support information and self-help tools for Microsoft products.

www.access-programmers.co.uk/Tips.htm is a Microsoft Access help centre providing many tips and a discussion forum and ideas.

www.smartcomputing.com/ has many pages of articles about Access, including a search facility.

Another very good site is www.tck-tips.com

'Allen Browne's tips for MS-Access users' offers lots of tips: users.bigpond.net.au/abrowne1/tips.html

'Tony's Main Microsoft Access Page' has a great number of Access links: www.granite.ab.ca/accsmstr.htm

Uncle Jim's Microsoft Access Tips claims to have 12 pages with over 1000 helpful tips for Access users of all levels: www.geocities.com/SiliconValley/Code/5046/access.html

www.bpro.com/Access/tips.htm has many useful tips.

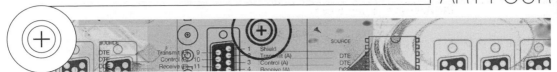

Appendices

Contents

Access glossary

Action query	An **action query** is a query that copies or changes your data. There are four types of action queries: delete, update, append and make-table.
Append query	An **append query** is an action query that adds the records from a query to the end of an existing table.
AutoExec	The **AutoExec** macro is a macro that runs automatically when a file is opened.
AutoFormat	An automatic format that can be selected when creating a form or report with a wizard. You can apply an **AutoFormat** to an existing form or report by clicking on the AutoFormat icon.
AutoNumber	A field data type that automatically gives a unique number to each record as it is created.
Bound control	A text box or other control on a form or report that gets its contents from a field in the underlying table or query.
Button	A **button** or **command button** is a control on a form or report. Click on the button to perform an operation, e.g. run a macro or apply a form filter.
Calculated control	A **calculated control** on a form or report is a control that displays the result of a calculation rather than stored data.
Calculated field	A **calculated field** defined in a query displays the result of a calculation rather than stored data.

Cascading delete	When a record in the primary table is deleted, all the related records in related tables are also deleted. This will only work if referential integrity is enforced between the tables.
Cascading update	When a record in the primary table is changed, all the related records in the related tables are updated. This will only work if referential integrity is enforced between the tables.
Check box	A **check box** is a small box in a table, form or report that can either be selected or not selected. Clicking on a check box puts a little tick in the box. This is called **checking**. Clicking again to remove the tick is called **unchecking**.
Combo box	A **combo box** is a control on a form. Clicking on the combo boxes displays a list of choices available to the user. One of these choices can be selected or the user can type in data. It can also be called a **drop-down box**.
Command button	See **Button**.
Continuous form	A **continuous form** is a form that displays more than one record on the screen in form view. You can set a form to be continuous using the form's default view property. A single form only displays one record on a form.
Control	An object on a form or report such as a text box, check box or command button. A **control** can display data or perform an action.
Control tip text	A brief description of a control that is displayed when the mouse moves the cursor over the control.
Crosstab query	A query that calculates a sum, average or count on records and then groups the result by two types of information.
Default property	Specifies the value a control or field will automatically take.
Default value	The **default value** is the value of a field that is automatically entered when a new record is created. For example, in a customer table, a company doing a lot of business in Derby can set the default value for the town field to **Derby**.
Delete query	A **delete query** is a query that deletes records from one or more tables matching the query criteria.
Design view	The mode that allows you to design a table, query, form, report or macro. You can create new objects or modify the design of existing ones.
Dialogue box	A **dialogue box** (or in American English a dialog box) is a box on the screen that enables the user to select choices and/or enter data.
Drop-down box	See **combo box**.

Dynaset	A **dynaset** is simply the table resulting from a query.
Event	An **event** is an action that takes place when a certain object is selected, for example, clicking on a command button. Microsoft Access can be programmed to run an event procedure when an object is selected.
Event procedure	An **event procedure** is a procedure automatically executed in response to an event such as clicking on a button.
Expression	An **expression** is similar to a formula – it can combine values, fieldnames and operators into a single value in a form, report or query. For example: =[Length of Lesson]*[Cost]
Expression Builder	A tool in Access used to create an expression. The **Expression Builder** includes a list of common expressions that you can select from.
Field	A **field** is a data item stored in a column in a table, storing details such as forename, surname, etc.
Field data types	The possible data types for a field in a table.
Field list	A small window listing all fields in the record source in the design view for a query, form and report.
Field selector	A small bar in datasheet view that you click on to select an entire column.
Filter	A **filter** selects only certain records based on certain criteria, such as all lessons for student whose ID number is 5.
Focus	The active control in a form. The control that is ready to accept data input.
Form	A **form** is a user-friendly way of displaying data from a table or query. It can also be used to enter data or as a switchboard. A form is fully customisable to suit the user.
Form design view	The **form design view** window is the window which is used to design forms.
Form footer	Space at the end of a form. It is used to display, for example, instructions for using the form, command buttons or unbound controls to accept input.
Form header	Space at the start of a form. It is used to display, for example, a title, instructions for using the form or command buttons.
Form properties	Features of a form that affect its appearance. Form properties are set in form design view using the properties window.
Form selector	A box in the top-left corner of a form in design view. Click on this box to select the form. Double-click on this box to open the form's property window.

Form view	A window that displays the form. One or more records can be displayed. Data can be edited and new data added.
Front end	A **front end** is the name given to a user-friendly interface that appears on the screen when the file is loaded. Usually it will give the user a menu of options. It can also be called a switchboard.
Global menu bar	A customised menu bar that replaces the built-in menu bar in all windows in your application.
Index	An **index** is used to speed up sorting of a table. The key field of a table is automatically indexed.
Input mask	An **input mask** controls which characters can be entered into a field, for example what format they are and how many characters are allowed.
Key field	The **key field** or primary key is a field which is unique for each record and is used to identify records.
Label	A **label** is a control on a form or report that displays descriptive text, such as a title or a caption.
Linked table	A table in a file outside the open database from which Microsoft Access can access records.
List box	A **list box** is similar to a combo box; a list box displays the choices available in a list format. The user can scroll down to see additional choices.
Lookup field	A field that displays data as a drop-down lists. It is either: ○ a list that looks up data from an existing table or query or ○ a list that stores a fixed set of values.
Macro	A **macro** is a program that stores a series of Microsoft Access commands so that they can be executed as a single command. Macros automate complex tasks and so save time by reducing the number of steps required to carry out a common task.
Macro group	A collection of related macros which are stored together under a single macro name.
Make-table query	An action query that creates a new table based on the results of a query.
Module	A collection of Visual Basic procedures stored together as one named unit.
Navigation buttons	Buttons in datasheet view and form view windows enabling you to move through the records.
OLE object	An object that allows object linking and embedding. An object from another program, for example, a JPEG image can be linked or embedded in a field, form or report.
OLE object data type	A field data type used to insert objects created in other applications in a Microsoft Access database.

One-to-many relationship	A relationship linking two tables. In the first table, the data appears once. This is usually the key field such as a video code in a table of videos. In a second table, such as the loans table, the video code will appear many times as the video can be borrowed many times.
Option button	An **option button** on a form is used for choosing from a list of options. You can select only one option button at a time. Also called a radio button.
Option group	An **option group** is a group of controls on a form such as option buttons. Only one option in an option group can be chosen.
Page footer	Space at the bottom of a page of a printed form or a report. It is used to display the date, page number, report summaries or any information you want at the bottom of every page.
Page header	Space at the top of a page of a printed form or a report. It is used to display titles, column headings or any information you want at the top of every page.
Parameter query	A **parameter query** is a query in which a user can enter one or more criteria values on which to select records.
Primary table	The **primary table** is the main table in the database. It will be the 'one' part of a one-to-many relationship.
Print preview	The **print preview** window is particularly useful in designing reports as it shows what the printed report will look like.
Property	A characteristic of an object such as a form or a control that can be set using the properties window.
Properties window	The **properties window** or **properties sheet** is the window in which you can view and edit the properties of tables, queries, fields, forms, reports and controls.
QBE	Query by Example. The method of setting up a query using query design view.
QBE Grid	A grid at the bottom of the query design view window, used for setting criteria.
Query	A **query** is a question about the data stored in your tables. It can bring together data from multiple tables and serve as the source of data for a form or report. See also **Action query**.
Query design view	The **query design view** window is the window which is used to design queries.
Record selector	The **record selector** is a small box or bar to the left of a record in datasheet view or form view that you can click on to select the entire record.

Appendices

Record source	In a database, the **record source** is the table or query that provides the underlying data for a form or report.
Referential integrity	Rules that preserve the relationships between tables when you enter or delete records.
Relationship	A **relationship** is a link between common fields in two tables.
Report	A **report** is a way of presenting data in a customised printed format. The information in a report comes from an underlying table or query.
Report design view	The **report design view** window is the window which is used to design reports.
Report footer	Space at the end of a report. It is used to display summaries and totals.
Report header	Space at the start of a report. It is used to display titles, dates or report introductions.
Report selector	A box in the top-left corner of a report in design view. Click on this box to select the report. Double-click on this box to open the report's property window.
Row selector	The **row selector** is a small box at the left of a row that when clicked selects an entire row in a table or macro design view.
Select query	A **select query** asks a question about the data stored in your tables and returns a result set in the form of a datasheet.
Scroll bar	The **vertical scroll bar** appears on the right-hand side of the screen, to enable the user to move up and down a table, form or report. The **horizontal scroll bar**, at the bottom right of the screen, enables the user to move to the right or left in a table, form or report.
SQL	Structured Query Language. A language used to set up queries. It is easier to set up queries using QBE.
Status bar	A horizontal bar near the bottom of the screen that displays useful information about a selected command or an operation in progress, e.g. the status bar shows whether CAPS LOCK has been pressed.
Subform/Subreport	Used to display data from more than one table on a form or report.
Tab order	The order in which the focus moves in a form from one field or button to the next as you press the TAB key.
Table	A **table** is a collection of data about a specific topic. A database will consist of several tables.
Table design view	The **table design view** window is the window which is used to design tables.
Text box	A control on a form or report that allows you to enter text.

Toggle button	A control that acts as an on/off button in a form or report. Click once to turn the item on. Click again to turn it off.
Toolbar	A **toolbar** is a row of icons, usually at the top of the screen. Additional toolbars can be added to suit the user.
Toolbox	A toolbar used to place controls on a form or report in design view.
Unbound control	A control that is not connected to any field in the underlying table or query.
Unbound object frame	A control you place on a form or report to contain an unbound object. An unbound object is an object, for example a picture, whose value isn't derived from data stored in the underlying table or query.
Update query	An action query that changes a set of records according to criteria specified by the user.
Validation	Checking data when it is entered to ensure that it is sensible.
Validation rule	A rule that sets conditions on what can be entered in a field.
Visual Basic	Microsoft **Visual Basic** is Microsoft Access's own programming language.
What's This icon	An icon on the Help menu. After you click on the **What's This icon**, the mouse pointer changes to the question-mark pointer. You can then click on an item to get help on it. Note: you can add your own What's This button to your forms and reports by using the WhatsThisButton property.
Yes/No data type	A field data type you use for fields that will contain only one of two values, such as Yes or No and True or False.
Zoom box	The **zoom box** is a box for entering expressions or text, where the original box is not big enough to see all the text.

Access toolbars

The Access toolbars that you are most likely to use are shown below:

Database

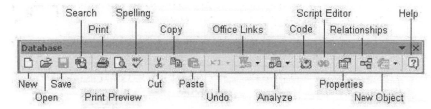

Figure 23.1

Table Design

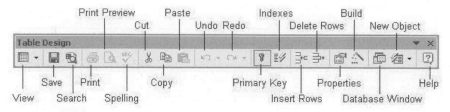

Figure 23.2

Table Datasheet

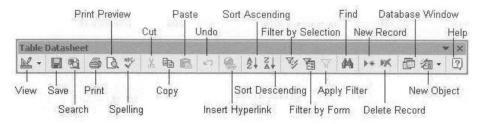

Figure 23.3

Query Design

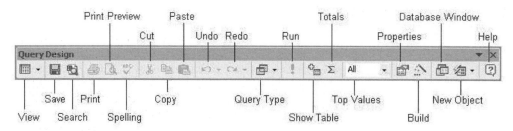

Figure 23.4

Query Datasheet

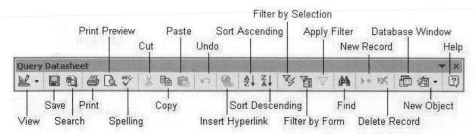

Figure 23.5

Form Design

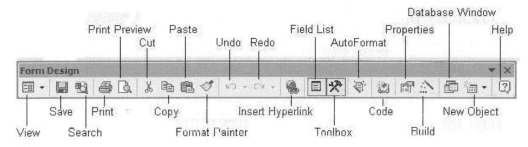

Figure 23.6

Form View

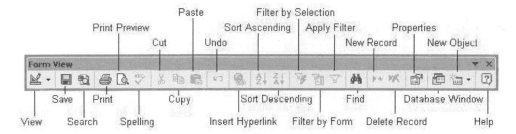

Figure 23.7

Formatting Form/Report

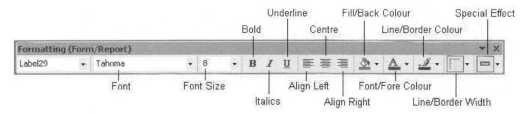

Figure 23.8

Report Design

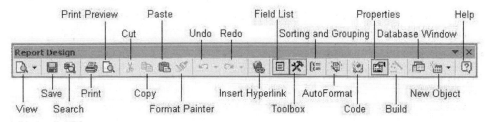

Figure 23.9

Report Print Preview

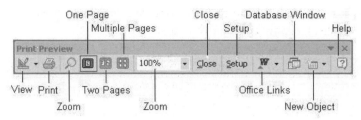

Figure 23.10

Toolbox

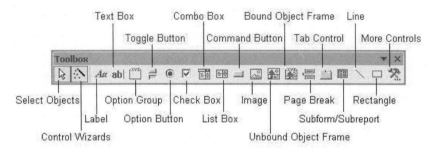

Figure 23.11

Macro Design

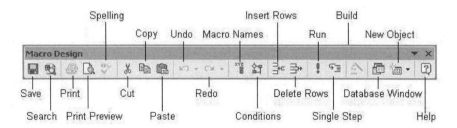

Figure 23.12

Keyboard shortcuts in Access

There are several keyboard shortcuts to help you move around the screen in Access and perform other common tasks. Here are some of the most useful.

KEYSTROKE	ACTION
HOME	Move cursor to the beginning of a field
END	Move cursor to the end of a field
PAGE DOWN	Move down one page
PAGE UP	Move up one page
CTRL + -	Delete current record
CTRL + ' (apostrophe)	Copy a field's value from the previous record to the current record
CTRL + :	Enter current time
CTRL + ;	Enter current date
CTRL + + (plus sign)	Add new record to table
CTRL + C	Copy
CTRL + F	Find
CTRL + F6	Cycle between open windows
CTRL + H	Find and replace
CTRL + N	Open a new database
CTRL + O	Open an existing database
CTRL + P	Print the current or selected object
CTRL + S or SHIFT + F12 or ALT + SHIFT + F2	Save a database object
CTRL + V	Paste
CTRL + W or CTRL + F4	Close the active window
CTRL + X	Cut
CTRL + Z	Undo
CTRL + PAGE DOWN	Moves right one page
CTRL + PAGE UP	Moves left one page
CTRL + SHIFT + 2	Copies the contents of a cell above into the current cell
CTRL + SHIFT + SPACEBAR	Selects the entire datasheet
CTRL + SPACEBAR	Selects current column
F1	Displays help
F4 or ALT + DOWN ARROW	Displays a selected combo box
F5	Switches from form design view to form view

Keyboard shortcuts in Access – *continued*

KEYSTROKE	ACTION
F6	Switches between the upper and lower parts of a window, e.g. in table design view
F7	Checks spelling
F11 or ALT + F1	Brings the Database window to the front
F12 or ALT + F2	Open the Save As dialogue box
SHIFT + ENTER	Instant save
SHIFT + SPACEBAR	Selects current row
SHIFT + F2	Zoom
TAB	Exits a combo box or list box
ALT + ENTER	Displays a property sheet in design view
ALT + F11	Switch to Visual Basic Editor and back
ALT + F4	Quit Microsoft Access, close a dialogue box, or close a property sheet

Taking screenshots

Screenshots of your system in action are vital both to prove that the system is working properly and to include in the user guide and technical instructions.

Using Windows Paint

To get a screenshot in Windows, press the **Print Screen** key on the keyboard. This puts the whole screen into the Windows clipboard.

You can then use **Edit, Paste** to paste the screen shot into your work.

The steps are:

1   Press the **Print Screen key** to capture the screenshot

2   Switch to **Windows Paint**

3   Click on **Edit, Paste**

4   You may be told your image is too big and asked if you would like to expand the image. Click on **Yes**

5   Save the image. (In *Windows 98* or later, you can save the image as a much smaller file by saving it as a **jpg** or a **gif**.)

6   Insert this image in your document.

If you only need to display part of a screenshot you will need to **crop** it. Cropping means cutting unwanted parts from the top, bottom or sides of a picture. Cropped pictures are smaller and so use less disk space.

Using Paint Shop Pro

Image manipulation software like Paint Shop Pro is ideal for screenshots, offering different options such as easy cropping and reducing to 16 or 256 colours to reduce the file size.

In Paint Shop Pro, the first step is to set up how the Screen will operate.

1   Click on **Capture, Setup**. Paint Shop Pro will open the **Capture Setup Dialog Box** shown below.

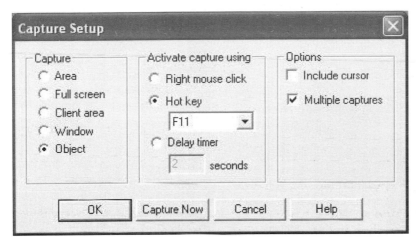

Figure 23.13

2   Click on the required **Capture** type.

The capture type determines which area of the screen will be copied:

Area   Select a rectangular portion of the screen
Full Screen   Copy the entire screen
Client Area   Copy the input area of the active window
Window   Copy the entire active window
Object   Copy a window feature or group of features

3   Click on the way you want the screen capture to operate.

Captures can be activated by using the right mouse button, setting up a Hot Key or setting a timer delay.

There is an option to include the cursor or not. If you choose to include the cursor make sure it is in the correct position before activating the capture.

4   Click on the **OK** Button to close the dialog box and save the capture set-up settings.

To activate the screen capture, choose **Capture now** from the Capture Setup box or Start from the capture menu.

Specification requirements

The table below briefly describes the requirements of some of the examination specifications. The information is only meant as a guide. Always refer to the full specification published by the examination board.

AQA A2 ICT out of 90	AQA A2 Computing out of 60	OCR A2 Computing/ICT out of 120	VCE ICT Unit 6
Analysis 18 marks	**Analysis** 12 marks	**Definition, Investigation, Analysis** 25 marks	**Analysis and design**
• Identifies an appropriate problem • Problem statement • Capabilities and limitations of the resources available • User requirements • Information flow and data dynamics • User's current IT skill level and training needs • Qualitative and quantitative evaluation criteria	• Identifies the problem and user • Reports on the problem • End-user requirements • Analyse the problem with data flow diagrams • State the objectives of the problem • Outline possible solutions and justify the chosen solution	• Defines the problem • Investigates the problem via interview, questionnaire • Analyses sample documents • Problems in the current system • Outlines the current system • End-user requirements • Analyses the problem with data flow diagrams • Specifies the hardware and software resources • Produces a detailed specification	• Design and analysis notes for the database • Detailed design and analysis notes that include graphic images to define the data model clearly and demonstrate that it is correctly normalised to third normal form • Draft design and final model shown correctly normalised to at least first normal form • Shows the entities, attributes, keys, relationships, and internally generated or processed data • Suitable data-input forms
Design 16 marks	**Design** 12 marks	**Design** 21 marks	**Implementation**
• Range of appropriate solutions • Compelling reasons for final choice of solution • Solution specified so that a third party could carry it out • Solution broken down into sub-tasks • Schedule and work plan • Designs including layout sheets, record structures, design for data-capture sheets, etc. • Testing plan	• Entity relationship models • Data dictionary including record or database structure • Validation routines • User interfaces • Screen layouts and data capture forms • Report layouts • Security measures and access control • Test strategy	• Entity relationship models • Data dictionary • Validation routines • Screen layouts and data capture forms • User interfaces • Report layouts	• A working relational database that allows users to append, delete and edit data, initiate queries and print reports • At least three related tables • Reports that make correct and effective use of queries, grouping, mathematical formulae and related tables • Effective use of validation and of automatic counter, date or time fields in data-input forms • User-friendly, well-laid-out screen data-input forms to enable data entry into multiple tables • Annotated printed reports and screen prints clearly demonstrating the operation of the database

Implementation 15 marks

- Design implemented unaided, in an efficient manner with no obvious defects
- Facilities of the software and hardware fully exploited
- Clear and thorough documentation

Testing 15 marks

- Effective test data to cover most or all eventualities
- Evidence of full end-user testing
- System tested with typical, extreme and erroneous test data
- Test outputs fully annotated

Technical solution 12 marks

- This section should document the implementation of the solution

System testing 6 marks

- Test plan and test data
- Hard copy of testing results cross-referenced to plan

System maintenance 6 marks

- Summary of package features used
- Samples of annotated design screens

Software Development, Testing and Implementation 35 marks

- Implementation evidence including evidence that the third-party user has used the system
- Implementation plan, including detailed stages of user testing
- Discussion of how the hardware and software available were suitable in solving the problem
- Develop a test strategy/plan
- Test the software solution with cross-referenced output to plan
- Results of end-user testing

Testing

- Annotated printed copy and test results for the database
- Test procedures, designed and implemented, that check reliable operation, including rejection of data outside the acceptable range

User guide 8 marks	User Manual 6 marks	Documentation 24 marks	User documentation
• A comprehensive, well-illustrated user guide • Deals with all aspects of the system – installation, backup procedures, general use and trouble shooting	• Description of the functions in the system • Sample screen shots • Error recovery advice	• Technical manual • User manual	• A user guide that enables novice users to make efficient use of the database • Clear and accurate definition in the technical documentation of database structure and data relationships, data dictionary range of acceptable data, example output from queries and reports, test procedures • Fluent use of technical language, good use of graphic images and use of annotated screen prints in user instructions and technical documentation

Evaluation 10 marks	Appraisal 3 marks	Evaluation 15 marks	
• Full range of qualitative and quantitative criteria • Solution fully evaluated • Evidence of end-user involvement	• Evaluate against objectives • Evaluate the user feedback • Identify limitations and improvements	• Evaluate against the specification • Evaluate the user testing • Identify limitations and improvements	

Report 8 marks	Quality of Report 3 marks	Report	
• Concise, well-written, fully illustrated, organised report	• Effective, clear, well-organised and written report	• Evidence of independent work and meeting agreed deadlines	

Visit the boards' websites for the full specifications: www.aqa.org.uk, www.ocr.org.uk, www.edexcel.org.uk